CLEAN ENERGY NATION

CLEAN ENERGY NATION

FREEING AMERICA FROM THE TYRANNY OF FOSSIL FUELS

Congressman Jerry McNerney, Ph.D.

and

Martin Cheek

American Management Association

New York • Atlanta • Brussels • Chicago • Mexico City • San Francisco
Shanghai • Tokyo • Toronto • Washington, D.C.

Bulk discounts available. For details visit:
www.amacombooks.org/go/specialsales
Or contact special sales:
Phone: 800-250-5308
E-mail: specialsls@amanet.org
View all the AMACOM titles at: www.amacombooks.org

This publication is designed to provide accurate and authoritative information in regard to the subject matter covered. It is sold with the understanding that the publisher is not engaged in rendering legal, accounting, or other professional service. If legal advice or other expert assistance is required, the services of a competent professional person should be sought.

Library of Congress Cataloging-in-Publication Data

McNerney, Gerald.
   Clean energy nation : freeing America from the tyranny of fossil fuels / Jerry McNerney and Martin Cheek
      p. cm.
   Includes bibliographical references and index.
   ISBN-13: 978-0-8144-1372-2 (hardcover)
   ISBN-10: 0-8144-1372-2 (hardcover)
   1. Power resources—United States. 2. Fossil fuels—Environmental aspects—United States. 3. Energy policy—United States. I. Cheek, Martin, 1966– II. Title.
   TJ163.25.U6M467 2012
   333.790973—dc22

                                                                              2008053754

About AMA
American Management Association (www.amanet.org) is a world leader in talent development, advancing the skills of individuals to drive business success. Our mission is to support the goals of individuals and organizations through a complete range of products and services, including classroom and virtual seminars, webcasts, webinars, podcasts, conferences, corporate and government solutions, business books, and research. AMA's approach to improving performance combines experiential learning—learning through doing—with opportunities for ongoing professional growth at every step of one's career journey.

Printing number

10 9 8 7 6 5 4 3 2 1

To Mary McNerney

The human race is challenged more than ever before to demonstrate our mastery—not over nature but of ourselves.

RACHEL CARSON (1907–64), AMERICAN BIOLOGIST
AND AUTHOR OF *Silent Spring*

CONTENTS

FOREWORD

Once before, America stood on the threshold of a renewable-energy revolution. In the late 1970s, wind farms were popping up in California. Companies making solar photovoltaic cells were attracting waves of new capital. Passive solar building designs, ultra-efficient windows, and energy-saving lamps were all very chic. Biofuels had strong supporters in the farm and forestry sectors, and national labs were exploring cellulosic ethanol and diesel fuel from microalgae.

President Carter had declared a goal of obtaining 20 percent of the nation's energy from renewable sources by the year 2000, and he had installed solar water heaters on the White House. New policies and funding would be needed to achieve the 20 percent goal, and I headed the federal laboratory charged with producing the policy roadmap. For reasons that still remain baffling, the Reagan administration was extremely hostile to renewable-energy sources. It ignored the policy roadmap and systematically crushed the wind, solar, and biofuel programs. President Reagan even ordered that the solar water heaters be ripped off the White House. For the last three decades, the renewable-energy industry has been something of a backwater in America.

Meanwhile, the rest of the world began waking up. Japan started pushing the envelope on solar electricity, and then Germany adopted a feed-in tariff that gave the industry a great shot of adrenaline. Worldwide solar sales have been growing 50 to 60 percent per year for the last decade. Denmark kept expanding the frontiers of wind technology; its innovations are now bearing fruit around the world. Enormous strides have been made in mapping and drilling deep for geothermal resources.

In the United States, we are finally beginning to elect some public officials with scientific backgrounds—and even a handful with personal experience in the renewable-energy field. At the head of that list is Congressman Jerry McNerney, an engineer with a Ph.D. in mathematics who has spent two decades working on renewable energy.

Representative McNerney and his coauthor, Martin Cheek, a Silicon Valley writer, have produced *Clean Energy Nation*, a timely, eminently readable assessment of the renewable-energy prospect. As suggested in its subtitle, *Freeing America from the Tyranny of Fossil Fuels*, it is a frank discussion by smart, experienced people who are not expecting any campaign contributions from Exxon or Peabody. *Clean Energy Nation* is provocative while not being hysterical; it is solidly researched but not laced with jargon and equations; it is hopeful but not naïve.

In *Clean Energy Nation*, McNerney and Cheek show readers that tomorrow can be much brighter if only the United States will seize back its former leading role and transform itself into a nation powered by the superefficient use of sustainable sources of energy. The impending peaking of the world's oil production, the boatloads of money being shipped to the Persian Gulf, and the myriad problems stemming from global warming should provide powerful motivation.

This inspiring book challenges its readers to become leaders themselves and to take personal and political action. The road ahead will not always be an easy one. But when humanity reaches the destination of genuine energy independence, the journey will have been well worth the effort.

Denis Hayes,
President of the Bullitt Foundation

A Declaration of Energy Independence

I n the summer of 1776, America stood at a crossroads. Inside the Pennsylvania State House in Philadelphia, the representatives of the thirteen colonies struggled among themselves in a debate just as hot as the heat wave then broiling the city. The members of the Second Continental Congress argued about the question of independence—specifically, on the issue of whether to cut the political cord tying nearly 3 million Americans to King George III's despotic government. They sought to achieve something never before seen in all of human history. To explain to the world why the colonies were determined to be "absolved from all allegiance to the British Crown,"[1] the Congress assigned five of its delegates to a committee set with the task of creating a document detailing the reasons the American people had a right to live in free and independent states. Serving on that committee was the thirty-three-year-old Thomas Jefferson, a Virginian. His brilliant genius for forging lofty phrases captured the American spirit in the Declaration of Independence. Jefferson's now-famous words, succinctly stating that ordinary people have the right to govern themselves and determine their own destiny, gave birth to a new nation founded on the principles of liberty and democracy. Ever since its creation on July 4, 1776, the United States of America has followed an often arduous but always rewarding road of constant protection and sometimes expansion of its citizens' freedoms, rights, and independence.

Today, America stands at a new crossroads. Inside the halls of the U.S.

1

Capitol Building in Washington, D.C., the representatives of the fifty states now struggle over the direction our nation must take on energy policy. We debate with the same passion that the Founding Fathers did in Philadelphia during the sweltering summer of 1776. Today's members of Congress now face the question of energy freedom—specifically, how to cut the cord tying more than 300 million Americans to fossil-fuel addiction. The question of how to achieve our energy freedom is complex and similar to the struggle faced by the signers of the Declaration of Independence. Our nation's success or failure in manifesting this necessary goal will determine what form our civilization will take in the future. We are facing a dual crisis. First, there is a limited supply of fossil fuels. With consumption growing every year, Earth's supply will start to dwindle, causing gross instability in the price of fuel. Second, the atmosphere has reached its limit to absorb carbon without causing a rapid increase of energy in the atmosphere and oceans. Either problem by itself is a daunting threat. Combined, they pose a massive challenge to modern civilization.

The approximately 9 billion people predicted to be living on our planet within two generations will face dramatic social, political, and economic upheavals without significant improvements in energy efficiency and the increased use of alternative fuel sources. Wars will arise as nations struggle with each other to compete for rapidly depleting oil sources and cope with shifting climate patterns. The global economy might very well collapse as industries fail for lack of power to manufacture their products or miss the means to distribute these goods in a transportation network once driven by oil-based fuels. Without power to pump water or operate farm equipment, people in urban regions might face mass starvation. Chaos could break out as desperate people resort to unlawful actions to survive in a world lacking the necessities that fossil-fuel-driven industry once provided. This is a harsh future we must not leave to our children and their children. We can avoid this dark fate and minimize the harm from climate change by taking the necessary steps now to build for ourselves and for posterity a future fueled by clean and renewable-energy sources in a clean and efficient economy.

One major barrier we must clear in dealing with our energy and climate challenges is that global climate change violates one of our basic assumptions. We presume that Earth's natural bounty will always be there for us. We know that people are fickle, that weather is unpredictable, but throughout history, our planet has rebounded and somewhere things are normal. Climate change challenges this presumption. Over decades, plains and savannas will become deserts. Polar and glacier ice will melt in the warming. Florida and New York City may disappear under ocean waves. The environment is going to change. But we can, too. We can take the steps—steps we *must* take—to mitigate the impact of global climate change. To do that, we must build an international consensus to organize and implement a plan of massive action. That in itself will be a huge social transformation. That's why we must think of this impending climate crisis not only as a major threat but also as a significant opportunity for motivating us all to achieve global energy freedom.

There will be considerable risks and failures involved in developing alternative fuel sources and in minimizing climate change. However, the rewards that will come from America's achieving its energy freedom will make us a much stronger nation and will strengthen the bonds with other nations, as well as provide the ingredients for a more stable world. Energy freedom will help secure our nation's natural environment as well by reducing the air and water pollution from toxic fossil fuels that now damages the health of many of our citizens. The innovative technologies generated in striving for energy freedom will also open wide the gates to economic prosperity for many Americans. New businesses will arise, providing significant opportunities for daring entrepreneurs, stock investors, and venture capitalists. Newly formed companies will generate good jobs for hardworking people. And if promoted globally, the new energy technologies and the accompanying economic prosperity they bring will create a ripple effect throughout the world, helping to stimulate economic development in foreign countries.

Of course, there are those critics who claim that investing in alternative energy is a waste of money because conventional oil is still "cheaper" in a free-market economy than clean and renewable sources of energy. That argument, however, is not credible if the hidden costs of oil are included in the calculations. If we consider the subsidies that big oil companies take from the U.S. taxpayers—at a time when those petroleum producers are making record profits—then we discover that the true cost of that oil is not "cheap." We might have learned an important lesson from the 1973 OPEC oil embargo, a period where we discovered firsthand how quickly our national economy can be manipulated and threatened by petroleum politics. If American policymakers had kept us on the course toward energy independence started during the Carter administration, we would not be facing our current crisis. Even so, there are still those politicians and pundits who fail to learn from history. Skeptics daily discourage us from aggressively reducing our dangerous dependence on fossil fuels, arguing that this action will irreparably hurt our economy and cause the "medievalization of the world."[2] Skeptics also claim that developing the technology and infrastructure to support clean and renewable energy across the nation is a task too costly and impractical to implement in any reasonable time frame. They insist the odds are impossibly high against success for energy freedom. These people fail to understand the American spirit. The United States is a nation that, from its very conception, has persevered against impossible odds—and has prevailed over those odds to achieve miraculous results. Despite facing the mightiest military power in the world, the American colonists achieved the impossible with a decisive victory against the British at the Battle of Yorktown in 1781. That triumph proved to be the turning point of the Revolutionary War. Eighty years later, the United States, led by President Abraham Lincoln, surmounted the grave challenge of a devastating civil war over the issue of slavery. With peace achieved in 1865, we underwent a painful rebirth as a nation dedicated anew to an expanded principle of freedom. In the 1940s, "the Greatest Generation" battled impossible odds to fight fascism and bring lasting liberty to Western Europe and Japan. In the last century, American patience and diligence helped us survive a forty-year threat of nuclear annihilation that ended with the fall of the Berlin Wall in 1989.

In today's America, we see daily the impact that our energy consumption has on our lives. The Deepwater Horizon oil spill made headlines in mid-2010 as it sullied the coastal beaches and damaged local economies of our states bordering the Gulf of Mexico. The recent Arab democracy movements in the Middle East to overturn dictators propped up by oil profits drove up crude oil prices and rippled throughout the world's economy. In 2011, we witnessed distressing evidence that non-fossil fuel sources of energy also have serious environmental and economic consequences. The catastrophic earthquake and tsunami that hit Japan severely damaged the Fukushima Daiichi nuclear power plant. The resulting release of radiation and the worldwide fears arising from potential reactor core meltdowns served as a reminder that gaining power from uranium atoms has risks. Public opinion shapes public policy. American citizens must understand that energy comes with costs, and a national conversation is needed on creating a comprehensive, long-term U.S. energy policy that takes into account the kind of future we want to see in America and worldwide.

Many of America's brightest minds are now working hard on the challenge of pursuing energy freedom. Almost daily, scientists and researchers are finding solutions that can transform our world. Humans are, by nature, resistant to transformative change until conditions are intolerable. We should look ahead and embrace change before we reach that point. The authors of this book realize and appreciate the challenge our nation and world face in meeting future energy needs. It is indeed difficult to imagine a future different from the present because our lives are utterly intertwined with fossil fuels. However, we challenge readers to share our vision of a clean and efficient America and a world with a sustainable-energy economy, with clean and quiet electric cars, with wind turbines gracing the landscape, with solar panels on our rooftops and solar plants in remote deserts, with prosperous family farms producing ecologically balanced biofuel feed stocks alongside food stocks, and with the nations of the world cooperating to manage global and local climates. We can transform our future, creating both jobs and energy in the process, and open up new chapters in human history. A bright tomorrow is indeed within our reach.

The vast majority of Americans truly want their nation to achieve energy freedom.[3] We believe our nation—with persistence and imagination—can realize that grand ambition. We understand that, united together, we must follow this course to energy freedom. Whether we call ourselves Republican or Democrat, or hold other political leanings, most citizens can plainly see the tremendous blessings that will come to them and their children if the United States makes the dream of energy freedom a reality. People want to live in a better and safer world. They want to be able to wake up in the morning and have no cause to worry that today there might be no usable energy to let them live their lives as they are accustomed to living. The social will always pushes the political will. That fact is certainly being felt today as a growing number of Americans encourage their local, state, and federal representatives to strive for energy freedom for the preservation of our nation's values.

As we progress further into the twenty-first century, America's leaders must face an important truth. They should recognize that our nation has a mandate to guide the rest of the world down a road promoting energy freedom through the development of new fuel-efficient technology linked with clean and renewable sources of power. The United States must begin making rapid progress in becoming highly efficient in replacing its widespread use of fossil fuels with energy from solar, wind, water, biofuel, geothermal, and hydrogen-based power sources. We live in an exciting time, a defining moment in human history, when we can and must take the steps necessary to achieve energy freedom that will benefit all humanity. If America is to fulfill the noble promise made by Thomas Jefferson in 1776, we must declare our energy freedom and attain that vital goal before we run out of time.

We now stand at the crossroads. Which road will we choose?

SECTION ONE

AMERICA'S ENERGY
PAST AND PRESENT

Before we can establish where we are going in our national energy journey, we must know where we now stand and understand how we got here. It's important to consider the past and present of America's energy story so that we can have the background knowledge we need to put into historical perspective the various issues we'll examine more deeply later in this book. In Chapter 1, we'll look at why we are facing the end of the fossil-fuel age and contemplate what it might mean for the future survival of our republic and our civilization. In Chapter 2, we'll explore the process by which the United States gradually became so dependent on fossil fuels for driving its economic, social, and political institutions. Finally, in Chapter 3, we'll analyze the various energy opportunities available to replace fossil fuels, and we'll examine the positive and negative aspects of their widespread use in American society.

CHAPTER 1

The End of the Fossil-Fuel Age

Imagine what your life would be like if the world suddenly lost its hydro-carbon power. If, for some reason, all the supplies of oil, coal, and natural gas on our planet vanished, you would be faced with life far different from the one you now know. Flick the light switches in your home and you would still be left in the dark. No matter how hard you pressed the buttons on the remote control of your TV set, *Survivor, American Idol,* and every other broadcast show would still fail to appear on the screen. You wouldn't be able to listen to music, from Bach to Bruce Springsteen, on your living-room stereo system. You wouldn't be able to surf the Internet, because your personal computer or laptop would sit on your desk as a useless piece of high-tech rubbish. And you wouldn't be able to call friends or family members, because the global phone system cannot function without energy. Your morning shower would be an unpleasantly frigid one, because no electricity or natural gas would be available to operate your hot-water heater. But most likely no water would come through your home's plumbing anyway, because it takes power to pump it to your neighborhood from the municipal reservoir or a well. Much of the food in your refrigerator and freezer would spoil after a few days, because there would be no electricity to run those kitchen appliances.

Whether you live in a small town or a major metropolis, your community could rapidly collapse into disorder without fossil fuels. After sunset, streetlights would stand useless, and crime could increase dramatically.

Local police departments would find it impossible to quickly respond to calls because patrol cars would sit idle without fuel. The same problem would be faced by other emergency services, such as fire departments and ambulances. The combustion engine of your car or truck most likely runs on fossil fuels, so unless you owned a horse or mule, you would be forced to travel only walkable or bikeable distances. If you are like most Americans who usually commute many miles by car to work, you would find it extremely difficult to get to your office or factory site. Not that it would matter. Without fossil fuels to operate the facilities, the factory or office building in which you work would be closed down, just like most other job sites around the world.

Without fossil fuels to generate electricity, public schools in every community across the nation could be closed. So you would need to find other ways to educate your children and help them spend their day. The doors of public libraries and community centers would be locked by city officials because there would be no way to supply patrons with heat, light, and other electric-powered services. Supermarkets and convenience stores would also soon be forced to lock their doors as they ran out of stock. If not quickly sold, perishable items would soon spoil as they sat defrosting on unrefrigerated store shelves. There would probably be enough food in warehouse storage to last for a short while, but the food must reach the markets, and that distribution depends almost entirely on petroleum. All the grain in the silos in Kansas will do little good for people in California and New York if it can't be shipped. Over a short time, most food production throughout the world would virtually stop because modern agriculture depends on oil and natural gas. The oil is used to plant and harvest crops. Most fertilizers are produced from natural gas. Chemicals to treat for pests and other problems come largely from petroleum. (In developing countries, more human and animal labor is used to grow crops, so they would be less vulnerable to the negative impact of food shortages.) Even more important than food, however, is drinkable water. Fossil fuels are used to process and pump this precious resource through canals and pipes all around our nation. Some water is shipped by trucks and that depends on oil. Within days, people would be desperate for clean H_2O. It's easy to see how law and order could quickly break down if food and water suddenly became scarce.

If fossil fuels were to suddenly disappear, our economy would quickly collapse. Stores would run out of merchandise because no diesel-powered trucks and trains could transport items down America's vast network of highways and railroads. Modern hospitals wouldn't be able to function. Without fossil fuels to move them, all the airplanes and trains in every nation on Earth would stand useless. Letters and packages could not be easily delivered across the span of distances because it takes petroleum energy to convey them by plane, train, or truck. After the fossil-fuel disappearance, national and international news information also could not be widely distributed by TV, radio, the Internet, or newspapers and magazines. When the winter months arrived, Americans in cold climates would find themselves shivering under blankets during blizzards or extreme freezing temperatures.

This scenario is hard to envision happening, but it's not just in the realm of imagined catastrophe. Although fossil fuels won't dramatically vanish in a frightening flash, our global civilization is right now facing a future where the limited supply of hydrocarbon energy from oil might indeed soon start to diminish or become prohibitively expensive. And concerns about the impending climate crisis and severe environmental changes from global climate change might put a political brake on coal use.

Already, we're facing growing political and social anxiety as the nations of the world awaken to the real prospect that we might be nearing the end of the fossil-fuel era. The fact is that the world economy is completely dependent upon fossil fuels. A sudden major, long-term shortfall in world oil supplies would result in unprecedented human suffering. Compounding the problem is the impending threat of global climate change. If the worldwide consumption of fossil fuels continues climbing at the maximum possible rate, the resulting climate changes will have the potential to completely disrupt civilization. Global warming's impact on water supplies could alter our current political systems, causing mass migrations, wars, and starvations. Unfortunately, global warming and the predictable sharp reduction of hydrocarbon fuel supplies will happen together, reinforcing the need to take action now while we still have the capability to effect changes that would result in a healthier, more prosperous society. So to better understand how we can face the society-changing challenges of our energy future, it is vital for us to know something about two major concepts directly connected to the topic of fossil fuels. They are Hubbert's peak and greenhouse gases.

HUBBERT'S PEAK

On March 8, 1956, Dr. Marion King Hubbert, a highly respected geophysicist who was just as cantankerous as he was brilliant, sat on a platform in a conference hall in San Antonio, Texas, preparing to drop a bombshell in a scientific research paper he would soon present.[1] In his report "Nuclear Energy and the Fossil Fuels," he intended to reveal to members of the American Petroleum Institute what he had mathematically calculated to be the future of U.S. oil production.[2] That fuel forecast was not a pleasant one.

Hubbert had grown up in central Texas and had earned his Ph.D. in geology and physics from the University of Chicago during the 1920s. After a period teaching as a professor, he had gone to work for Shell Oil Company, where he led a major research laboratory devoted to oil exploration and production. At Shell, he was known for his feisty attitude when it came to arguing technical details. This persona quickly inspired a saying among his colleagues that "Hubbert is a bastard, but at least he's our bastard."[3] During his years of researching the intricacies of oil, he had provided the world of geology with several significant discoveries. Early in his career, for example, he demonstrated mathematically that the tremendous geological pressures deep in the planet's crust cause rock to exhibit plastic characteristics much like clay.[4] This accomplishment and many others gained the geophysicist wide esteem in the scientific community, as well as in the oil industry.

On that March day in 1956, as San Antonio's mayor gave the conference's welcoming speech, someone signaled to Dr. Hubbert to come to a nearby phone. With minutes to spare before Hubbert was supposed to go up to the podium to address the audience, a public relations man back at Shell's head office in Houston started pleading with the scientist to withdraw or at least tone down his gloomy vision of oil's future. Hubbert refused to budge. He believed in his findings and bluntly told the PR man his intentions to go through with his presentation. After hanging up, he soon delivered what is now considered one of the most influential speeches in the history of the oil industry. Hubbert showed the audience a graphed bell-shaped curve he had created by using a complex math formula. It illustrated the stages of growth of oil extraction in the lower forty-eight American states over a span of many decades. This graph was based on an estimated total U.S. reserve of between 150 billion and 200 billion barrels—an approximation geologists at that time believed was accurate. Hubbert showed the people attending the meeting how the top of the graph projected that oil would peak in the lower forty-eight states sometime between 1965 and 1971.[5] After that, oil production would begin a steady decline as the nation's reserves started to diminish. See Figure 1-1.

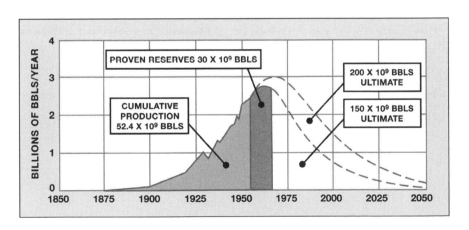

U.S. Oil Peak Graph prepared by Bob Snow at Design Factory Graphics based on Dr. Marion King Hubbert's original graph published in the 1956 report "Nuclear Energy and the Fossil Fuels."

Understanding the important consequences of Hubbert's findings if they proved to be accurate, members of the U.S. petroleum industry immediately went into action. They began a denial campaign to refute the geophysicist's prediction. It was partly an emotional reaction to Hubbert's presentation. After all, billions of future dollars were at stake. Many of the oil industry's geophysicists also began to challenge the figures that Hubbert had used to make his calculations, saying the United States still had many more oil discoveries waiting to be made—such as in the frontier of Alaska.[6] Some even suggested that Hubbert was a doomsday crackpot. They said that other scientists had prophesied the end of the oil supply as far back as 1900, incorrectly proclaiming the United States had only a decade or so before the nation's fuel tank would hit empty. But those scientists had used a different mathematical formula from Hubbert's. They had divided America's known petroleum reserves by an annual rate of production. Instead, during the course of the twentieth century, more oil fields were discovered, allowing the industry to continue its highly profitable boom years.[7]

Reality, however, eventually confirmed Hubbert's calculations were correct. By November 1970, America's oil production did indeed reach its peak point and began a consistent decline that continues today, just as Hubbert predicted in the 1950s.[8] No one really knew the exact time the actual pinnacle moment occurred until a couple of years later, when data demonstrated that the United States was indeed undergoing a steady decline of production in its oil fields. That moment, often called Hubbert's peak, marked an important milestone for America and the world. It also provided us with a cautionary message that a nation that derives nearly all its energy requirements from fossil fuels is living on borrowed time.

In the 1970s, Americans started to wake up to the fact that they faced an uncertain oil outlook. One of the loudest alarm clocks went off when service stations began to run out of gasoline and the economy was severely hurt following the oil embargo by the Organization of Petroleum Exporting Countries (OPEC) in the fall of 1973. As chaos disrupted the country, elected leaders began to truly comprehend the major impact of the oil peak in the United States. Hubbert was invited to speak to a congressional subcommittee on the environment on June 6, 1974, and there, as a senior research geophysicist with the Department of the Interior's U.S. Geological Survey, he discussed how he derived his equations and data. He then presented the forecast date when his calculations showed the planet's oil production might crest. During his testimony, he informed the members of Congress that "the peak in the production rate for the world, based upon the high estimate of 2,100 billion barrels, will occur about the year 2000."[9] That same month, a *National Geographic* article quoted the geophysicist as saying, "The end of the oil age is in sight."[10]

Unlike his U.S. projection, Hubbert's estimate of world oil production's peak did not hit a bull's-eye. His theory requires inputting accurate oil reserve estimates into the calculation, and the data are often unverified by outside sources. It can also change as new oil fields are discovered or as geopolitical situations reduce the consumption of petroleum (as occurred during the energy conservation movement in the United States during the 1970s and 1980s). Also, many OPEC nations tend to overinflate their estimates of oil reserves, adding to the uncertainty of the data. Most significantly, advanced oil exploration and drilling technology developed in the thirty years following Hubbert's testimony helped to more efficiently extract the crude out of Earth's crust. Even Hubbert himself pointed out that his famous curve is not a crystal ball but only an indicator based on mathematical statistics requiring a reliable estimate of Earth's reserves for an accurate prediction. A computation is only as accurate as the numbers plugged into it.

But Kenneth S. Deffeyes, a professor emeritus at Princeton University, believes that Hubbert came close enough in his original estimate of the year 2000 for when global oil production could peak. Deffeyes, who worked under Hubbert's supervision during his years at the Shell lab, believes his colleague would have no doubt revised his prediction based on more accurate estimates of Earth's oil reserves. Calculations today, made by some petroleum experts using Hubbert's methods and more accurate data than Hubbert had, predict that the world's oil production will reach a peak sometime around the year 2010.[11] Some oil experts believe that if it hasn't done so yet the world is close to hitting that historic mark, forecasting it will probably happen between the years 2005 and 2020.[12] We won't know the exact time frame it occurs until perhaps a year or two after it happens, when there is statistical evidence of a marked decline in global oil production. But we do know that when the world reaches the top of the bell curve in oil production and begins its inevitable plummet, it will prove to be a dramatic transition point for humankind. It will mark the moment when we must acknowledge that unless we develop other sources of energy to replace petroleum, our civilization is living on borrowed time.

Some oil experts point out that the world still has plenty of petroleum just waiting to be found underground. It's true that trillions of barrels of oil still remain to be extracted out of nonconventional sources such as oil sand and oil shale. "Oil sand," also known as tar sand, is a bituminous (organic liquid) mixture consisting of sand or clay, water, and extra-heavy crude oil. Currently, the northeastern section of Alberta, Canada, is the largest supplier of this type of petroleum product, according to the Alberta Department of Energy. "Oil shale" isn't really oil or shale but a fine-grained sedimentary rock that holds a solid mixture of organic compounds called kerogen that can be processed into a liquid hydrocarbon much like petroleum.[13] The global deposits of oil shale—including a massive reserve in America's Green River Basin covering Utah, Wyoming, and Colorado—theoretically could make up the equivalent of up to 1.8 trillion barrels of potentially extractable petroleum product, according to the U.S. Department of Energy Office of Petroleum Reserves. These nonconventional fossil fuels, however, are much more expensive to extract and process into a usable energy source than the "easy" petroleum traditionally pumped from oil fields. They also pose significant environmental challenges. Their extraction will pollute groundwater, and the methods used to process them into a usable form will add considerable amounts of toxic pollution and greenhouse gases to the atmosphere.

When it comes to the world's easily extractable oil, it is evident that we are definitely facing a climax. Mexico's Cantarell oil field is the world's second largest petroleum production complex—after the Ghawar field in Saudi Arabia. Set in the Gulf of Mexico near the state of Campeche, Cantarell produces about 60 percent of Mexico's petroleum. It is a mature field that peaked in production at the end of 2004, with an output of 2.1 million barrels a day.[14] Since then, it has begun a steady drop in the quantity it produces. With Mexico's economy so heavily dependent on its nationalized oil industry, a steady decline in production ability at Cantarell and other oil production sites will have major political and social consequences. Mexico's problems stemming from its oil peak will also almost certainly spill across the border. Mexico is the second largest petroleum supplier to the United States after Canada, according to statistics on U.S. imports by country of origin kept by the U.S. Energy Information Administration (EIA). A steady drop in our neighbor's oil reserves could seriously affect our own economy. Mexico's Cantarell is no doubt an indicator of how, one by one, other oil fields across the world will eventually hit their production peak and force an industrial civilization to rethink how it uses petroleum.

Adding to the problem of peak oil is the growing consumption of this fossil fuel throughout the world. To power cars, homes, and industries, the United States, with around 4 percent of the human population, uses about 21 million barrels of oil a day, according to the EIA. America's voracious consumption of the planet's oil has set what many consider a wasteful example for the rest of the world, and other countries are fast catching up to our nation's lavish lifestyle. The most prominent of these are China and India. With nearly 2.5 billion people combined (based on 2010 data in the Central Intelligence Agency World Factbook), China and India make up roughly one-third of the planet's population. With the globalization and modernization of their economies over the last few decades, these Asian countries are steadily developing consumer-driven societies that require a growing supply of fossil fuels to keep their economies expanding. Of course, this mounting industrialization of the world's nations, combined with a growing number of people on the planet, is creating an immense army of consumers, all of whom require energy to meet their modern lifestyle needs. But at some point soon after the peak oil point is reached, the industrial world will be forced to face an unpleasant question dealing with the basic facts of economic supply and demand. How will all these burgeoning consumers get the energy they demand when the global supply of oil rapidly starts its unavoidable decline?

Our world obviously cannot continue going down this path without massive negative consequences. It is up to us to use Hubbert's famous predictions to make some important decisions on how to survive in an uncertain world of oil decline. Given a finite supply of oil reserves, one of the crucial components of Hubbert's peak is the time factor. On the decline side of the peak, we will face and have to cope with more and more competition for less and less petroleum. Like the passengers on the ill-fated *Titanic* after it hit that iceberg in the North Atlantic one April night in 1912, we stand on a sinking ship. In the first hour after the damage was done to the great ocean liner, many of those unlucky passengers remained unaware of the grave danger they faced. Today, many Americans deny the reality of the danger we face as we cross over to the other side of Hubbert's peak. We will surely confront tragic consequences if we do not find other sources of energy to sustain our way of life. Hubbert's peak gives us an admonition that the end of the fossil-fuel age is upon us. It is up to us to now heed the warning.

PEAK COAL AND GREENHOUSE GASES

Some people say that the peak oil problem can be easily solved. All we need to do is simply ramp up our use of coal to replace oil. Indeed, technology exists to turn coal into an oil-like substance. When Nazi Germany's petroleum supply started to fail during World War II, German scientists developed a method called the Fischer-Tropsch process to convert coal into a type of liquid fuel that could run military equipment such as tanks. And in the nineteenth century, some major American cities burned coal in ovens to make a natural gas that lit street lamps and homes.[15] People who advocate more coal usage often point out that the United States has enough coal reserves to last for at least 250 years, a figure derived in the early 1970s. This number has been downgraded, however.[16] The World Coal Institute estimates that the proven reserves of coal on our planet will last for about a century and a half. But a 2007 National Academy of Sciences (NAS) report found that our nation lacks adequate data to accurately estimate for policymakers how many years of coal reserves we really have left. Furthermore, coal excavation and production will become harder on the environment and more dangerous for miners after we tap out our current supply of easy-to-reach ore, the NAS found. At the present rate of production, America can meet its coal needs through at least 2030, the report stated, and there will be "probably enough for 100 years."[17]

Better data about our country's coal reserves and whether they can meet increasing demand and consumption will enable us to more wisely evaluate our future use of this fossil fuel. According to U.S. Department of Energy projections, the world's coal consumption will grow at an annual rate of 2.5 percent a year through 2030.[18] And if two published studies prove to be correct about our current usable supply of this hydrocarbon in relation to growing global consumption, we might hit a "peak coal" period in the next two decades. One study published in March 2007 by the Energy Watch Group, an organization of scientists who supply information and analysis to the German Parliament, warns that global coal production might "peak around 2025 at 30 percent above present production in the best case," and if this prediction comes to pass, the production will "reach a plateau and will eventually decline thereafter."[19] Another study released in February 2007 by the Institute of Energy, which supplies scientific information for the European Commission's Joint Research Center, warns that the growing global consumption of coal might overwhelm its production. "The immense growth in coal consumption since 2000, driven mainly by China, has not been matched by a corresponding development of proven coal reserves, despite the increase in world coal prices," the study said.[20]

If indeed the end of the fossil fuel era looms, in view of the potential peak of oil and coal production in the next couple of decades, as some experts suggest, we must prepare ourselves for a major transformation of our global economy and society. And it comes at a time when we must aggressively address another serious problem related to the production and consumption of fossil fuels. Burning these energy sources—particularly coal—produces a massive quantity of the greenhouse gas carbon dioxide, which significantly contributes to the heating of the planet. Al Gore, in his book *An Inconvenient Truth,* has raised awareness about global climate change that puts billions of people and many of the world's living organisms in peril.

Carbon dioxide is not the only molecule that contributes to the warming of Earth. Water vapor, methane, chlorofluorocarbons, and nitrous oxide also contribute to the "greenhouse effect."[21] However, carbon dioxide from burning fossil fuels makes up 82 percent of the greenhouse gas emissions from human sources, according to the EIA. The term *greenhouse effect* was coined as far back as 1822 by Jean Fourier, a French mathematician who wanted to make an analogy of Earth's atmosphere to the glass in a botanical conservatory.[22] Like greenhouse glass, the planet's atmosphere allows the sun's rays to pass through it to be absorbed by land, water, and air. And just like thick greenhouse glass does, the atmosphere also can hinder the escape of this radiant heat energy back into space. Thus, much like a garden greenhouse works, only on a much smaller scale, the thin layer of air that spreads over the globe helps to retain an average temperature of 59 degrees Fahrenheit (15 degrees Celsius) across the entire planet. This comfortable heat range makes our world hospitable for life. Without the greenhouse effect, Earth would be like Mars—a cold, dead world. But the atmosphere could also contain an overabundance of greenhouse gas so that it holds in too much of the sun's heat. Similarly to what happens if the glass enclosing a greenhouse is too thick and doesn't allow enough heat to radiate out, too high a concentration of greenhouse gases accumulates and keeps in heat energy. On a global scale, the effect makes the world's ambient temperature increase and thus causes the climate to severely change. The planet Venus is an example of a place in the solar system where the intensity of greenhouse gases has made it far too hot for life to exist.

Over the last two centuries since the start of the industrial age, tremendous population growth combined with modern civilization's increased use of fossil fuels has created changes to the chemistry of our planet's atmosphere. To feed and house people throughout the world, we have cut down millions of acres of forest trees and set them ablaze, thus releasing billions of tons of carbon dioxide into the air. Burning fossil fuels such as oil and coal over the last 200 years has also increased the carbon dioxide content in the atmosphere. Long ago, when these fuels were produced by nature through the decomposition of prehistoric plant and animal life, nature sequestered much of our planet's carbon safely underground. As we are learning, the burning of these ancient energy sources comes with a steep cost. Once released into the atmosphere, carbon dioxide can remain there for as long as a century.[23] The more of this heat-absorbing molecule that we pour into our planet's atmosphere, the more sun-radiated heat Earth will retain.

The scientific evidence demonstrates that global warming is a real danger that jeopardizes our planet's health and possibly even humanity's survival. The science is solid. Some elected political officials, however, refuse to take this threat to our biosphere seriously. They call it a "hoax,"[24] despite the massive amounts of documented and peer-reviewed evidence provided by scientists showing that the climate crisis is indeed a genuine phenomenon that is changing our planet in ways that might not be pleasant for the people on it.[25]

The problem of global climate change has also produced some interesting radical solutions, including one suggested by Nobel Prize–winning physicist Paul Crutzen of the Germany-based Max Planck Institute for Chemistry. He described a proposal for using high-altitude balloons to drop sulfur dust into Earth's stratosphere, simulating the way dust from a massive volcanic explosion would be thrown high into the atmosphere. The sulfur particles might then act like miniature mirrors and reflect the sun's rays back into space, thus dropping the planet's overall temperature. In a *National Geographic* article, Crutzen explained that this extreme and untested experiment in atmospheric reengineering should be attempted only as a last resort to combat global warming, adding, "I hope that my experiment will never have to take place."[26]

This planet reengineering experiment might indeed be taking place, although not intentionally. Scientists working in Israel during the 1980s and 1990s found that the sunlight that reaches Earth has been growing dimmer. The soot and dust particles released high into the atmosphere from burning coal and other fossil-fuel sources reflect some of the sunlight back into space. Ironically, this "global dimming" phenomenon has helped to slow down the effects of global warming. Unfortunately, it might have also helped to mask the true impact of global warming on our planet's rising temperature. Some

scientists estimate that if we decrease the impact of global dimming by reducing the particle pollutants in the atmosphere, Earth might see a 2- to 3-degree
Celsius (about 5-degree Fahrenheit) increase in its planetwide temperature
by the year 2050.[27]

In April 2007, Dr. James E. Hansen, the head of NASA's Goddard Institute for Space Studies, in New York City, shared with the House of Representative's Select Committee on Energy Independence and Global Warming
his views of human-made interference with our planet's climate. Hansen is
a world-renowned expert on climatology, and his work has brought much
public attention to the issue of global climate change. His remarks to House
members were sobering. In summary, he stated that scientific data and analysis "reveal that Earth is close to dangerous climate change, to tipping points
of the system with the potential for irreversible deleterious effects."[28] This
global tipping point might be reached as early as 2016 if greenhouse gas emissions are not substantially reduced, he predicts.[29] After this point, catastrophic
global climate change would become an unstoppable occurrence. As Hansen
has described, dramatic effects would include the complete melting of all
summer ice in the Arctic regions, thus devastating the wildlife and people
living there; water shortages in America's West and other parts of the world;
and drought conditions that could cause the collapse of agriculture throughout the world. According to Hansen, the "greatest threat" to humanity from
global warming would come from the obliteration of the West Antarctic ice
sheet, as warming ocean water and surface melt liquefy it. "There is increasing realization that sea level rise this century may be measured in meters if
we follow business-as-usual fossil fuel emissions," he told congressional representatives during his testimony.

Hope, however, still exists to save the planet from this climate catastrophe, Hansen added. The key is for the United States to take quick action. At
the top of the list of recommended measures, he suggested, "First, we must
phase out the use of coal and unconventional fossil fuels, except where the
CO_2 is captured and sequestered. There should be a moratorium on construction of old-technology coal-fired power plants."[30] Hansen also recom-
mends a "fee-and-dividend" policy to regulating carbon emissions. With this

approach, the government charges an escalating fee for fossil fuels at their point of entry (such as an oil well, a coal mine, or a seaport) into the economy. This would increase the cost of carbon fuels, stimulating innovations in clean-energy sources. One hundred percent of the money raised would be given as dividends to American households on an equally divided basis to offset the increased energy costs consumers will face during the national transition to clean energy. Consumers who lower their energy bills through energy efficiency and by installing renewable-energy sources such as solar, wind, or geothermal can pocket the difference between their bills and their dividends.

If scientists like Hansen are correct in their projection of global warming's effect on our planet, what we decide to do about humanity's annual release of billions of tons of greenhouse gases into the atmosphere is an important question that *must* be answered. And we must answer it quickly before climate changes cause even more drastic damage to our world. Because reducing our use of fossil fuels is the obvious crucial component in tackling this epic challenge, we will discuss in more detail in later chapters the role of energy independence in dealing with the issue of climate change in our future.

FACING OUR FUEL FUTURE

Luckily, we are not helpless. We have options. The decisions we make about our energy independence during the course of the next ten to twenty years may determine whether our civilization—and maybe even the human race itself—will survive into the twenty-second century. We are a smart species and have successfully faced problems in the past that have threatened our survival. We have adapted and thrived. We know we have some time left to prepare for the inevitable day when fossil fuels will not be as easy to obtain as they have been for the last 200 years. But we must start preparing today. The longer we wait to take action, the harder it will be to face the major social and political problems that are building like a massive tsunami heading toward us.

Adding to our dilemma is the unavoidable fact that the world's population is growing rapidly and is expected to reach more than 9 billion people by the year 2050. This will put a heavy burden on our planet's resources as the demands grow exponentially for a dwindling supply of fossil fuels and other reserves. The greatest concentration of this population boom will be in China and India, which might hold more than 3 billion people when the twenty-first century hits the midway mark. These two nations are also rapidly urbanizing their societies. Sustaining the highly industrial infrastructure they are quickly building will require the consumption of even greater quantities of depleting fossil fuels. Although these nations also see the crisis at hand and are taking steps toward developing clean and renewable fuels to alleviate its impact, as developing countries, they also see their economic futures in stark terms. They know that America's economy was developed on fossil fuels and believe that the United States bears significant responsibility for the current levels of greenhouse gases in the atmosphere. Many public officials in the United States, on the other hand, believe that reducing our fossil-fuel consumption will have a strong negative impact on our economy, and that Americans should not have to reduce their greenhouse gas generation as long as the developing countries are generating just as much as we are. This kind of political calculus is preventing the cooperation and agreement needed to reduce fossil-fuel consumption and greenhouse gas emissions. We must overcome it to achieve real progress. And we can.

We live in an extraordinary age of technological achievement. The scientific advances that have occurred in the last two centuries have created a standard of living for many of us that greatly surpasses anything human beings have experienced in previous eras. But most of us take for granted that our modern society exists in large part thanks to the power contained in ancient fuels. Without the energy stored millions of years ago in nature's reserves of oil, coal, and natural gas, today's global civilization would be far different from the one we know. Now we must start facing the fact that this hydrocarbon energy supply is not an unlimited one.

We still do not yet fully understand how every individual on Earth will be personally impacted if the world's power from fossil fuels runs dry and we fail to adequately prepare alternative energy sources. As we face a future when the supply of hydrocarbon fuels starts to become economically impractical to extract out of our planet's geology, the United States must now meet its moral obligation and make major changes to its social and technological infrastructure to prepare for this new world. If we fail to take action to ignite an energy independence movement now, the price we'll pay will be a rapid decline of our modern civilization in the coming decades. If we succeed in creating a clean-energy nation, the prize of peace and prosperity we'll earn will be well worth the effort.

CHAPTER 2

How to Become Dependent on Fossil Fuels

Although fossil fuels are found deep underground in many locations on the planet, the energy they contained originally came from a source about 93 million miles (150 million km) away from Earth. That source is a 4.6-billion-year-old star we call the sun. Although it is a fairly ordinary celestial body compared with the 200 billion or so other stars in the Milky Way galaxy, the sun plays a special role for virtually all life forms on our tiny blue world. It gives us the light and heat that's so vital for sustaining our existence. In fact, the sun is so important to the creation and continued survival of life on our world that many humans in the ancient past, including the Egyptians, Greeks, and Romans, considered it to be a deity.

To understand how the sun creates energy, let's take a journey in our imagination across the vacuum of space to our star. In our mind voyage, we approach the bright sphere and are overwhelmed by its vast size. About 1.3 million planet Earths could fit within its volume, and it contains more than 99.9 percent of the mass in our solar system. As we get closer, we can see more details, including the enormous arc of a solar flare leaping from the sun's illuminated surface. Nearby, we notice a relatively dark patch or two, which we recognize as sunspots. These are regions where intense magnetic fields cause the temperature to be somewhat cooler than the rest of the massive orb's surface. We pass through one of these spots and continue our imagined travels by voyaging deeper down through thousands of miles of hydrogen

27

and helium gas. When we reach the sun's core, we find a hellish place where the temperature is a staggering 28.1 million degrees Fahrenheit (15.6 million degrees Celsius), and the pressure is 340 billion times the air pressure at sea level on Earth.[1]

No doubt the extreme conditions at the core would quickly incinerate any astronaut who would venture into it. But this environment provides the perfect state for sustaining an ongoing thermonuclear reaction that has enabled the creation of all life back on our home world—including us human beings. Our very survival depends on what happens here at the heart of a star. In the core region of our sun, the tremendous pressure and temperature continuously fuses together the nuclei particles in hydrogen atoms to form the element helium. During every second of this fusion process, great reservoirs of heat and radiation are released in an ongoing series of reactions that would make all the nuclear weapons on Earth pale significantly in comparison.

This thermonuclear furnace at the sun's core produces not only heat but also radiation as light particles that scientists call photons. At the moment of their creation, the photons begin following a chaotic path as they bounce in a bedlam bumper-car ride among the densely packed hydrogen atoms. They take thousands of years to make their way to the sun's surface. Once freed from their solar labyrinth, the light particles forever leave the place of their birth, traveling at 186,282 miles per second (299,792,458 meters per second) through the vacuum of space. Because our sun is a relatively far distance away from us, the vast majority of the photons never reach our planet. That's a good thing. If the bulk of them did pour down upon our world, Earth soon would be fried by the heat and radiation, and life here couldn't exist. Luckily, our home planet orbits the sun at what scientists call a "Goldilocks zone"—a safe distance where it receives not too much, not too little, but just the right amount of solar energy to give us a comfortable climate.[2]

Once photons reached Earth, many of these particles were converted long ago into fossil fuels. To understand that process, it is important to know how green vegetation stores light. Think of Earth's trees, grass, and other plant life as solar-powered batteries. Instead of using an alkaline acid to store energy, as your common Duracell household battery does, the plant cells contain a chemical substance called chlorophyll. In a process called photosynthesis, this green-colored material absorbs the photons that travel from the sun. It stores their energy to help keep the plant alive and growing.

In case you don't recall the biology-class lessons about photosynthesis from your school years, here's a quick refresher course. Inside the cells of a plant's leaves, chlorophyll uses the sun's light to actively bond carbon dioxide molecules obtained from the air with the hydrogen obtained from water molecules drawn up from the soil through the roots. During this solar-powered chemical bonding process, photon energy is first absorbed by the chlorophyll and used to split the water molecules into their respective hydrogen and oxygen atom components. The now-freed oxygen atoms are a by-product in the process. The green plant releases them back into Earth's atmosphere, where, conveniently enough, people and other animal species can breathe them into their lungs to sustain life. Meanwhile, the plant's chlorophyll continues using the sun's photon energy, this time to chemically bond the carbon dioxide molecules with the freed hydrogen atoms. This process forms a new molecular compound called a carbohydrate. The photon energy is stored within the chemical bonds of this carbohydrate, awaiting future use by the plant as a food (such as a sugar or starch) or as a fibrous building material (such as cellulose).[3] Sometimes animals such as bugs or bunnies or people come along and munch on a vegetable leaf or a tree's fruit. In the process of digesting this starch or sugar, they absorb some of the sun's energy that the plant has previously stored. Thus, virtually all life on Earth is "solar powered," even people.

Plants have been manufacturing carbohydrates using sunlight since the first green algae formed in ponds and lakes more than 2.5 billion years ago. But the time frame we need to focus on to understand the creation of fossil fuels doesn't go back that far. Coal came from plants that grew between 286 million and 360 million years ago, an age known as the Carboniferous Period. During this time, our planet's land masses were covered with great tropical swamps, out of which grew massive trees, ferns, and large leafy plants. Oil and natural gas formed 144 million to 213 million years ago when the oceans, lakes, and inland seas swarmed with bacteria; tiny photosynthetic organisms with silica cell walls called diatoms; and mats of algae, a green gooey substance made up of microscopic plants, especially algae, living together in colonies. All this life kept absorbing the photons from the sun and bonding it with carbon atoms and water molecules to form the organic carbohydrate compounds. On occasion, the organic material would be covered by successive layers of sediment caused by landslides or mud slides or massive sandstorms. These events trapped the carbohydrates in anaerobic conditions under mud, sand, and rock that kept them from decaying. During hundreds of millions of years, this natural process pulled carbon dioxide out of Earth's atmosphere and stored these molecules deep inside the planet. The removal of this greenhouse gas gradually cooled our world's overall temperature, making it a hospitable place for human beings, who came along much later.[4]

Gradually, over long spans of time, the dynamic forces of earthquakes, volcanoes, and continental drift changed Earth's geological formation. If, watching from outer space, you could view our planet's last 360 million years as a time-lapse movie, you would observe the various continental land masses of North and South America, Europe, Asia, Australia, Africa, and Antarctica break apart, smash together, and drift apart again. When some of these land masses crashed into each other—such as India plowing into southern Asia— you would witness from this continental collision the geological formation of massive mountain ranges, such as the Himalayas. Powered by the great ocean of molten magma churning miles beneath our feet, our planet underwent a slow but never-ceasing process of transformation over the course of millions of years. During that time, the buried carbohydrates descended deeper into our planet's crust because of these geological forces. Cooked by the great pressure and heat under tons of rock, the oxygen molecules making up this organic material were gradually released. The baked carbohydrates thus formed into a new compound called a hydrocarbon. This molecule is the building block of petroleum oil, coal, and natural gas and is much more volatile than carbohydrates. Hydrocarbons hold the ancient sunlight energy captured in their chemical bonds in a much more compacted form than carbohydrates. When fossil fuels are burned, their fire releases a much more concentrated energy than would be available in a similar amount of the carbohydrate compounds.

Because they were made from the fossilized remains of ancient plants and animals, hydrocarbon energy sources are often called fossil fuels. These fuels are of different states depending on what type of life originally produced them, as well as the geological conditions that "cooked" them. As the sediment solidified into rock, coal formed from the accumulation of partially decayed land plants transformed under the great pressure and high temperatures. Crude oil was created when fine mud covered the microscopic plants in the world's oceans and they decomposed under the increasing pressure as, over the ages, this biomass sank deep under the seafloor. And natural gases such as methane are made up of the lightest hydrocarbon molecules that are released as petroleum oil in underground reservoirs slowly decays.[5]

EARLY HUMAN HISTORY OF FOSSIL FUELS

Like buried pirate treasure, all the accumulating fossil fuels lay hidden in Earth's crust for hundreds of millions of years. Over the ages, mountains rose and fell, and new seas were born and disappeared, covering the hydrocarbon deposits deeper under the rock. Eventually, in their *Jurassic Park*–like world, *Tyrannosaurus rex* and the other antediluvian species walked the land far above these massive stores of energy. The age of those great reptiles ended 65 million years ago when, scientists theorize, an asteroid the size of a small city hit our planet in what's now the Yucatán Peninsula and brought doom to the dinosaurs. Freed from the tyranny of their carnivorous predators, nocturnal rodentlike animals began to evolve into a variety of new and unique species. The age of the mammals had begun.[6]

Among the more sophisticated animals that emerged during evolution's millions of years of mammalian experimentation was a primate that possessed an innate curiosity for the world. It evolved to walk upright on its legs, thus freeing its forelimbs forever from mere locomotion. It also learned how to conquer its animal fear of fire and thus discovered it could use the flames of burning trees and bushes to cook meat, light the dark night, and protect itself from hungry enemies. The clever creature eventually also discovered how to use stones to make tools and weapons that would help it survive and even thrive in a harsh natural world. That primate was our early human ancestor. As its descendants, we have inherited the quality of curiosity that has led us to experiment with other energy sources besides wood and brush. We humans eventually found we could ignite the strange black rocks of coal and the smelly liquid pools of petroleum. We learned that these flaming fuels could provide us with heat, light, and protection from wild animals.

Humans have used petroleum for at least 5,000 to 6,000 years, and no doubt longer. Egyptian tombs from as far back as 4,000 years ago contain pictures of people using oil for food production. In what is now Iraq, the ancient Sumerians, Assyrians, and Babylonians collected the crude oil and asphalt (called "pitch" in the Bible) that seeped up from some locations along the Euphrates River. The Greek historian Herodotus mentions that the Babylonians even used asphalt in constructing the walls and towers of their great cities. And crude oil was used by the ancient Persians and Egyptians as a medicine for wounds, as well as fuel to light the homes of the nobles in their society. As far back as 8,000 years ago, natural gas played a religious role in the Baku region of present-day Azerbaijan. Gas seeps, probably initially set on fire by lightning strikes, burned as "eternal flames" that were worshiped by the ancient Persian people.[7]

In what is now France, coal was used by people as a combustion source for fire and light many thousands of years ago. In ancient Britain, during the Bronze Age, people used coal for religious and other purposes. Archeologists have found traces of this hydrocarbon burned in funeral pyres from this ancient period.[8] And in the first century, one Roman traveler wrote of viewing a brazier of burning coal on the altar of Minerva in the town of Aquae Sulis, where the modern British city of Bath now stands. The Chinese also found practical uses for fossil fuels and may have been the first civilization to use coal to change the chemical composition of ores and metals. Some historians believe that as far back as 3,000 years ago, coal from northeastern China's Fushun mine was burned in primitive furnaces to smelt copper, and 2,500 years ago, the Chinese might have been the first to use natural gas for practical purposes by piping this hydrocarbon from wells and igniting it under large pans of seawater to evaporate the liquid to produce salt.[9] Ancient

Chinese and Japanese records also allude to natural gas being used to heat and light imperial palaces and the homes of nobles. And more than 500 years ago, people in China began to drill wells using bamboo and iron bits to reach oil reservoirs 2,000 feet below ground.

Fossil fuels were also used in North America during ancient eras. Archeologists have determined that during the 1300s, the Hopi Indians living in what is now the American Southwest dug up coal and burned it to cook their food, heat their homes, and bake hard their clay pottery. Some Native American tribes also used pitch to waterproof their canoes and as a medicine. In 1510, Christopher Columbus found asphalt on the island of Trinidad. On his way back to Mexico during his exploration of the New World, the Spanish conquistador Hernando de Soto passed through the Texas Gulf Coast region in 1543 and discovered asphalt, which he used to waterproof his expedition's boats. In 1627, near present-day Cuba, New York, the Franciscan priest Joseph de la Roche d'Allion witnessed a *fontaine de bitume* (a fountain of oil) and described this wonder in his journal. When the Europeans came to North America for exploration and settlement during the sixteenth century, they charted the New World's wilderness and, among its vast resources, found other fossil fuels, such as the coal deposits discovered by Louis Joliet and Father Jacques Marquette along the Illinois River. These resources in North America were not exploited except for a few coal mines in the 1700s. The start of the industrial revolution during the second half of the 1700s, however, quickly changed that situation as fossil fuels began playing an increasingly important role in empowering our young and ambitious American nation with new technology.[10]

THE BIRTH OF THE FOSSIL-FUEL AGE

A Scottish engineer and inventor named James Watt played perhaps the most important role in creating the modern fossil-fuel age. As a young man in the eighteenth century, he made mathematical calculating instruments for wealthy amateur scientists. But in the year 1764, the destiny of the world was dramatically changed when one of his patrons asked him to repair a broken model of a Newcomen steam engine. A practical-minded fellow, Watt carefully analyzed the design and realized it was highly inefficient because it lost enormous amounts of steam energy during operation. With his knack for finding ways to improve gadgets, Watt worked on making the device much more productive in its power output. In 1769, he received his first patent for his energy-efficient steam engine design. (Today, the "watt," a unit of measurement for electrical power, is named in honor of this father of the industrial revolution.) Putting scientific discovery to industrial use, Watt began to manufacture his newly improved steam engines on a commercial basis. Among his initial customers were the owners of Cornish copper mines, who used his device for pumping water from out of their underground operations. Soon flour, paper, cotton, and iron mills and whiskey distilleries also began widely using his revolutionary machine.

Long before Watt's steam engine, much of England's verdant woodlands had been cut down for use as charcoal to fuel iron making in blast furnaces as well as for building homes and sailing ships. Facing an impending fuel crisis, England discovered its abundant coal deposits could serve as an alternative energy source to wood. By the year 1700, the island-nation annually produced 2.7 million tons of this fossil fuel. A hundred years later, Watt's steam engine significantly increased the yearly need for coal production in England to about 10 million tons. During the first half of the nineteenth century, Watt's coal-powered contraption found many new practical uses, including as a power source for ocean-crossing ships and locomotive trains that raced on rails crisscrossing England, Europe, Asia, Australia, and the Americas. Watt's steam engine helped usher in a new age of invention, spawning technological innovations that required a cheap and easily obtainable source of energy for manufacturing and power. The large deposits of coal buried underground in Europe and the United States helped power the first stages of the industrial revolution.[11]

Widespread coal usage also helped lead to the growing consumption of petroleum oil as a fossil fuel around the midnineteenth century. Ironically, oil became popular with the public for a reason today's environmentalists would probably applaud. During this time, humans hunted thousands of sperm whales in the world's oceans and slaughtered them merely for the natural oil these leviathans contained. The fuel obtained from these cetaceous creatures was sold as a product to light lamps in American and European homes. But as the whale population became depleted due to unregulated hunting, the price of this biologically produced oil became prohibitively expensive for most people. The cost of a gallon of whale oil reached an astronomical high of $1.77 in 1856 (about $44.56 at today's consumer price index value).[12] People also began to worry about the impending fuel crisis that would come when the last whale was taken from the seas.

A Canadian geologist named Dr. Abraham Gesner came up with an ingenious solution to this crisis. He discovered that refined petroleum oil could substitute for whale oil. Up until that time, petroleum oil was a major nuisance for most people when they found the sticky substance seeping up from the ground on their property. But Gesner saw the energy possibilities in this annoyance. In 1849, he applied techniques similar to those used by whiskey distillers to refine this fluid hydrocarbon and manufacture a new product he called keroselain. (Over time, it would be more commonly known as kerosene.) The public quickly took to this new alternative energy source because it proved much cheaper to purchase than whale oil; it did not spoil, as whale oil did; and it did not have whale oil's offensive odor when it burned in a lamp. Gesner's popular invention of kerosene started a petroleum boom in the 1850s. By 1860, the United States had thirty petroleum refineries distilling kerosene to illuminate American homes.[13]

At first, most petroleum used in the kerosene-manufacturing process was produced by skimming the fossil fuel off of ponds and lakes where it floated on the water's surface. But the rising public demand for kerosene grew so great that this production method quickly became inefficient. A better technique to produce commercial quantities of petroleum oil was needed. An enterprising American named Edwin Drake came up with it. He believed that oil could be found buried deep in reservoirs, much like water is retained in underground aquifers. And just like water, a well could be drilled through the soil and rock to procure the petroleum. Although some people scoffed that Drake's "oil well" idea was an impractical one that would never work, he persisted in his goal of digging for the liquid fossil fuel. On August 27, 1859, near the town of Titusville in northwestern Pennsylvania, Drake struck "black gold" in the world's first commercially successful oil well.[14] That date marked the birth of America's modern petroleum industry.

With Drake's find, America's oil rush began in earnest. Many speculators saw a means to get rich quick in the burgeoning new energy business. Wherever there was a major oil find, boomtowns sprang up seemingly overnight around the site. Soon, Pennsylvania's landscape was dotted with towering derricks that gushed fountains of black crude. Many daring entrepreneurs made big bucks from the boom, but even more lost their investment money. Among the thousands who failed to strike it rich was a young actor named John Wilkes Booth, who in 1864 lost his money after unsuccessfully speculating in Pennsylvania oil. Six months later he would assassinate President Abraham Lincoln.[15]

Following Lincoln's death and the end of the Civil War, the American nation turned to the task of rebuilding itself and healing the shattered lives of its people. Many citizens saw the growing new oil industry as their financial salvation. In January 1865, speculators discovered a major oil reservoir in Pennsylvania near an area now known as Oil Creek Valley. A community with the peculiar name of Pithole soon sprung forth there, and by September of that year it had a population of about 15,000 people. Pithole would go down in history as America's biggest oil boomtown. Two years later, as oil strikes grew increasingly infrequent and there were few prospects for a solid financial future in petroleum, the town's population dropped to about 2,000 citizens.[16] The story of Pithole symbolizes the problems that a limited supply of fossil fuels can bring to a local economy. Fueling the dream, however, some individuals did strike it rich in petroleum. Among the few U.S. entrepreneurs who became financially wealthy from the nineteenth century's newly emerging oil industry, none is more famous than John D. Rockefeller. More than any other individual, this ambitious man set in motion the expansive growth of America's big oil business.

BIG OIL

In 1858, at the age of nineteen, the scrupulously puritanical Rockefeller started on his path to a massive fortune. With a neighbor friend named Maurice Clark, the highly serious young lad formed a business enterprise selling grain, hay, meat, and other goods. Rockefeller's natural mercantile talent, along with his mental acuity with numbers, led to their company's becoming a thriving success supplying food and general goods items to the Union Army during the Civil War. But Rockefeller realized that with the war's end, his winning business model would also terminate. So in 1863, he decided to venture into the newly emerging petroleum oil industry. Seeing the boom and busts of the oil towns, he wisely chose to go into a segment of the business he believed would be much more financially stable—refining the oil that other people drilled.

Forming a team of business partners, Rockefeller set up a company that stood on the cutting edge of oil-refining technology. The company built refineries that were much more efficient at producing kerosene than their competitors. It owned the oil-barrel-making plants, as well as its own New York City warehouse and boats to transport the petroleum to customers. Expanding its business enterprise even wider, the company became the first to ship petroleum oil products by using tank cars on railroad lines. And Rockefeller found ways to generate even greater wealth for his company by using and selling the various "waste" products that came from manufacturing kerosene. Among these by-products was a high-quality lubricating oil sold to grease the nation's machinery, the cleaning fluid benzene, and paraffin wax used to manufacture candles and waterproof paper. Another derivative product called gasoline, which Rockefeller's company sold as a cheap fuel, would years later create a far more lucrative market for the oil industry than kerosene ever could.

So successful did Rockefeller's oil-refining business grow that on January 10, 1870, he formed the Standard Oil Company of Ohio. At the time of its creation, the company controlled only about 10 percent of the world's oil business. But over the next decade, by using the company's influence with the railroads in transporting its product throughout the United States, Rockefeller and his ruthless business partners forced many smaller oil companies to merge with Standard Oil. The company thus grew into a monopoly that held almost complete control of America's oil production and refining. This tremendous control that Standard Oil maintained over our nation's petroleum fuel worried many citizens, including President Theodore Roosevelt, who worked to increase the federal government's regulatory power over monopolistic business practices. After years of legal wrestling between the federal government and Rockefeller's corporate lawyers, in 1911 the United States Supreme Court ruled that Standard Oil's stranglehold on the petroleum industry was illegal. The justices then ordered the company divided into thirty-four new business operations.[17] Among the oil companies formed were Standard Oil of New York (which eventually became Mobil), Standard Oil of New Jersey (which later became Esso and then Exxon), and Standard Oil of California (which is now Chevron).

ELECTRIFYING THE WORLD

Modern civilization has become highly dependent on coal as well as oil, and it is in part due to the knowledge Benjamin Franklin gave the world when his famous kite-flying experiment proved that lightning was electricity. For many years after Franklin's famous discovery of the phenomenon of moving electrons, electricity was viewed by the general public as a mere scientific curiosity without any real practical application. That all started to change when Samuel Morse invented the telegraph and Alexander Graham Bell invented the telephone, thus proving there were commercial uses for electricity as a means of long-distance communication. But it was the American-born inventor Thomas Edison and the Serb-American electrical engineering genius Nikola Tesla who truly electrified the world for the benefit of all humanity.

Edison's technical improvements of incandescent electric light (the idea was half a century old by the time he got around to tackling it) helped to spark the public's imagination to the true potential offered by modern conveniences powered by electricity. On New Year's Eve in 1879, "the Wizard of Menlo Park" publicly demonstrated his electric light by illuminating his New Jersey laboratory to the amazement of his holiday guests. But it would take several more years for Edison to fully give birth to the electric industry by building the world's first commercial power station. Located in New York City's lower Manhattan district, the plant went into operation on September 4, 1882. Powered by burning coal that turned steam turbines, the electricity generated at this prototype plant provided electric power and light to customers within a one-square-mile area around Pearl Street.

Electricity over the next decade made a slow but steady climb in public use. Its real boost in popularity came in 1893 in Chicago, at the World's Columbian Exposition. There, nearly 28 million people (at a time when census records show the total U.S. population was 62.6 million) saw for the first time how electricity could bless their lives with comfort and convenience. Also called the Chicago's World Fair, the great gathering provided Americans with a central location where they could see exhibits demonstrating many modern wonders of the world. Electricity was the star of the show. Searchlights created ornamental electric "fountains" that astonished drop-jawed visitors. Massive pavilions showed off the potential of the latest in electric gadgetry, including electric home appliances, electric burglar alarms, an electric coat-thief detector, and an electric chair. But the real revolutionary history made at the exposition was hardly noticed by most visitors. The fair served as the proving ground for Tesla's alternating current (AC) system, which provided a more efficient way than Edison's direct current (DC) system to power electric products. This first large-scale demonstration of AC power, as well as the practical technologies that it could be applied to, helped inspire the public to imagine the potential benefits electricity could give America and the world.[18]

After the Chicago's World Fair, the surge to electrify the United States began in earnest. Accompanying it was an increasing demand for more fossil-fuel production to satisfy the public hunger for electric power. This growing need proved to be a financial boom for the coal industry, which sold much of its ore product to the thousands of power plants being built throughout America. But the popularity of the electric light also brought a decline in profits for the petroleum oil industry. The American public no longer wanted to deal with messy and highly flammable kerosene lamps when, at the flick of a wall switch and with no unpleasant kerosene odor, they could enjoy the ease of electric illumination in their homes and offices. Oil companies faced an uncertain future as the demand for kerosene steadily declined with electricity's rapid rise. However, a new invention called the horseless carriage would soon bring the petroleum industry a business bonanza opportunity.

AUTOMOBILES AND AMERICA

When Karl Benz patented a design for his three-wheel automobile in Mannheim, Germany, in 1886, he set in motion major technological changes that would dramatically shape the political and social world. At first, the public saw cars powered by combustion engines as too unreliable for practical purposes. Automobiles were considered luxury toys only the very rich could afford. But then Henry Ford, a self-educated engineer who once worked for the Edison Illuminating Company, took up the hobby of tinkering with his own automobile and devoted his spare time to improving on the concept of engine-propelled vehicles. On June 4, 1896, Ford test-drove his first automobile design—a conveyance he called the Quadricycle—on the streets of Detroit. It was essentially a gasoline-powered four-wheel cart, but this odd-looking contraption proved to be the prototype for more technically sophisticated vehicles in the near future.

The Detroit inventor formed his Ford Motor Company in 1903 with the intention of mass-producing inexpensive cars for ordinary people. By 1908, his factories were cranking out the Model T, which sold for $825, a price affordable for the average American. By 1914, more than half a million of these popular cars were churning up the dust of American roads.[19] The cost of the vehicles kept falling as assembly-line production methods were significantly refined and as parts-manufacturing techniques improved. Ford's idea for selling low-cost automobiles revolutionized the world of transportation as millions of ordinary

Americans purchased his cars in ensuing years. For the first time, ordinary people could enjoy the newfound freedom of being able to travel wherever the dirt roads of early-twentieth-century America would take them. City dwellers could ride in Ford cars into the country to enjoy an afternoon picnic, while farmers and ranchers could travel into town more easily than by horse and buggy to sell their agricultural goods and pick up supplies. And Ford's factories also created job opportunities for the millions of workers across the nation who provided the raw materials necessary for manufacturing these newfangled horseless carriages. America began revving up its engines in both a literal and an industrial sense.

About the same time that electric-powered lighting reduced kerosene demand, the petroleum companies saw Ford's mass production of the automobile as their financial salvation. The vehicle's combustion engine could run on gasoline refined from oil, so the increasing need for gasoline caused a surge in the need for petroleum production. Not only was petroleum refined into gasoline fuel, but it also began to be widely used in laying down asphalt for city streets and country roads throughout the United States. American automobile drivers and passengers could now roll smoothly along on their travels without the inconvenience of navigating through dust and mud.

The development of modern factory-based car production methods and the construction of better roads across the United States also had another significant impact on the rising use of fossil fuels in America. Other businesses borrowed Henry Ford's assembly-line system and began mass-producing goods more cheaply and reliably than they ever could by individual hand labor alone. Those factories needed coal power to operate their equipment and machinery. Those mass-produced consumer products also needed to be transported by rail and over roads to America's towns and cities. The newly emerging national distribution system also created a greater need for oil to run in vehicle engines. And popular home products such as washing machines, radios, and other appliances also dramatically increased the need for electricity generated by coal. America suddenly found itself with an exponentially growing appetite for fossil fuels.

OIL OUT WEST

Pennsylvania was the oil industry's most productive state during the last half of the nineteenth century, but the American West came to rule in petroleum production during the first half of the twentieth century. Oil had been drilled in Texas since 1866, but the amounts produced from these sagebrush wells were relatively minor compared to those of East Coast strikes. In 1888, a crew of drillers near the Texas town of Nacogdoches struck an oil field that produced up to 300 barrels a day, helping to attract other oil speculators to the state. Among them was Patillo Higgins, a self-taught geologist who had only one arm because, as a young man, he had lost the other in a shoot-out with a sheriff's deputy. Higgins saw the future potential of petroleum for America—and for himself. He noticed a salt-capped hill that the locals in the dry southeastern region of Texas called Spindletop. Around this site, sulfur springs flowed and natural gas seepages ignited in flames when lit by a match. Spindletop might have a huge pool of petroleum under it, Higgins reasoned, so he and other investors created the Gladys City Oil, Gas, and Manufacturing Company for the purpose of exploiting the site. For more than a decade, they drilled exploratory holes, losing money and having little to show for their efforts. Finally, on January 10, 1901, the company drilled to a depth of 1,139 feet and a gusher of oil shot 100 feet to the sky. It took nine days to control the well as its seemingly endless supply of crude formed a large black lake near the derrick. Known as the Lucas Gusher, after one of the company's investors, the well produced more than 100,000 barrels a day—a world record at that time. More important, it proved that the Lone Star State had huge reserves of petroleum under its immense real estate. That fact lured other money-eyed speculators. Only two years after Higgins's famous Spindletop strike, hundreds of other oil companies were formed in Texas, and several of them would eventually become big-name players, such as Texaco, Amoco, and Exxon (which originated as the Humble Oil Company and was consolidated in 1959 with Standard Oil Company of New Jersey).[20]

California also became a major oil industry player during the first half of the twentieth century. The famous La Brea Tar Pits in Los Angeles had long given evidence that petroleum might indeed be found in that basin area. The first oil well, however, was drilled by hand in 1861 in Humboldt County, in the far northern reaches of California, although it was in the southern portion of the state where major oil strikes subsequently occurred, in Ventura and Los Angeles counties. In 1896, America's first offshore oil well was drilled from piers built over the Pacific Ocean in Santa Barbara County. It wasn't until 1899, however, when the discovery of a vast oil field in Kern County, in California's Central Valley, made the Golden State a serious national contender in oil production. In 1900, California produced about 4.3 million barrels of oil each year. Five years later, it reached 34 million barrels a year. With the car-driving public's unquenchable demand for gasoline growing only greater, the state's annual production leaped to 103.4 million barrels a year by 1920.[21]

Besides automobiles, the technology of modern warfare also generated an increasing demand for fossil fuels. The great global conflicts of World War I and World War II required vast supplies of petroleum and coal to power military airplanes, tanks, jeeps, and ships, as well as to provide energy to run the factories that manufactured military equipment. The start of the cold war between the Soviet Union and the United States, along with the rise of the military-industrial complex following World War II, raised the national thirst for fossil fuels to ever greater levels.

After World War II, many of America's GIs came home from the European, North African, and Pacific fronts with a desire to start families and successful careers. With the major population boom that followed their return, large tracts of suburban homes were quickly built. New families began filling their houses with the latest in shiny electrical appliances and parking in their garages the latest models of gas-guzzling cars. American service people who had been based in Europe thought it would be pleasant to drive their new automobiles down wide highways, similar to the modern Autobahn they had seen in Germany. Led by President Dwight D. Eisenhower, the federal government began building the Interstate Highway System that connected many of the nation's cities and towns with multilane paved roads. The development of passenger jet planes in the 1950s, as well as wide-body jumbo jets such as the Boeing 747 (which first came into service in January 1970), linked through commercial air travel the cities of America with the rest of the world. These airplanes burned millions of gallons of petroleum-based jet fuel. At no other time in human history did a civilization become so overwhelmingly dependent on a limited source of energy.

IMPORTED OIL

The nation's growing dependency on fossil fuels put in peril our way of life, however. In the postwar years, many people in the United States came to realize the vital necessity of preserving American oil production for future military use and economic strength. Politicians also knew that America's oil fields were limited, and so they cast an eye toward creating a strong U.S. presence overseas. America had started down the road that led to a growing reliance on oil from foreign sources.

Another major factor added tension to America's growing imports of foreign oil. The Organization of Petroleum Exporting Countries (OPEC) came into existence in September 1960, when Iraq's government invited representatives from Saudi Arabia, Iran, Kuwait, and Venezuela to Baghdad to discuss the production of oil and the mutual coordination of petroleum prices for maximum profit. Over time, OPEC added other nations, such as Qatar in 1961, Indonesia in 1962, the United Arab Emirates in 1967, Algeria in 1969, Nigeria in 1971, and Angola in 2007. The OPEC member nations now control two-thirds of the world's oil reserves, placing the United States in a severe political handicap because of our economic dependence on its supply.

Currently, the OPEC cartel produces about 42 percent of the oil required by the world's industrial nations. Much like the monopoly that U.S. oil tycoon Rockefeller's Standard Oil Company had a century ago, OPEC's control of so much of the world's supply of petroleum has given it a powerful stranglehold on the global economy for the last several decades. The result for the United States has been costly political and social consequences. We first saw the influence of OPEC's power over the world's energy supply on October 17, 1973, when its Arab nation members imposed an oil embargo against Western nations in retaliation for several European countries and the United States providing Israel with military supplies during the Yom Kippur War fought against Egypt and Syria. The embargo resulted in a five-month "energy crisis," during which the price of oil doubled virtually overnight and continued to rise with reduced supply.[22] The effects of this crisis quickly rippled through the U.S. economy, causing the costs of gasoline and electric power to rise. Higher manufacturing and transportation costs resulted, creating a major recession in our economy that caused many Americans to lose their jobs. Suddenly, Americans truly began to realize the frightening fact that a major dependence on fossil fuels from foreign sources could severely jeopardize our quality of life.

During this crisis period, Americans began discussing earnestly the use of non-fossil-fuel sources such as wind and solar power. But once OPEC lifted the embargo and the supply of oil from the Middle East returned to a normal flow, public talk of alternative fuels quickly waned. The crisis wasn't an anomaly, however, and we now know that unless we develop clean and renewable-energy sources, we will continue to live under the tyranny of fossil fuels. Because of the unstable politics in the Middle East, our nation has been hit by several more energy crisis situations since 1973. The Iranian Revolution of 1979 and the Gulf War in 1990 both jeopardized our nation's supply of oil and thus hurt our economy. In recent years we've also learned that it isn't only foreign oil sources that can put at risk our nation's economic well-being. There are domestic threats, too, related to the energy industry. For example, in 2001 California endured a statewide electricity crisis because of the failure of deregulation and the unethical business practices of energy companies such as Enron Corporation. And in the near future, our nation's oil supply faces an ever-growing threat as the availability of economically viable petroleum diminishes at the same time that demand for oil in industrializing China and India dramatically increases.

The challenges we have undergone in the past will almost certainly be viewed as relatively minor compared to what we will face in the future if we, as a nation, fail to take greater control over our energy needs. Fortunately, this looming crisis comes at a time when we are now developing technologies that will enable us to take advantage of non-fossil-fuel sources of energy. We Americans possess two valuable resources—our intelligence and our imagination—that will enable us to develop realistic solutions to our energy problems. We can and must use the innovative spirit our nation has long cherished to deal with our present fossil-fuel challenge. In the 1850s, American entrepreneurs invented a practical way to distill petroleum to manufacture kerosene, solving our first "oil crisis" at a time when the nation's supply of whale oil became threatened by overhunting. And in our present energy crisis here in the first decades of the twenty-first century, we have even more sophisticated methods at hand that will enable us to take advantage of energy sources that are cleaner and more reliable than fossil fuels. We'll take a close look at those alternative energy solutions in our next chapter.

CHAPTER 3

The Dawn of a New Energy Era

At the dawn of the twentieth century, few Americans could have imagined the technological marvels future generations would enjoy ten decades later. In the early 1900s, most people traveled along dirt roads in horse-drawn vehicles that averaged about 5 miles an hour. Today, we think nothing of motoring cross-country on paved highways at more than 65 miles an hour. A hundred years ago, Orville and Wilbur Wright were still test piloting their pioneering flying machines. Today, people board jumbo jets daily to fly in comfort at 30,000 feet above oceans and continents. A century ago, telephones were fairly primitive contraptions that required callers to first contact a human operator at a switchboard before being connected. Today, affordable cell phones stored in our pockets and purses not only provide us with instant voice communication but also serve as cameras and connect us to the information on the Internet. A century ago, humans dared venture on celestial journeys only in Jules Verne and H. G. Wells stories. Today, rockets regularly launch satellites and people into Earth's orbit, and robotic probes bound across the vacuum of space to land on and explore neighboring planets. At the dawn of the twentieth century, while many physicists thought humanity had reached the limits of scientific discovery, a patent clerk in Switzerland tinkered with the revolutionary notion that matter and energy were interchangeable. Albert Einstein's research provided the basis for modern nuclear reactors and atomic weapons. And the integrated circuits inside much of the digital technology that we take for granted today, such as computers and global positioning systems, are based on the principles of quantum mechanics that ingenious physicists discovered during the last 100 years.

We now enjoy the technological fruits of the most inventive time in all of human history. But the possibilities for ever more phenomenal advances are even greater in the next hundred years. If we can continue our amazing streak of innovation—and there does not yet seem to be any practical limit to what our minds can achieve if we can only imagine the possibilities—our children and grandchildren will enjoy a world of wonders now seen only in science fiction stories.

The only real certainty we have for predicting future marvels is that just as technological progress in the last hundred years needed energy to operate, tomorrow's advanced gadgets and gizmos will also require a reliable supply of power to function. Our children's and grandchildren's world will need energy—and plenty of it. And it is highly unlikely that this energy will still be produced by consuming oil, coal, and natural gas at the accelerating rates we are presently experiencing. The more encouraging scenario is that in the future the world will have greatly expanded its use of environmentally friendly, renewable-energy sources to replace dwindling supplies of fossil fuels. By setting a realistic course for developing a clean-fuel infrastructure today, people in the not-too-distant future will benefit greatly from the power provided from the sun, wind, water, biofuels, and geothermal energy, and possibly from controlled fusion power.

Let's now consider the various alternative energy sources that could potentially help us achieve our energy independence, examining them on a historical and scientific basis, as well as where they technologically stand in their present development. We'll also discuss the positive and negative aspects of each technology as a form of power for today's America, as well as for our nation in the near future.

SUN POWER

On a scorching day in summer, sidewalks can be baked so hot by mid-afternoon that you can literally fry an egg on them. And the water inside a garden hose, if it's left directly in the line of the sun's radiation, can get so hot it can scald your skin. The amount of sunshine striking the surface of our planet annually provides more than 10,000 times the amount of energy that all of humanity can use in a year. If we could harvest only a fraction of that solar radiation, human civilization could easily end its dependence on Earth's fossil-fuel reserves. Sun power dramatically impacts our world in many ways. Every day, it affects the lives of everyone on our planet by holding sovereign reign over our weather, our crops, our economy, and the course of human civilization. But we tap into only a tiny bit of this cornucopia of energy streaming from the sun. Solar-produced electricity makes up less than 1 percent of the world's production of power. Yet the solar-energy industry is starting to emerge as technology makes leaps in improvements. Over the last fifteen years, solar-energy production has increased by 30 percent annually while the price for photovoltaic (PV) power has dropped an average of 4 percent a year during that time period. The energy source is also seen in a positive light by many Americans. A 2007 Roper Center for Public Opinion Research survey found that 87 percent of Americans believe newly constructed houses should offer solar panels as a feature to home buyers.[1]

People have long employed the energy of the sun. The power from our star has been used over the centuries to dry clothes, to dehydrate animal meat and fruits to preserve them, and to keep homes warm in winter. In Greece during the second century before the common era, the sun's power might have been used as a powerful "death ray" weapon against the Roman fleet intent on invading the city of Syracuse on the island of Sicily.[2] The brilliant Greek mathematician Archimedes is alleged to have invented a giant mirror that concentrated the sun's heat energy into a beam that set afire the sails of enemy ships as they approached. Although this story is no doubt apocryphal, it shows that the ancients understood the strength of the sun's radiant power and how it might be used for practical purposes of national security.

Today, solar energy is still at the early stages of its modern technological development. We as a nation are just beginning to understand how to plug into the power of the sun for the benefit of civilization's near-term and long-term future—by building homes and offices that are designed to use solar power based on the principles of architecture and by incorporating construction material manufactured to absorb and retain the sun's radiant heat. We have examples from ancient cultures of these "passive systems" of solar-power use. The Romans 2,000 years ago were particularly ingenious in building mansions and bath houses that used the sun's rays to heat them. And the ancient Anasazi people, who lived more than a thousand years ago in what is now the Southwest region of the United States, brilliantly constructed "cities" tucked into the recesses of cliffs that remained cool when shaded in summer months and were warmed by the sun's energy in the winter.[3]

In the last few decades, as fossil fuels have become more costly to produce, we have seen a steadily rising popularity in the use of "active systems" to exploit solar energy. One of the most common uses of this harvesting of sun power is to heat water in homes and swimming pools. Many American homes now have flat-plate solar collectors that raise the temperature of water by harvesting the sun's energy. In these devices, cool water passes through a web of tubes in thin metal plates that are painted black to more efficiently absorb the sun's radiant heat. The solar heat is then absorbed by the water and the liquid's temperature rises up to 180 degrees Fahrenheit (82 degrees Celsius). This hot water is transferred to an insulated tank, where it is stored for later use.

One exciting development in solar energy incorporates the concentrated heat principles credited to Archimedes' legendary "death ray" device. Engineers in locations with sunny climates, such as Italy, Spain, France, and California, have designed and built giant versions of the Greek scientist's famous mirror invention. Instead of applying the sun's rays for battle purposes, however, the sunshine collected is used to generate electricity in a large solar power plant. Hundreds of flat mirrors are set in an arrangement that aims the sun's light onto a central receiver mounted on a tower. The receiver is filled with synthetic oil that absorbs the sun's energy and raises the liquid's temperature to more than 1,100 degrees Fahrenheit (600 degrees Celsius). The hot oil is then pumped to another location in the plant where its energy is used to boil water and thus produce steam to mechanically drive a turbine linked to an electric generator. A 2008 study suggested that this type of thermal technology could provide up to 90 percent of America's electricity needs, including running a national fleet of electric cars.[4]

Another major innovation in solar energy comes to us as a gift from midtwentieth-century space exploration. Scientists needed to find a way to provide power for communications and military satellites that NASA planned to rocket into Earth's orbit. Fossil-fuel-powered satellites would be impractical because of their exceptionally heavy weight at launch and very limited life span. Nuclear-powered satellites might work better, but they came with an unacceptable danger of contaminating land and oceans if a launch failed or when the satellite eventually plunged back to Earth. The scientists reasoned that the best solution to their satellite-fuel problem was to use the sun to provide a free and steady source of energy. Bell Labs researchers invented PV cells (also called photoelectric cells) that absorb direct sunlight to generate electricity. Employing a manufacturing process similar to that used for computer chips, these cells are made from a large crystal of silicon that is sawed into thin circular wafers. Today, PV technology originally developed for satellites is used in other, more commonplace applications, from ordinary pocket calculators to roadside-emergency call boxes. In recent years, the cost to manufacture PV cells has dropped considerably, so they are increasingly becoming a feature of modern office buildings and suburban homes. And as the price for manufacturing these energy-producing devices drops even more in the near future, it might become unremarkable to one day see many acres of glistening PV panels installed across America's desert regions to generate electricity and transmit it to communities through power lines. A key to achieving commercial success with PV cells is for mass-manufacturing techniques to steadily improve and thus drive the costs of these devices down. The cost of producing PV modules, in constant dollars, has fallen from $50 per watt in 1980 to as little as $3 per watt today, according to the U.S. Department of Energy. With an accelerated rise in competition for this potentially huge market, we'll see continuing price reductions, making it more and more affordable in coming years.

Besides photovoltaic technology, there are other exciting new developments now being produced by scientists working in solar-energy innovation. Some are low-tech and low-cost, such as a "solar pond" concept, whereby the sun's heat is trapped in a layer of saltwater and later used to warm buildings and generate electricity. Another possible development, one that still awaits invention, is a process using tiny nanotechnology "power plants" to absorb the sunlight in a chemical reaction. Much like the process of photosynthesis, which occurs in the chlorophyll of green vegetation, this artificial process might one day collect the sun's photon energy and store it for later use by human beings.[5] It might also conceivably be a way to pull carbon dioxide out of the atmosphere and thus help reduce the effects of global warming. Although no one has yet practically achieved this system, we know it is possible. If it is a process that already exists in nature, then scientists can also surely discover the secret.

Another futuristic use of solar energy sounds like something right out of a James Bond movie. Some scientists have proposed launching a series of 50-square-kilometer sun satellites in geostationary orbit 36,000 kilometers over the planet's equatorial region. The PV panels on these satellites would collect the sun's energy and beam it down as microwaves to a ground-based receiving station. This system would have the benefit of generating energy twenty-four hours a day—with an occasional lapse whenever a solar eclipse would shut down its operation for a short time.[6] At this point in history, however, this highly advanced system would be extremely expensive to implement because it would require many rocket and space vehicle launches to carry astronauts and material into orbit to build and maintain it.

Solar energy has its pluses and minuses. Its greatest benefit is the fact that sunshine comes to us free from the star that our planet orbits. Also, no one has any political or economic monopoly on solar energy, and it is an environmentally friendly power because it is nonpolluting and involves no combustion of fuels here on Earth. It also comes from a source that won't become depleted anytime soon—the sun has been streaming out energy into space for about 4.6 billion years and scientists estimate it will continue to do so for another 5 or 6 billion years. Another benefit to solar energy is that in sunny environments such as Australia and equatorial Africa, it can be used in remote locations where it is too impractical to install transmission lines to power plants.

The use of solar energy on a wide scale, however, does have several drawbacks at this present time in its technological development. The chief problem is the fact that it is not yet cost-competitive with fossil-fuel energy. The PV cells and the infrastructure to support them still have not reached a crucial price threshold to make them competitive with fossil-fuel-generating plants. That situation, however, will change in the next decade as fossil-fuel costs rise and mass-production techniques for PV cells bring their costs substantially down. Another problem with solar energy is that its use depends on the seasonal climate and weather of a location. Geographical places that do not receive much sunlight during the year won't be able to make as much use of solar energy as sunnier spots. A third problem is the obvious fact that sun power can be produced only during daylight hours. During nighttime, solar-energy production ceases until the coming of the new day's dawn. So to use solar power effectively after sunset, it will be necessary for society to develop more efficient and cost-effective energy storage systems and ways to transport power in a specific region. (Solar thermal appears to be close to being cost-competitive and can store heat energy for periods when the sun does not shine.) Despite the significant obstacles, the future for solar power looks bright as scientists and researchers continue to tackle the technological challenges that need to be solved before we can achieve commercial-scale solar-power generation. Human beings are on the verge of devising exciting innovations that will soon result in the dawning of a widespread solar-energy age for America.

WIND POWER

With their fists firmly holding the string of a kite as it soars in an afternoon sky, many children have gained a direct knowledge of one of the world's most abundant energy resources. Although to a youngster's mind it might seem as if some magical force invisibly keeps the aerodynamic toy suspended in the air, the phenomenon is actually based on physical science. The energy producing that kite-lifting breeze originates from the sun. Wind is solar powered. About 2 percent of the sun's energy received by our planet is converted into air motion that varies in force from a light wisp of air to the intense gale of a hurricane or typhoon. No matter what its strength at any given location or moment, the wind is created because the sun's radiation heats the air surrounding our planet. The variation in temperatures causes convection currents that result in the creation of high- and low-pressure zones. Nature always strives to balance its books, so air rushes in from the high-pressure area to the low-pressure area to equalize the two zones. The resulting airflow causes the phenomenon that allows children all over the world to fly their kites.[7]

For many thousands of years, people have made practical use of the wind as a power source. Among its first major applications in ancient times was to power water transportation. Boats and sailing ships caught the wind's energy in their billowing canvases and used it to push people and cargo across lakes, rivers, and oceans. Without the energy from wind to move their vessels, European adventurers would not likely have voyaged to North and South America until many centuries after Christopher Columbus's famous voyage of 1492. Humans have also long used wind energy for agricultural purposes. Recorded evidence of windmills used for milling grain goes back to Persia in the year 644. Like the sailboats that inspired them, these early windmills used giant canvas sails fastened to a radial arm that turned around a center axis. This axle connected to the various gears that mechanically transferred the wind's energy into a movement that turned a heavy grinding stone. Even today, many farms and ranches in the United States continue to employ windmills as a cost-effective way to pump water up from underground aquifers. Take a country drive in almost any American agricultural county and you will still see these relics standing as graceful guardians over pastures and fields.

With the dawn of the industrial revolution, the popularity of wind power began to hit the doldrums. With the convenience and reliability of coal power, factories and farms in Europe and America gradually moved away from windmills and instead used cheap fossil fuel to generate steam that powered the pistons and gears of machinery. Even the sailboat technology that had proved the wind's worth since ancient times was eventually replaced by coal-powered steamboats and steamships. Wind power seemed as if it might be a quaint but outdated technology of the past, but the energy crisis of the mid-1970s helped spark a surprising resurgence in modern times. With the OPEC oil embargo, many Americans awakened to the fact that the industrialized world had developed an unhealthy dependence on fossil fuels. The crisis pushed us to rediscover other resources, and wind power came back into fashion as a clean-energy alternative to hydrocarbons. Scientists, including many at NASA, looked at the old-fashioned windmills and realized these energy-gathering devices could be made much more efficient in harvesting the energy produced when nature stirs the air. Inspired by modern airplane design, innovative scientists developed aerodynamic turbine blades that made more efficient use of the wind to generate electricity.

The last quarter century has witnessed a dramatic revolution in wind-turbine technology around the world, and we are only in the early stages of developing systems to take advantage of this clean and virtually limitless natural energy resource. The United States today gets a little over 1 percent of its electric power supplied by wind energy, which is equal to energizing about 4.5 million homes. We are bound to see this number increase as the number of megawatts provided by wind grows substantially every year. The United States at the start of 2010 was the global leader in total wind power installed, with slightly more than 35,000 megawatts, according to the American Wind Energy Association (AWEA). China was third after Germany on the list, producing just over 25,000 megawatts of wind power at the start of

2010. China is ramping up its wind manufacturing, however, and in 2009 it passed the United States in new installations and in manufacturing of wind turbines. If our nation continues to develop turbine technology and builds a sufficient number of wind farms at locations favorable for this energy source, we could dramatically reduce our fossil-fuel consumption. In theory, the wind flowing over the plains of North Dakota could provide up to 33 percent of America's electric needs.

Something as basic as the breeze will play a key role in helping America achieve its freedom from fossil fuels. Already, great technological strides have been made in harnessing the wind, and more innovations will come in future years, resulting in lower costs for producing power. A study done in 2001 concluded that if the United States installed about 250,000 new turbines across the country, we could produce the equivalent of two-thirds of the electricity generated by our coal plants.[8] Currently, a 1.5-megawatt wind turbine costs about $2 million to set up and as much as $30,000 a year in maintenance costs, so a project of this sort would require a substantial capital investment. But when environmental and health costs are brought into the equation, it is actually cost-competitive with fossil-fuel power. Wind energy will actually save the United States money in the long run compared to the total price of coal power plants.

Like solar power, energy from the wind has its benefits and disadvantages. Because it originates from the sun, the wind is free for every nation to harvest for a long time. Earth will have breezes coursing through its atmosphere for the next several billion years. Wind power also produces no pollution that might contaminate our planet's air and water. Wind turbine towers can be built for people who live far from the electric power grid, thus allowing developing countries with scattered villages to benefit. Rural regions in extremely windy sections of the United States, such as North Dakota and Texas, can greatly gain from constructing wind farms where hundreds of turbines stand in pastureland leased out by farmers. Agricultural counties throughout America could find more local job opportunities and generate additional revenue to build schools and roads as they generate cheap electricity.

Wind power, however, is not a perfect energy solution. Because it is produced by the sun's radiation and its strength is often based on geological location, wind comes inconsistently throughout the day and during various seasons of the year. This intermittence must be made up by other energy sources. Potential wind farm sites are also often far from urban areas, where demand is greater. This means that a substantial amount of money is required to construct transmission lines and substations to bring the wind-generated electricity to customers. Power harvested from the wind must also overcome several common misperceptions the American public has developed about using it. Many people believe that wind turbines are noisy and disturb nearby neighborhoods. Indeed, older turbine technology in the 1980s created a loud racket as the blades turned and gears churned, but that problem has been solved by better and more efficient turbine designs. Most of today's wind turbines make a light whooshing sound that is all but drowned out by ambient wind noises. Despite the lower decibel levels from modern wind turbine technology, residents living near proposed wind-energy developments have expressed to their local government officials their concerns about how the sound of the rotating blades and the sight of the tall towers might lower their quality of life and property values. Another misperception about wind turbines is that they slaughter a high number of bats and birds that unfortunately get caught in the path of the spinning blades. It is true that flying animals are killed by turbines, but the number is quite low. In 2002, the National Wind Coordinating Committee (NWCC) made an analysis of research documents dealing with various causes of avian mortality. Their comparison study found that collisions with spinning wind turbines resulted in about one death for every 10,000 birds killed by collision caused by human activity. Far more birds die by flying into buildings, communication towers, and vehicles. Many more birds are also killed by farming pesticides and house cats allowed to run free outside.[9]

Wind as an energy resource for the United States and the rest of the world will continue to see major growth opportunities as turbine technology improves and mass production reaches a critical cost-effective level.

Although the technology was initially developed in America, the governments of countries such as Germany, Denmark, Spain, and England have provided decades of consistent incentives for wind power, with the result that the technology developed in the United States is being widely manufactured by those countries with all the economic benefits being realized overseas. There's still a huge opportunity to develop wind power as a source of energy in America. Even someone as crazy as the fictional Don Quixote, famous for tilting at windmills in the La Mancha region of Spain, might see the tremendous potential benefits that wind will provide the world.

WATER POWER

Of all the planets in our solar system, Earth is *the* water world. Almost three-quarters of our globe is covered by this versatile liquid substance, most of it in the great oceans that plunge several miles into deep trenches at some points. Powered by the sun's heat and Earth's gravity, all this water is constantly cycled through our global weather system. It evaporates, rising high into the sky, then condenses into clouds and falls back to the ground as rain and snow to eventually course through the channels of rivers and creeks on a never-ending journey.

Human beings long ago learned how to tap into the energy of our planetary water cycle. They discovered that hydropower provided a much more efficient energy alternative compared to muscle power from people and animals. More than 3,000 years ago in the Near East and in Asia, people invented waterwheels and built canals to move river and creek water and thus irrigate crops and drive mills grinding grain.[10] In the last century, massive dams have been constructed throughout the United States and the rest of the world that use the potential energy stored in lake reservoirs to generate electricity. In this system, floodgates in the dams are opened, allowing gravity to pull the reservoir water down a sloping channel where it passes through massive turbines that quickly spin owing to the continuous flowing force. The spinning turbines create an electric current that is sent through transmission lines to homes and businesses in communities miles away.

About 24 percent of the world's electric power is currently produced by hydropower. In America, it makes up 12 percent of the generated electricity and equals about 75 percent of all electricity generated by renewables. There is great potential for even more use throughout the world—especially in South America, Africa, and Asia, which have regions holding large quantities of water. As China industrializes, it sees the opportunities of providing energy for its multitudes from water power. That nation's massive and environmentally controversial Three Gorges Dam, a 1.4-mile (2.25-km) structure along the Yangtze River, is its hallmark hydroelectric power project. Five times as big as Hoover Dam, it created a reservoir that supplies the water for twenty-six generators that can produce as much as 84.7 billion kilowatts' worth of electric power every year.[11]

Despite the many benefits, hydroelectricity has several substantially negative aspects as a power source. The massive dam structures necessary to hold back water are expensive and time-consuming to build. They also require continuous maintenance to make sure they are safe from a calamitous failure that could kill people living downstream. The world has seen several dams give way because of inherent structural faults, and these disasters have caused many people to lose their lives and property. The famous Johnstown Flood of 1889 happened because a Pennsylvania dam broke; the resulting deluge killed 2,209 people.

Dams also have a severe impact on the natural environment, often disrupting the ecology of plants and animals in a location. For example, to provide a water supply for San Francisco, the Hetch Hetchy Valley in the Sierra Mountains was flooded by the O'Shaughnessy Dam, finished in 1923. This valley, a natural wonder of California rivaling nearby Yosemite, was submerged under a large reservoir, much to the lament of environmentalists then and today. Although Hetch Hetchy generates electricity and water for San Francisco's needs, some people have called for the dam to be taken down and the glacial valley to be allowed to return to its natural state. Another environmental impact that might add slightly to global warming comes shortly after a reservoir fills. The resulting lake completely covers the trees, grasses, and shrubs growing in a dammed valley. Methane gas produced by decaying vegetation slowly bubbles up to the surface and mixes into the atmosphere. Like carbon dioxide, methane is a substance that traps the sun's heat in the atmosphere, thus adding to our current climate crisis.

One challenge with hydroelectricity is that it is highly dependent on location and available water sources. Dams generating electric power can be built only where there is enough water to fill a large man-made lake. But in recent years, "run-of-the-river system" sites called microhydro plants have been built that supply electricity to local villages and businesses.[12] These have a much lower construction cost compared to the grand engineering marvels built in the past. Because they don't require the construction of a massive dam project, they also have minimal impact on the natural environment and less capital costs, making them attractive for developing nations, where they can provide power to small towns and villages.

Hydroelectric dams are not the only way to generate power from water. In recent years, engineers have dreamed up other technologies to exploit the energy carried in sea waves. One of the most interesting hydropower concepts is a system that uses the ocean's mighty throbbing to produce electricity. If you have ever stood along the coast and watched the waves crash into the rocks and explode in great blossoms of white spray, you've seen the ocean's potential as an energy storage system. One Department of Energy estimate projects that, theoretically, the ocean wave forces could produce up to 2 terawatts of electric power—equal to 2 trillion watts. Although it is still difficult to harvest this power on a commercial level with present-day technology, several ingenious systems have been devised that, in the near future, might prove economically viable. One method uses air compression produced inside a tubelike chamber whenever an ocean wave passes along. As the water level naturally rises, the air pressure builds up and is forced through a turbine at the top that turns rapidly to generate electric current. When the wave recedes, air is drawn back into the chamber and again passes through the turbine, continuing the production of electric power.[13]

Another invention for an ocean-powered energy source applies the gravitational energy from the rise and fall of the tides. This natural effect is created twice a day by the pull of the moon's mass on the surface of Earth. The celestial attraction lifts up on the water so that a bulge is formed and the tide rises in that location. One technology designed to take advantage of this phenomenon uses large turbines resembling underwater windmills that are placed at channel locations where the tidal current is strong. Pushed by the incoming or outgoing tide, they turn in a continuous cycle and thus generate electricity. A small prototype of this system is being tested in New York City's East River by Verdant Power, a sustainable-energy company, and the power generated is being used by a nearby supermarket. Another proposed tidal-powered system uses a series of damlike barrages that store the water supplied by the incoming tide. After the moon passes along on its orbit around Earth and the daily tide falls to its lowest level, the water held behind the dam is released to pass through turbines for electricity generation. Engineers have suggested that the Severn Estuary in the southwest region of England would be an ideal location for such a tidal dam. They have conceived a design for building a long barrage barrier across the basin that would use 216 turbines to provide about 5 percent of England's electricity needs.[14] The high cost and the considerable environmental impact to the region have kept this project from being approved by England's government.

The future will possibly see even more exotic ways to harvest ocean energy. Right now, these inventions are still in their pioneering stages. With enough research and development, however, they might provide an important energy resource during the coming decades. One novel technology, called ocean thermal energy conversion (OTEC), works on the principle that the sea collects much of the sun's energy that shines on it. As a result, the temperature of the surface water rises. In tropical regions, the surface can be a balmy 68 degrees Fahrenheit (25 degrees Celsius) while the ocean depths a mile (1.6 km) below stay chilly at 36 degrees Fahrenheit (20 degrees Celsius). The OTEC's generator uses the warm seawater to boil liquid propane, which has a low boiling point. This propane steam then turns a generator turbine that creates electricity. Next, the propane gas is cooled and condensed using the cold water that is pumped up to it through a long intake tube reaching down deep into the darker regions of the ocean's depth. The cycle continues with the warm upper-layer water boiling the propane into steam again. An experimental OTEC plant in Hawaii generated up to 50,000 watts of electric power in May 1993. The OTEC system, unfortunately, has a limited use range and can be used only in waters near the equator located near land sites that make it economical for electricity production.[15]

LIFE POWER

Consider a battery that collects energy from the sun and stores it in a system that creates no pollution and costs zero dollars to build. This system has the added benefit of renewing itself and taking carbon dioxide out of Earth's atmosphere, thus reducing global warming. This amazing mechanism also adds visually to the beauty of our nation's cities, towns, and rural areas. This "battery," of course, is green vegetation, the source of all biofuels.

When most people hear the term *biofuels* they usually think of the ethanol and biodiesel that they can pump into their cars in place of petroleum-based gasoline. But on a broader definition of the term, humans have been using biofuels for thousands of years. Historically, one type of "biofuel" was the grain and grass fed to working farm animals such as horses and oxen that plowed the farm fields. A hundred or so years ago, when travel by saddle or horse-drawn carriage was still a common means of getting from one place to another, the hay market provided a profitable source of biofuel. In fact, you and all other human beings are powered by the energy of biofuels. The cells of our bodies break down the chemical fuel that's inside the tossed vegetable salad or meatloaf you might have eaten last night. This fuel is metabolized by your digestive system into energy for you to do activities such as walking across the street, washing the dishes, or reading this book.

Americans are increasingly looking at the biofuels ethanol and biodiesel as alternatives to fossil fuels. Ethanol is an alcohol made from crops such as sugarcane and corn. The plant matter goes through a fermentation and distillation process very similar to how beer and liquors are made. The result is a fuel that burns cleanly and makes engines run smoothly and quietly. Ethanol also has performance power, as demonstrated by the Indy Racing League, which runs the Indianapolis 500 and switched in 2007 from methanol to 100 percent ethanol to fuel its race cars. For thirty years, the U.S. government has kept a cap of a 10 percent ethanol blend in gasoline sold for ordinary vehicles. In October 2010, the EPA raised this to 15 percent for use in cars with a model year of 2007 or later. The agency's concern is that some older cars built before that year face the potential problem of having their engine and fuel system seals eaten away by ethanol, thus damaging these vehicle components. Another problem with ethanol is that it provides less energy per gallon than gasoline, making it potentially more expensive to burn per mile. Biodiesel, on the other hand, is a vegetable oil made from oil-seed crops including canola and soybean. It can be used in most diesel engines with little or no alteration. In fact, back in the 1890s, Rudolf Diesel originally designed his namesake engine to run on peanut oil, a type of biodiesel.[16]

Another large source of biofuels might be found as close as your kitchen sink's waste disposal unit. There's energy gold in the garbage that Americans throw out every day. The millions of tons of vegetation-based refuse produced daily in homes and as industrial waste from food-manufacturing plants is another major source of alternative energy that has not yet been truly tapped. Over time, the vegetable matter breaks down and releases methane, as well as carbon dioxide gases. Modern landfill sites are now starting to be built with a buried web of perforated pipes that collect the methane and carry it to a power station, where it is burned to generate electricity for nearby communities. Farm waste from animals is another important source of biofuel that is only now starting to be better utilized in the United States. America's chicken and turkey farms, for example, produce millions of tons of poultry litter annually. Instead of having to deal with the problem of discarding this dry waste product, our nation's farmers can sell it to power plants as fuel. In Benson, Minnesota, a 55-megawatt power station uses about 500,000 tons of poultry litter and other biomass a year to produce power for about 40,000 homes. The production also provides a fertilizer by-product that can be sold to farms to nourish soils.[17]

Combustible biogas made from the decomposing remains of plants is another biofuel source that is well worth considering for America's energy independence. The remains of vegetable crops and wood can be processed to create a fuel that's a mixture of methane and other gases. This gas is scrubbed clean to rid it of pollutants, then burned to turn an electric turbine. Another system to create biogas uses the humble anaerobic bacteria (microorganisms that can't live in oxygen) to break down animal waste and water-rich vegetation waste. Living in an enclosed metal container kept at a tropical temperature, these microscopic organisms feast on the waste, releasing methane gas as a by-product over a period of a week or two. The gas is then burned to power a generator that produces electricity. The remaining sludge is also put to good use as an environmentally friendly fertilizer sold to farms.[18] Algae might also one day be used on an extensive scale to produce biodiesel for our energy independence. These tiny plants could be grown in vast acres of ponds where they could be harvested for the natural oil they produce.[19] These algae oil farms might be placed next to coal-power facilities where the electricity-producing plant's carbon dioxide exhaust could be pumped into the water and thus absorbed by the tiny organisms.

The wide use of biofuels would provide significant economic benefits to America's farmers and help considerably in weaning ourselves off of foreign oil. It would also help in cleaning the environment by minimizing the release of pollutants contained in fossil fuels. And although burning ethanol and biodiesel fuels does release the greenhouse gas carbon dioxide, it releases approximately as much carbon as was absorbed during the plant growing season and is thus considered carbon neutral because it does not contribute additional carbon to the atmosphere, as fossil fuels do.

Currently, the primary problem with biofuels is that many farmers are not yet using cost-effective techniques to grow crops that can be used as energy feedstocks. Money to pay for the water, fertilizer, and diesel fuel for tractors and harvesting equipment adds to the price of production and makes biofuels—especially corn-based ethanol—less competitive compared with fossil fuels. Another potential problem is that if forests are destroyed to produce feedstocks for biofuels, then more carbon dioxide is released in the forest destruction than could be captured by the biofuel, thereby aggravating the global-climate-change problem. We need to make sure that we are determined to prevent this type of activity. With more efficient technology and better processing methods, we can achieve an increase in mass production of ethanol and biodiesel that will make these biofuels cost-competitive with petroleum products.

Another concern with biofuels is that they might lead to food shortages. Critics warn that competition in using cropland to grow corn and other products for fuel will reduce the availability of food and raise prices at the supermarket. This is a legitimate problem to address. One possible solution is for American farmers to grow hearty prairie grass that requires less water and can thrive in highly degraded and infertile soil while leaving better soil for food production. According to a ten-year study done by University of Minnesota scientists, "prairie hay" harvested on unfertilized ground yielded as much or more new usable energy per acre as did corn for ethanol grown on fertile farmland.[20] Overall, much more research and development needs to be done to implement the large-scale production of biofuels for our nation's transportation needs. But in the next few decades, these fuels will almost certainly help America gain its energy independence from fossil fuels while strengthening our nation's agricultural economy.

NUCLEAR POWER

Billions of years before our solar system came into existence, the early universe was a vastly different place. During this time, hydrogen and helium were the only elements in existence, and these two gases clumped together to form trillions of stars that, over time, produced the heavier elements through the nuclear processes going on deep in their cores. When these stars exploded in spectacular blasts that astronomers call supernovas, they spewed into space vast quantities of various elements of the periodic table, including gold, iron, and—most important for our discussion of nuclear power—uranium. This mixture of star-born elements eventually formed into a vast number of planetary bodies scattered throughout the universe. Among these celestial spheres is the world we call Earth.

The element uranium can be found extensively throughout our home planet. It is just as widespread as tin and 500 times more plentiful than gold.

Our oceans contain uranium in their surging waters, and it is also found in the granite that makes up the mountains that rib Earth's crust. The big problem, however, is that these supplies provide only extremely tiny amounts of uranium per volume. It is presently far too expensive to commercially harvest uranium for energy production from these sources. In certain sites throughout the world, however, nature has accumulated uranium ore in more condensed levels. One such deposit site in what is now Gabon, West Africa, once held so much concentrated uranium that the nuclear forces began a fission chain reaction that generated 100-megawatt levels of heat energy for about 150 million years. Various other locations in Australia and Canada contain uranium in large quantities suitable for humans to mine for electricity generation in nuclear reactors. The uranium is processed into concentrated fuel pellets and placed into rods made of zirconium alloy or stainless steel. These rods are then put into a nuclear reactor's core, where the fission process can be controlled. As the uranium atoms naturally split apart inside this core, they release heat energy. This heat is used to boil water, converting it into steam that is used to turn turbines that generate electric power.[21]

The world's first nuclear power plant went into operation on June 26, 1954, in the Soviet Union, generating 5 megawatts to provide electricity for homes and businesses in the city of Obninsk. A modern plant today produces about 1,000 megawatts of power to supply electricity to 400,000 homes. About 439 nuclear reactors in thirty-one countries are now in operation, producing 16 percent of the world's electric power. The United States has 104 operating reactors, more than any other country, and they produce about 20 percent of our nation's electricity. France, with 59 reactors, comes in second in terms of the number of nuclear power plants, but they generate a total of 78 percent of that country's electricity.[22]

Fifty years ago, Americans dreamed of a nuclear-powered future where they might enjoy cheap and limitless energy released from the atoms. There was talk of energy too cheap to meter. For many reasons, both political and technological, the promise of cheap, abundant nuclear power was never fulfilled. Nuclear power as it stands today, in its fission-reactor state, has its positive and negative aspects. Scientists figure a typical 7-gram pellet of uranium can produce the equivalent of 3.5 barrels of oil, or 1,780 pounds of coal, so a small amount of nuclear fuel can produce a huge amount of energy compared with fossil fuels.[23] Another benefit is that nuclear power releases no air pollution or carbon dioxide or sulfur dioxide gas into our atmosphere during the reaction process. Therefore, it does not directly add to our climate-crisis problem or the threat of acid rain. However, massive amounts of coal and oil are consumed in the mining and processing of uranium, and also in manufacturing the concrete and steel required to construct nuclear-reactor facilities. Nuclear reactors also use large quantities of water, which is itself an energy product.

Nuclear power is also a political hot-button issue in the United States. Although there are many proponents for building more reactors for our future energy needs, Americans have grown wary of nuclear power over the years. Our original optimism for nuclear energy has changed into a cautious concern about its widespread development as an alternative fuel source to hydrocarbons. Much of the public's worry about the potential dangers of fission reactors developed after the 1979 nuclear accident at Three Mile Island near Harrisburg, Pennsylvania, that resulted in a partial meltdown. Compounding these concerns was the disastrous 1986 reactor meltdown at Chernobyl in the Soviet Union. Although modern designs for nuclear reactors promise to provide potentially greater safety than older nuclear plants, scientists and the government still need to work out the details of disposing of the radioactive waste produced in the reactor cores so that future generations of Americans won't face unintended release of radioactive waste into the environment.

Another drawback to nuclear energy might be the overall cost to commercially produce it in the future. A proposed third reactor for Maryland's Calvert Cliffs nuclear power plant, for example, would cost between $2.5 billion and $3 billion for design and construction—and that's if the job gets finished on schedule. Add to this bill another $290 million to $370 million for decommissioning and cleanup costs, as well as for storing the radioactive waste, and the price of fission power rises even higher.[24] Much of this money must come from government subsidies paid for by American taxpayers. In reality, if the history of building nuclear plants is an indicator, the cost over-runs for building new power plants might make them costlier than first estimated—especially if innovative technology is used. "New nuclear reactors represent novel and complex technology that will retain a risk of high costs," according to a 2007 study of nuclear power in America. "From the start of commercial nuclear reactor construction in the mid-1960s through the 1980s, capital costs (dollars per kilowatt of capacity) for building nuclear reactors escalated dramatically."[25]

Another problem with nuclear energy is the potential national security threats we face in a world so dramatically changed by the tragic attacks of September 11, 2001. FBI Director Robert Mueller told Senate members that reactors are an aim of potential terrorist action. "[An] area we consider vulnerable and target rich is the energy sector, particularly nuclear power plants," he said in testifying before the Senate Committee on Intelligence in February 2005. "Al Qaeda planner Khalid Sheikh Mohammed had nuclear power plants as part of his target set, and we have no reason to believe that Al Qaeda has reconsidered."[26] A nuclear power plant could be an attractive target for a terrorist strike, and America's plants in the past have severely failed in regard to security protection. Nuclear Regulatory Commission (NRC)–supervised security exercises found that about 50 percent of our nation's nuclear power-plant facilities that were tested were unable to prevent a simulated attack. "The NRC's mock terrorist exercises severely limit the tactics, weapons, and explosives used by the adversary, yet in almost half the tests they reached and simulated meltdown and catastrophic radioactive releases," according to Paul Leventhal, president of the Nuclear Control Institute.[27] Also, an increase in spent nuclear waste increases the chances that some of this radioactive material can get into hostile hands that could use it for making "dirty bombs" or for building a nuclear device that might threaten a major American city.

A big question regarding the use of nuclear-fission material is how to dispose of the spent reactor fuel so that it is not a hazard to public safety or to the environment. In 1987, Congress chose Yucca Mountain, located on the Nellis Military Operations Area in Nevada, as a long-term solution to storing the waste material produced by America's reactors. This location has generated tremendous controversy because of the environmental impact of transporting radioactive material across the country and storing it in vaults deep inside the desert mountain. This question of where to store the nuclear waste remains unanswered after the Obama administration cut funding to develop Yucca Mountain.

A final consideration for nuclear energy as an alternative energy source is the fact that commercial-grade uranium exists in limited quantities on our planet. The Energy Watch Group released a study in 2006 that calculated production of economically mineable uranium will peak by the year 2035. "Even if we take into account that uranium prices will rise dramatically and that this will raise interest in exploiting previously uneconomical uranium mines, our uranium reserves will be fully depleted in seventy years at the latest," Dr. Werner Zittel, an author of the report, said in a public statement.[28] A report by the International Atomic Energy Agency suggests that, depending on the world's demand for nuclear power in the coming decades, production "deficits" in known uranium resources might be experienced between the years 2026 and 2035. Optimistic energy experts, however, suggest that the future technological development of breeder reactors will help the world extend its nuclear-energy potential for thousands of years.[29] In the national discussion about how the world can gain its energy independence, some American politicians advocate that the United States must increase its development of nuclear-fission reactors to replace fossil fuels whereas other leaders remain cautious about such a plan. No doubt the debate will continue for many years.

The future might hold a nuclear option that will make that abundant-energy dream come true later in this century. For many decades, scientists and researchers have been working on developing a special type of nuclear-energy plant called a fusion reactor. If implemented, it would generate power by fusing the nuclei of hydrogen atoms. This is the same natural principle that produces energy at the heart of our sun. If humans can find a way to safely and economically sustain a nuclear fusion reaction where the nuclei of hydrogen are forced together to release heat, we could potentially have access to massive reservoirs of energy existing inside the hydrogen atoms that are so abundant in the universe. The hydrogen in ordinary water—such as what you get from your kitchen tap—could provide every American with an adequate supply of energy. The problem at this point in time is that an industrial fusion reactor is far from reality. Humans have not yet come up with the technology to commercially create the high temperature of 100 million degrees Fahrenheit (56 million degrees Celsius) to overcome the electrical forces that hold atoms together and thus fuse the nuclei in hydrogen to release the atomic energy. Although it holds tremendous promise for humankind, fusion power appears to be decades away. On an optimistic note, however, perhaps we should bear in mind a failed prediction made by Albert Einstein, a man who knew a thing or two about energy. With regard to the possibility of nuclear reactors, he commented in 1932, "There is not the slightest indication that nuclear energy will ever be obtainable. It would mean that the atom would have to be shattered at will." Time and technology proved him wrong.

EARTH ENERGY

Miles below our feet lies a vast ocean of energy that has barely been tapped by human beings. Inside our planet's mantle surges a reservoir of molten rock reaching temperatures of up to 1,652 degrees Fahrenheit (900 degrees Celsius). This magma was heated during the formation of our planet from the decay of radioactive elements such as uranium, potassium, and thorium. The eruption of volcanoes, the jarring of the land by earthquakes, and the natural hot springs and geysers give evidence to the tremendous geothermal energy supply kept submerged deep within our world.

Since ancient times, people have used this Earth energy for practical purposes. Some aristocratic Romans heated their mansions and baths using hot springs. Almost certainly the ancient Romans would be proud to know that Italy was the nation that brought the commercial development of energy from Earth's interior into the modern world. In 1904, that Mediterranean country first generated electricity produced from underground steam in the city of Larderello, in southern Tuscany. Today, the world annually produces about 8,000 megawatts of electric power from geothermal energy, out of which the United States taps 2,800 megawatts, and California leads the way with 47 geothermal plants producing 2,626 megawatts, with the geological potential to generate up to 4,000 more megawatts to meet the state's electricity needs.[30]

Once a geothermal power station is constructed, the energy it produces is relatively low cost. Geothermal power plants are also usually small, so they have less of an impact on the environment. These plants are also good for the natural world because the steam generated at these sites is not created by burning any type of combustible fuel but, rather, comes from the heat yielded by the planet's molten mantle. The primary downside to geothermal energy is that power plants can be built only in specific regions of our planet where molten rock is near enough to the surface to heat water. Another major concern is that geothermal power stations might trigger seismic activity along earthquake fault lines. A 3.4 tremor near the Swiss community of Basel, for example, was attributed to a "deep heating mining" project (now discontinued) that would have drilled a hole deep into the earth and pumped water to the hot rock below. And environmentalists have pointed out that drilling holes to tap the subterranean steam might release pollutants such as hydrogen sulfide as well as toxic minerals into the environment, which could contaminate lakes and rivers and kill aquatic animals and plants.[31] Geothermal plants also release the greenhouse gas carbon dioxide, but at a level of about one-thousandth of an equivalent to a coal-burning power station. With technological advances from more research and development in geothermal systems, Americans might one day soon safely and economically tap into the energy of the tremendous heat found in the heart of our planet.

HYDROGEN

By far, the most abundant element in the universe is hydrogen. It makes up about 75 percent of the universe's elemental mass, so it's no surprise that our planet has a great quantity of this most basic of all the atoms. Most of it is stored, bonded with the element oxygen, in a liquid form in our world's oceans, lakes, and other water sources. In a gaseous state, hydrogen can be combusted to run turbines to generate electricity. It is important to realize that hydrogen in and of itself is not a source of energy. We should think of it more as an "energy carrier" that is commercially produced from other fuel sources.

In recent years, significant technical advances have been discovered that might one day make the production of hydrogen out of water a practical way to supply the world with alternative energy to fossil fuels. Using a renewable power source such as solar or wind energy, an electric current can be sent through water, thus separating the oxygen molecules from the hydrogen. These two elements can then be liquefied to allow for easier storage and transportation to a site where they can be used in a fuel cell, a device that recombines the oxygen and hydrogen to produce electricity.[32] This technology is environmentally friendly because it emits only water vapor and no air pollution. It can also be used as an energy storage medium for homes, businesses, and transportation. In 2007, automaker Toyota tested a prototype fuel-cell vehicle that journeyed a distance of 350 miles (563 km) from Osaka, Japan, to Tokyo on one tank filled with hydrogen. Other carmakers such as Hyundai Motor and General Motors are also planning environmentally friendly fuel-cell cars projected for mass production by the year 2012.

Using the simple life forms of algae and anaerobic bacteria, research scientists have found another method to produce hydrogen for energy use. Some species of algae can naturally split water molecules under certain conditions, thus releasing the hydrogen atoms from the oxygen. Scientists at the University of California at Berkeley are looking into genetically developing these algae forms so that in the future, ponds of green gunk might produce commercial quantities of hydrogen. Other scientists and researchers are looking into different types of bacteria that can break down organic material such as waste from food-manufacturing plants, thus releasing the hydrogen contained in the carbohydrates. One day, food manufacturers might make extra financial profit by selling the hydrogen once disposed of in their industrial waste. Such a system would also allow food manufacturers to easily get rid of much of their product waste and thus save them the cost of transporting it to a dump site.[33]

Hydrogen as an energy medium provides many benefits. It is a nonpolluting substance and does not contribute to any greenhouse effect. It can be produced virtually anywhere because the water from which it can be derived is plentiful on our planet. The problem with hydrogen, however, is that during the process of electrolysis, energy is needed to separate it from oxygen into a free-floating gas state. In addition, there is no existing infrastructure to commercially store and distribute hydrogen as a fuel for wide public use. A great deal of money will need to be spent to construct hydrogen-production plants and also to equip the cars and buses of the world with fuel cells or hydrogen-burning engines, along with a vehicle fuel tank that can safely store hydrogen. Another challenge that hydrogen faces is the public concern about its potential volatility. Many people bear in mind the horrific newsreel images of the hydrogen-filled passenger airship *Hindenburg* bursting into a fireball on May 6, 1937, at Lakehurst, New Jersey, killing thirty-six people. However, because hydrogen has a higher ignition temperature than gasoline or natural gas, it is less flammable than these fossil fuels. Hydrogen gas has been safely used in industry and manufacturing for many decades.

The various alternative energy sources to fossil fuels that we have just described provide many options for America to consider in reaching a national goal of energy independence. As we've seen, no energy source is 100 percent perfect as a solution. Some of the alternatives, such as corn ethanol and fission-based nuclear power, have political and social challenges stemming from their potential threat to the environment or other public health and safety issues. Other clean- and renewable-energy sources also come with their share of technological hurdles in terms of near-term implementation. But if the history of science serves as a reliable guide, the technical challenges will be met if given enough research time and innovative development. America, of course, must not look for a single "silver bullet" solution. We must instead consider the whole package of sustainable-energy sources and develop a sound national energy policy that takes advantage of all our potential clean power and fuel supplies, while also reducing our energy demand through efficiency and conservation efforts in all public and private sectors.

AMERICA'S ENERGY ISSUES

Most Americans don't often consider the direct and very real impact that energy use has on them as individuals. Whatever form it might take, energy use affects virtually every aspect of our lives, twenty-four hours a day, seven days a week, 365 days a year. Energy issues abound all around us, both in dramatic ways, such as the rising price at the gasoline pump, and in subtle, often unrecognized ways, such as the electric power required to clean and distribute our water supply. In this section, we will examine in depth eight of America's most important energy issues to better understand why it is so essential for our nation to gain its freedom from fossil fuels.

In Chapter 4, we'll look at why clean energy will help us preserve our democratic form of government. In Chapter 5, we'll consider our national security and how achieving our energy independence can help make Americans significantly safer from foreign threats. In Chapter 6, we'll examine how clean and green energy can enable us to become better stewards of the natural world and fulfill our moral obligation to protect the environment. In Chapter 7, we'll consider how America's economy can grow more robust and secure as we develop sustainable-energy industries that will create hundreds of thousands of green-collar jobs. In Chapter 8, we'll find out how enhancing the efficiency of our nation's vehicles and transportation systems is absolutely vital for achieving our energy independence. In Chapter 9, we'll learn why our nation's food supply is so closely intertwined with fossil fuels and how energy independence can help our country's farmers provide the agricultural products needed to sustain our modern civilization in future years. In Chapter 10, we'll analyze how achieving a sustainable-energy society will help improve the health and well-being of all Americans. Finally, in Chapter 11, we'll gain an understanding of how building America's brainpower by improving our schools and educational systems is an absolutely necessary component to achieving our energy independence.

Some of the chapters in this section will deal with potential calamities that might come about in the twenty-first century because of the peaking of global oil production and the climate changes resulting from global warming. We must accept the fact that modern civilization will pay a heavy price if we continue traveling down the hydrocarbon highway. We must not sugarcoat the truth about our present energy situation and ignore the catastrophic harms our addiction to fossil fuels might bring.

On the other hand, we must not let these potential troubles discourage us from moving forward and finding solutions—and taking action to avert their impact. Instead, we must use the threat of these doom-and-gloom projections to motivate us to step up our efforts to gain energy independence. We are not helpless in shaping our destiny. There are viable solutions for a better future for all of us, which we'll learn about in the third section of this book. As you read about America's energy issues, please bear in mind that we can avoid the brunt of many of the possible trials and tribulations by implementing a vigorous national energy policy that will lead to a sustainable-energy society. We all have a bright future ahead of us if we can keep up our courage and take action to achieve it.

CHAPTER 4

Energy and Good Government

n 1921, President Warren G. Harding appointed Albert Fall, a Republican senator from New Mexico, to manage the nation's public lands as the head of the U.S. Department of the Interior. In his new political position, Fall soon persuaded U.S. Secretary of the Navy Edwin Denby to give the Department of the Interior control of the Navy's emergency petroleum reserves in the Elk Hills of California and at a Wyoming site known as Teapot Dome. Soon after gaining jurisdiction of the land, Fall began making leasing deals for the reserves with corporate executives Harry Sinclair of Mammoth Oil (later Sinclair Oil) and Edward Doheny of Pan American Petroleum. Although no competitive bidding was done, these agreements were considered perfectly legal based on the federal statutes of the time.

In exchange for his participation, Secretary of Interior Fall secretly received various gifts from the oil executives, as well as no-interest personal loans that amounted to over $400,000 (the equivalent of about $4 million today). When the U.S. Senate started to investigate the questionable contracts in 1922, Fall took action to conceal all the incriminating evidence of his bribery from the oil companies. He almost got away with his crime, too. But late in the investigation a document surfaced proving that in November 1921, Fall had received a $100,000 loan from Doheny. After a sensational court trial, Fall was found guilty of accepting bribes. He was fined

sational court trial, Fall was found guilty of accepting bribes. He was fined

77

$100,000 and served one year in prison. He has the dubious distinction of being the first former cabinet member to go to a federal penitentiary.[1]

The infamous Teapot Dome scandal gives us a dramatic history lesson on corruption. Unfortunately, the problem did not end in the 1920s. In recent decades, we've witnessed a scandalous parade of elected and appointed public officers whose ethical behavior has been tainted by the financial pressure of the fossil-fuel industries. Members of both political parties receive election contributions from oil businesses, but the vast majority of this money has gone to Republican candidates or Republican Party organizations. During President George W. Bush's administration, the oil and natural gas industry gave 80 percent of its political contributions to Republicans, according to the Center for Responsive Politics. More than $393 million was spent by the oil and gas industry on lobbying the federal government during the Bush years.[2]

Less than two weeks after his 2001 inauguration, President George W. Bush tapped Vice President Richard Cheney to chair a task force called the National Energy Policy Development Group, initiated to establish an energy policy for the new administration. According to a *Washington Post* investigation in 2005, influential people who met behind closed doors with Cheney or his staff and helped shape America's energy future included Red Cavaney, the president of the American Petroleum Institute; James J. Rouse, then ExxonMobil's vice president; Jack Gerard, an official with the National Mining Association; and Kenneth Lay, the CEO of Enron. In a token gesture, on April 4, 2001, the energy task force staff did meet with members of various U.S. environmental organizations, such as the Friends of the Earth and Defenders of Wildlife, in an unproductive one-hour photo-op session that Cheney did not attend. This was the only meeting the task force held with environmentalists, although forty or more meetings had been held in which Cheney or his staff listened to fossil-fuel industry and fossil-fuel interest group officials.[3] Cheney never revealed the identities of the people who met with him and the task force staff, claiming executive privilege for his nondisclosure of names. Lawyers for Sierra Club and the public interest group Judicial Watch sought legal access to the task force records but failed in court to make the vice president provide the documents.[4] Much like Teapot Dome, the administration's infamous energy task force's secret meetings demonstrate the unbalanced influence the fossil-fuel industry has had in manipulating our nation's energy course.

CLIMATE CHANGE

When he first ran for the White House, George W. Bush pledged to voters in Saginaw, Michigan, on September 29, 2000, that he would work to deal with the climate crisis the world faced from the burning of fossil fuels. "We will require all power plants to meet clean-air standards in order to reduce emissions of sulfur dioxide, nitrogen dioxide, mercury and carbon dioxide within a reasonable period of time," he said.[5] Bush, whose ties to the oil industry are well established, failed to keep his promise when he stepped into the Oval Office. Claiming that taking the crucial action needed to reduce industrial carbon dioxide emissions would hurt our nation's economy, the Bush-Cheney administration refused to join with all the other nations of the world and sign the Kyoto Protocol. Helping to make this energy policy decision were the fossil-fuel company executives who would experience potential loss in profits if the country lowered its coal and oil consumption. The insidious conflict of interest in the federal government's dealing with the fossil-fuel industry might have major consequences for the future of all humanity. If we let this political situation continue to pervade in the halls of our nation's capital, it could seriously stall the United States from taking proper action to mitigate the effects of global climate change.

At the same time as the U.S. public was growing increasingly concerned about how climate change will damage our planet in coming decades, the Bush administration took pains to cast doubt on the potential catastrophe our nation faces from this impending environmental crisis. Its political appointees often challenged or suppressed scientific documents that might provide political ammunition to environmentalists to push for substantial limits on greenhouse gas emissions. Bush's staff even engaged in active censorship of government scientists who could have provided their valuable expertise about what potential climate-change damage might result in coming years if we fail to find wiser ways to consume fossil fuels. To find out how extensively the administration's political goals might be hampering climate-science data from freely reaching the media and other public information sources, the Union of Concerned Scientists and the Government Accountability Project, both nonprofit nonpartisan groups, conducted a 2006 survey of climate-focused scientists at seven federal agencies. Their report found that during a five-year period, at least 435 incidences of "political interference" occurred over climate-related scientific findings. About 46 percent of the survey respondents said that they had personally been pressured by bureaucrats to remove terms such as "global warming" and "climate change" from their documents. Two in five scientists who responded said that their communications had been edited to change the meaning of their scientific findings. "Policy should be based on sound science," the report stated, quoting one anonymous scientist at the U.S. Department of Agriculture. "Results of science should not be diluted or . . . adjusted to justify policy. This particular administration has gone beyond reasonable boundaries on this issue. To be in denial on climate change is a crime against the nation."[6]

After being warned by their bosses not to talk publicly about climate change, some government climate scientists have resigned from their jobs on the principle that the American people must know the truth about what problems fossil-fuel-induced warming presents for our planet. James Hansen, the director of NASA's Goddard Institute for Space Studies and one of America's top climate-science experts, publicly condemned the Bush-Cheney administration for putting its political goals ahead of global climate problems. "In my more than three decades in government, I have never seen anything approaching the degree to which information flow from scientists to the public has been screened and controlled as it has now," Hansen said in testimony to the House Committee on Oversight and Government Reform in March 2007.[7]

Luckily, much of this political suppression of climate science has been brought to the public's attention. One outrageous example of tampering with scientific information on global warming received significant press coverage in 2005, when the *New York Times* revealed that Philip A. Cooney, the chief of staff in the White House Council on Environmental Quality, had made sweeping alterations to climate-change-related science studies published in 2002 and 2003.[8] Before being employed by the White House, Cooney worked as a lobbyist with the American Petroleum Institute. Cooney edited "The Strategic Plan for the United States Climate Change Science Program" and other science reports to "exaggerate or emphasize scientific uncertainties"[9] and thus create a perception of doubt about global warming's potential effects on the world's environment. Among his more notable adjustments of science was the deletion of text describing how rising temperatures increase the melting of ice and snowpack. He handwrote on the document that this information wandered "from research strategy into speculative findings/musings."[10]

Cooney did this editorial tampering despite the fact that he lacks the necessary scientific expertise to make such changes (his academic background is a bachelor's degree in economics). He was outed in his document fiddling by Rick Piltz, who had served as a senior associate with the U.S. Climate Change Science Policy Office. The House Oversight and Government Reform Committee investigated and found that President Bush's administration had indeed "engaged in a systematic effort to manipulate climate change science and mislead policymakers and the public about the dangers of global warming."[11] To protest how politicians were distorting scientific research, Piltz quit his job with the government and founded Climate Science Watch, a nonprofit organization "dedicated to holding public officials accountable for the integrity and effectiveness with which they use climate science and related research in government policymaking." In a memo to climate-change officials written soon after he left government work, Piltz stated: "Politicization by the White House has fed back directly into the science program in such a way as to undermine the credibility and integrity of the program in its relationship to the research community, to program managers, to policymakers, and to the public interest. The White House so successfully politicized the science program that I decided it was necessary to terminate my relationship with it."[12] Shortly after the media started investigating the matter of the edited reports, Cooney resigned from his White House position. He quickly found a job with ExxonMobil.[13]

Using a classic tactic from the tobacco industry, the oil industry in the last decade has reframed the scientific debate about global climate change in order to promote its own political agenda. By manipulating media information describing how our planet's average temperature is rising owing to man-made greenhouse gas emissions, it has worked to create a cloud of doubt in the public mind about climate science. Starting in the late 1990s, ExxonMobil set up a disinformation campaign strategy intended to mislead the American public and lawmakers about climate-change facts and thereby raise doubts about the validity of scientific research dealing with worldwide global warming. According to a 2007 report by the Union of Concerned Scientists, between 1998 and 2005, the big oil companies channeled about $16 million to underwrite "research papers" intended to manufacture uncertainty about even the most incontrovertible scientific evidence for climate change. The oil industry provided funding to forty-three organizations that sought "to confuse the public on global warming science." Many of these groups had "climate contrarian" scientists who could cherry-pick scientific data to write documents refuting legitimate climate researchers. Through its educational foundation, ExxonMobil, for example, gave $630,000 to the George C. Marshall Institute, an organization that has over recent years churned out contrarian reports designed to cast doubt on the scientific evidence that global climate change is caused by human-emitted greenhouse gases.[14] This organization, which promotes itself with the motto "science for better public policy," has produced a number of reports and essays designed to generate uncertainty of the scientific findings of climate change. In pondering what the George C. Marshall Institute's real agenda might involve in shaping science for public policy, we should consider the high potential for conflict of interest that comes from the fact that William O'Keefe, a former executive vice president and chief operating officer for the American Petroleum Institute, served on the institute's board of directors. From 2001 to 2005, O'Keefe also worked as a paid lobbyist for ExxonMobil.[15]

Oil companies such as ExxonMobil routinely attempt to manipulate public opinion on energy issues because it benefits their bottom line. If they can shape significant doubt in the American people's opinions about climate change, they can influence political policy relating to this issue. Public doubt serves to solidify the justification given by some American politicians that our nation must wait to act to ease possible effects of this environmental emergency until "all the science" confirms climate change is a serious threat to humankind. In their effort to be "fair and balanced" in their news reporting, the American media also unwittingly help power the information-laundering machine. The media often mention these pseudoscientific findings in print and broadcast reports, thus putting them on equal footing with legitimate science. This coverage causes the public to question legitimate research about climate change. Journalists should report which organizations are providing subsidies for these papers so that their audience can determine if there might be a conflict of interest.

Not just the oil companies but also various politicians understand the strategy of reframing the issue of climate change to instill doubt and un-certainty in the American public's mind. Many politicians benefited from a private memo titled "Straight Talk" written in 2002 by GOP political consultant Frank Luntz to instruct them in this reframe tactic. (Luntz also did public polling for the "Contract with America" manifesto that propelled the Republicans to gain control of the House of Representatives in the election of 1994.) In his memorandum, Luntz advised politicians to encourage Americans to doubt the issue of a scientific consensus about the causes of climate change. Luntz's memo stated: "The scientific debate remains open. Voters believe that there is no consensus about global warm-ing within the scientific community. Should the public come to believe that the scientific issues are settled, their views about global warming will change accordingly. Therefore you need to continue to make the lack of scientific certainty a primary issue in the debate, and defer to scientists and other experts in the field." Because people tend to trust scientists more than politicians, the Luntz memo advocated that politicians raise doubt about legitimate climate-science reports by being "more active in recruiting experts who are sympathetic to your view and much more active in making them part of your message."[16]

STATE GOVERNMENT

It's no secret that the politics of energy and climate change has become a hot-button issue in the United States. And nowhere can the heat be felt more than in the trials and tribulations some of America's state governments have faced in trying to significantly reduce vehicle-caused greenhouse gas emissions. Frustrated with the failure of the federal government under the Bush-Cheney administration to provide real leadership to decrease these heat-trapping gases emitted from the tailpipes of cars and trucks, various states have stepped up to take action themselves. California took the leading role, a significant one because it has more than 32 million registered vehicles. Leaders in the Golden State decided in 2005 to get assertive in tackling the problems of climate change. The state legislators and Governor Arnold Schwarzenegger used the federal Clean Air Act to try to set more stringent limits on the greenhouse gas emissions of cars, trucks, and SUVs. The state sought to reduce tailpipe emissions by 30 percent by 2016, starting with vehicles produced in 2009. This effort would reduce greenhouse gas pollution to a level equivalent to 6.5 million cars being taken off the road. Sixteen other states making up 45 percent of America's auto sales also joined in supporting and adopting California's higher fuel efficiency standards, thus potentially reducing greenhouse gas emissions by the equivalent of 22 million cars and cutting gasoline use by 11 billion gallons a year.[17]

A mandate in the Clean Air Act required the state government to request a waiver from the Environmental Protection Agency (EPA) to regulate the pollution from its vehicles. The state of California filed its request in December 2005. Concerned about how such a massive market might force it to include potentially expensive energy-efficiency improvements in its vehicles, the auto industry submitted documents to the EPA to block the granting of the waiver. For two years, administrators at the EPA dragged their feet in announcing a decision. Frustrated by the long delay, California filed a lawsuit in November 2007 to prompt the agency to move forward. On December 19, 2007, the same day that President Bush signed a law submitted by Congress to raise fuel efficiency in cars, light trucks, and SUVs to 35 miles per gallon by the year 2020, EPA Chief Stephen Johnson denied California's request for raising its own fuel efficiency standards. In the four-decade history of the Clean Air Act, it was the first time the federal government refused to grant a state a waiver.

In denying California its request, Johnson patently ignored advice from his own staff. On October 17, 2007, he had received an e-mail memo from Margot Oge, the director of the EPA's office of transportation and air quality. It clearly addressed the importance of granting the waiver. "From what I have read and the people I have talked to, it is obvious to me that there is no legal or technical justification for denying this [request]," Oge wrote Johnson. "The law is very specific about what you are allowed to consider, and even if you adopt the alternative interpretations that have been suggested by the automakers, you still wind up in the same place."[18] Other internal memos at the EPA showed that staff members feared the agency's credibility might be damaged by Johnson's waiver denial.

In January 2008, in an attempt to have Johnson's decision reversed, California filed a lawsuit against the EPA. Fourteen other states joined California in this legal pursuit. At first, Johnson explained that he denied the waiver because the new fuel-economy standards set by Congress and signed into law by President Bush were stricter than California's standards. "The Bush administration is moving forward with a clear national solution, not a confusing patchwork of state rules," he said in a conference call set up for news reporters. "I believe this is a better approach than if individual states were to act alone."[19] Later, when his opinion was shown by the California Air Resources Board to be untrue, he issued another justification in a forty-seven-page document. In it, Johnson said that in the past the EPA had granted waivers only in cases that dealt with air pollution problems for a specific location. Climate change, he argued, affects not only California but also the rest of the United States. Thus, he held, the state does not satisfy the requirement of "compelling and extraordinary conditions" that would allow it to set its own vehicle regulation standards.[20]

The same month that California filed its lawsuit, the U.S. Senate's Environment and Public Works Committee requested documents from the EPA to analyze the process by which Johnson made his decision to deny California's waiver request. Although the documents were not considered classified information and did not deal with national security, the EPA had oddly covered over much of the text with white tape to conceal the information. The Senate staff was forced to have EPA employees watch over their shoulders as they pulled off the tape and transcribed these documents. California Senator Barbara Boxer, the committee's head, scolded Johnson for the EPA's failure to cooperate and told him that he went against the agency's mission in his zealousness to protect special interests. "The EPA has failed to fully respond to our request for information. . . . I've never seen anything like it," she said during a committee hearing. "The people who pay the administrator's salary have a right to know how he came to a decision that is so far removed from the facts, the law, the science, the precedent, state's rights, and all the rest that goes with it."[21]

On May 20, 2008, Johnson came before the House Oversight and Government Reform Committee, which sought to find out from him how much influence the White House had played in shaping his decision to deny California its waiver. Johnson repeatedly refused to provide the committee members with any information or subpoenaed documents about his meetings with Bush administration staff or even the president himself that detailed conversations about this important issue. Committee Chairman Henry Waxman told Johnson he was a "figurehead" for the administration. "The president apparently insisted in his judgment and overrode the unanimous recommendations of EPA scientific and legal experts," Waxman told Johnson. "You reversed yourself after having candid conversations with the White House."[22]

The former EPA head officer's extraordinary political maneuverings to deny the waiver demonstrated a deepening crisis that sabotages the agency's mission to protect human health and the environment. It also signaled that the motives at the EPA during the Bush-Cheney years might have been more about political ploys than environmental protection. The crisis within the EPA is apparent from a study released by the Union of Concerned Scientists in April 2008, detailing that many EPA scientists believe their research findings are being "suppressed and distorted" for political reasons. The report states that 889 scientists—about 60 percent of those surveyed—"personally experienced at least one type of political interference in the past five years." And 232 EPA scientists—about 18 percent of those surveyed—said their work had experienced frequent or occasional "changes or edits during the review that changed the meaning of scientific findings."[23] The political interference at the EPA and the federal government's resistance in dealing with California and the other states over vehicular carbon dioxide emissions highlight how much the Bush-Cheney administration's allegiance to fossil fuels put in peril the integrity of our American democratic political process.

The Teapot Dome scandal in the 1920s and the blatant conflicts of interest we have seen in Washington, D.C., during the first decade of the twenty-first century provide us with lessons on the importance of upholding fairness, openness, and truthfulness when creating national energy policies. Americans want leaders in government who refuse to show favoritism toward special interests when they are creating and managing our nation's public policy. Our nation's people want leaders with integrity who follow the rules of ethics and consider the facts of science when making their decisions on energy and environmental issues. Our citizens want lawmakers who understand that their job is to secure liberty for all Americans now and in the future. As Thomas Jefferson said in 1809, "The care of human life and happiness and not their destruction is the first and only legitimate object of good government."[24] A clean-energy nation requires a clean government. Clean government is good government.

CHAPTER 5

Energy and National Security

As Theodore Roosevelt stood watching, four squadrons of U.S. Navy battleships and their escorts came to the end of the most historic voyage in American history since Christopher Columbus's voyage in 1492. Accompanied by U.S. military officers, the Rough Rider president saluted America's "Great White Fleet" as it steamed into the port of Hampton Roads, Virginia, on February 22, 1909. The oceangoing vessels had just finished a fourteen-month, 43,000-mile (69,200-kilometer) journey circumnavigating the globe, the first battle fleet in history to do so. A primary purpose of this ambitious naval undertaking was to prove to the world that the United States would be *the* military power of the twentieth century. The voyage had been an overall peaceful one. Thousands of people in foreign ports had greeted the fleet's 14,000 sailors and officers with good wishes and grand pageantry. In his speech welcoming the fleet back to its American port, Roosevelt extolled the accomplishment of the sailors and marines by proclaiming, "Those who perform the feat again can but follow in your footsteps."[1] The triumphant voyage marked the start of America's rise as the most powerful military force in history. It could, however, never have been achieved without an assured supply of coal and oil. By the end of the twentieth century, after the Soviet Union collapsed under the weight of its own bureaucratic and military inefficiencies, the United States stood out as the world's most formidably armed superpower.

A hundred years after the Great White Fleet's voyage, fossil fuels continue to play a vital role in providing twenty-first-century America with the energy we need to keep us safe from the threats of hostile foreign nations and terrorist activities. Our military guzzles down 5.46 billion gallons of oil per year, making it the world's largest single user of fossil fuels.[2] Our national defense requires that the United States produce and consume massive amounts of coal and petroleum oil to build and propel its military machines across the seas, over the ground, and through the skies. Because airplanes, tanks, ships, and other defense equipment run on fossil fuels, protecting our supply of this energy resource is vital to America's national security interests. But, as we shall see, the social and political burdens that will come from global climate change and increased competition for oil in the future also put our national defense at risk.

To quench the nation's never-ending thirst for oil, we must get our crude increasingly from foreign sources. In 1973, America imported 30 percent of its oil. That figure doubled to 60 percent by 2007. Around the year 2025, energy analysts forecast, we will grow dependent on foreign oil reserves for at least 70 percent of our supply.[3] Much of that oil will come from nations with which America has had tense political relations. Among them is the Kingdom of Saudi Arabia, which holds the world's largest reserves of conventional oil, at an estimated 267 billion barrels.[4] Testifying before a Senate Committee in July 2005, Under Secretary of the Treasury Stuart Levey warned that certain groups and individuals in Saudi Arabia covertly provide many millions of dollars—much of it oil money—to fund violence against the United States. "Wealthy Saudi financiers and charities have funded terrorist organizations and causes that support terrorism and the ideology that fuels the terrorists' agenda," he told senators. "Even today, we believe that Saudi donors may still be a significant source of terrorist financing, including for the insurgency in Iraq."[5]

Next door to Iraq, the country of Iran possesses an estimated 90 billion barrels of proven oil reserves, according to GlobalSecurity.org. Iran's President Mahmoud Ahmadinejad routinely whips up anger and hatred against the United States. By going against United Nations Security Council resolutions

calling a halt to Iran's uranium enrichment actions, Ahmadinejad has also bran-
dished a blunt atomic threat toward the United States by continuing to develop
his nation's nuclear program. Meanwhile in the Western Hemisphere, the South
American nation of Venezuela, run by President Hugo Chavez, has become a
hydrocarbon headache for the United States. Holding the world's seventh largest proven reserve of petroleum, Chavez takes delight in playing this "oil card"
in a high-stakes game against America. He has threatened to withhold Venezuelan oil from us on several occasions. "It is a card that we are going to play
with toughness against the toughest country in the world, the United States,"[6]
he once boasted. It's a dangerous ploy. If Venezuela does cut off its oil production for a long period of time, the resulting price hike could drive a major global
recession.

The world's growing dependence on Arab, Persian, and Venezuelan oil
will only intensify as demand rises while the global supply shrinks. The National Energy Policy that President Bush released in May 2001 recommended
that we diversify our foreign oil sources to reduce our Middle East dependence. Canada and Mexico are friendly suppliers of oil we can trust. But
Bush wanted us to also purchase more oil from politically volatile nations including Angola, Russia, and Nigeria.[7] The reality of geology shows, however,
that failing to gain our energy freedom means we will be increasingly obliged
to Middle Eastern countries to satisfy our escalating petroleum consumption. Member nations of the Organization of Petroleum Exporting Countries
(OPEC) produce about 40 percent of the world's oil exports and hold approximately 80 percent of the proven conventional oil reserves on our planet.[8]
About 85 percent of OPEC's reserves are under the sands of the Middle East.
Unless we can cut down on our wasteful fossil-fuel consumption and develop
cleaner sources of energy, America's growing dependence on Middle East oil
in the coming years could force us to continue our presence in that unstable
region of the world to protect our economy and business interests. During the
Iraq War, the United States spent more than $100 billion a year in direct costs
protecting Persian Gulf interests, and our addiction also results in billions of
dollars in lost government revenue and domestic investments, as well as the
loss of more than 2.2 million U.S. jobs as capital flows overseas.[9]

TERRORISTS

If our increasing dependence on foreign oil stretches our military infrastructure and troops to a breaking point, the United States won't be able to respond to a potential conflict with nations such as Iran or North Korea that will see us as highly vulnerable. Our weakened defense would give our adversaries the confidence to test their power against America's infrastructure. Our dependence on foreign oil also makes us more vulnerable to terrorist strikes that are designed to annihilate our economy and thus destroy our democratic system. Our nation's energy house of cards could easily come tumbling down if terrorists strategically target our weakest links.

Although media reports have raised awareness of the security of nuclear facilities and the electric grid, the American public should recognize that the worldwide oil-transport infrastructure also remains at risk. The famous Trans-Alaska Pipeline stretches virtually unprotected for 800 miles (1,287 km) through isolated wilderness from the North Slope to the port of Valdez.[10] Coordinated bomb attacks on vulnerable portions such as bridges would contaminate the beautiful Arctic environment and could close down this important oil artery for several weeks—or maybe even months, if weather conditions prevented repair. In 1988, the Trans-Alaska Pipeline hit its peak at 2.1 million barrels a day. That has decreased, and in 2007, about 740,000 barrels a day passed through the pipe, about 3.5 percent of America's total daily consumption at the national consumption rate of 21 million barrels a day. An attack on the pipeline would hit America in its monetary heart by promoting fear on Wall Street about the vulnerability of our nation's domestic oil supply.

But terrorists don't have to strike an at-risk section of the nearly half million miles (804,672 km) of oil and natural gas pipe arteries within our borders. They can damage pipelines in the Middle East—and they often do. In February 2010, as one example, attackers bombed an Iraqi oil pipeline in Rashidiya, near Baghdad. The damage cut oil production at Iraq's Dora refinery from 140,000 barrels a day to 70,000 barrels a day. Terrorists can also go after the more than 4,000 oil tankers that, according to the U.S. Department of Transportation's Maritime Administration, cruise the world's waves. These large and lumbering vessels make up the most vulnerable component of the oil supply chain to the United States—and terrorists know it. Tankers docked at loading facilities have been targeted by Al Qaeda suicide attacks. In one such incident in October 2002, a small boat with explosives torpedoed into the French supertanker *Limburg* at a port in the nation of Yemen. The resulting explosion killed one crew member and created a large breach along the tanker's side that spilled about 90,000 barrels of crude into the Gulf of Aden.[11] The oil caught fire and took thirty-six hours to put out. That damage was relatively minor compared to what a more ambitious strike could accomplish. If a terrorist organization really wanted to choke the world's oil supply chain, it could assault a supertanker at a vulnerable shipping point to block other tankers from passing through. We can conceive of one scenario where terrorists might secretly plant an atomic explosive device—most likely a compact "suitcase bomb"—deep inside the hull of a supertanker. The thousands of barrels of oil that would surround it would prevent its radioactive detection. With a blast charge of one kiloton—about the amount of 1,000 tons of dynamite—the device would blow up the ship and spread radioactive material. If the attack came at a critical point for oil transport, such as the Suez Canal, the Strait of Hormuz, the Red Sea, the Panama Canal, or the Strait of Malacca, it could impede the flow of much of the Middle East's crude. That would strike panic in the world's markets, quickly causing a major financial recession or even global economic depression.

Oil goes to ports on all of America's coasts, so we are vulnerable in many areas. But the biggest strike would be to the deepwater Louisiana Offshore Oil Port (LOOP) in the Gulf of Mexico, "the largest point of entry for crude oil imports" into America, which processes about 13 percent of the U.S. imported crude that comes by ship.[12] A strike at this major port would severely cut our oil artery and bleed the productivity of many of our nation's industries. The potential outcome could be that America's economy would collapse and millions of our citizens would suffer financial upheaval.

GLOBAL CLIMATE CHALLENGES

In October 2003, two Pentagon analysts released a report with the rather bland title "An Abrupt Climate Change Scenario and Its Implications for United States National Security." The information this document contained was scarier than the frights found in a Stephen King horror story. The authors, Peter Schwartz and Doug Randall, envisioned global climate change bringing our planet massive food shortages and reductions in freshwater supplies, losses in land owing to rising seas, and diseases devastating large human populations. Taking a look at the history of warfare, the authors described how the strained carrying capacity of an environment has served as the breeding ground for conflict between various tribes or nations. When people have plenty, they live peacefully. But when diminishing resources threaten their survival, they go to battle. If Earth's carrying capacity for humans is abruptly lowered because of quickly changing climate conditions, we could see far more violent conflicts between the world's nations. "Today, carrying capacity, which is the ability of the Earth and its natural ecosystems including social, economic, and cultural systems to support the finite number of people on the planet, is being challenged around the world," the Pentagon report read. "With 815 million people receiving insufficient sustenance worldwide, some would say that as a globe, we're living well above our carrying capacity, meaning there are not sufficient resources to sustain our behavior."[13]

Human civilization couldn't exist long without a stable climate. The invention of agriculture came about at least 10,000 years ago as the last major ice age ended. The warming climate provided humans with the opportunity to end their hunt-and-gather lifestyle and put down roots in organized settlements where they could cooperate in growing crops and raising livestock. Ancient agricultural technologies provided the food resources and social stability for people in the past to evolve their simple villages into large cities, such as those in ancient Sumer, where Iraq now exists. Although Earth's warming led to the birth of civilization, that doesn't mean continued warming of our planet is a good thing. There is a window of climate comfort that allows us to live happily between the borders of a frigid ice age and a sweltering planetary warming age. We're now crossing that line into uncharted territory. If we go too far in heating up the planet, we'll see a progressive breakdown of civilization as natural necessities such as food and water become increasingly scarce and a mild climate environment vanishes.

If the report by Schwartz and Randall doesn't sound an alarm for America about climate change and its impact on our national defense, we should consider the opinions about this challenge from retired American admirals and generals. The CNA Corporation, a nonprofit organization, interviewed former officers from various branches of the armed forces and issued a 2007 report of its findings titled "National Security and the Threat of Climate Change." The officers warned that the "threat multiplier" effects of climate change will cause a growing political instability as basic social foundations start to crumble. Governments around the world might fail due to the stress of major environmental changes on the population. As the military superpower of the world, the United States might find itself drawn into an ever-increasing number of conflicts and wars around the globe. "Economic and environmental conditions in already fragile areas will further erode as food production declines, diseases increase, clean water becomes scarce, and large populations move in search of resources," the report said. "Weakened and failing governments, with an already thin margin for survival, foster the conditions of internal conflicts, extremism, and movement toward increased authoritarianism and radical ideologies."[14] In short, climate change may create a breeding ground for despots and dictators whom America might be forced to confront with armed action.

Climate change will compel the U.S. military to radically adapt to changing conditions on an ongoing basis for the next several decades. One logistical nightmare might come as many of our naval bases—especially those on low-lying islands in the Pacific Ocean—will have to be retrofitted as sea levels start to rise. In the Middle East, dwindling water supplies will generate social unrest that will add to our troubles in that region. Mass migration of humans will also force our military to adapt to deal with political instability in certain regions. Another report issued in November 2007 by Dan Smith and Janani

Vivekananda outlined a tragic scenario where environmental refugees must cross international borders as their own lands become swallowed by rising seas. Their report, "A Climate of Conflict," sees a world in which forty-six countries—equaling about 2.7 billion people—will be at high risk for armed conflict as humans start to clash for food and water and also political power to control those resources. An additional fifty-six countries with a total of 1.2 billion people will suffer "a high risk of political instability" due to climate changes reducing resources.[15]

PEAK OIL PROBLEMS

Besides climate-change challenges, we also need to factor into the equation of global political instability the decline of the world's oil product and our military's increasing dependence on that fossil fuel. Petroleum is a primary resource without which our modern armed forces could not exist. Because our nation's military consumes a vast amount of petroleum in its daily operations—everything from jet fuel for planes to diesel for tanks and trucks—the U.S. Army, Air Force, Navy, and Marine Corps will be forced to find even more ways to be more fuel efficient as the precious stuff becomes rarer. A September 2005 Pentagon report titled "Energy Trends and Their Implications for U.S. Army Installations" warned of the future problems America's military will have to face as world oil production starts to drop: "We shall continue to face geopolitical risks and uncertainties and concerns about energy security will continue to rise," it said. "Petroleum will remain the most strategic and political energy commodity with natural gas running a close second." The report also included this rather ominous statement: "Oil wars are certainly not out of the question."[16]

Twelve retired generals and admirals followed up on the perils of our reliance on foreign oil energy and protecting America's national security with a CNA Corporation report released in May 2009. "Powering America's Defense: Energy and the Risks to National Security" stressed how our society's high dependence on overseas petroleum reduces U.S. leverage with other nations, funds organizations and individuals who seek to harm America, and places our troops in dangerous regions of the world. It also undermines America's foreign policy by entangling the United States with "unstable and hostile regimes," the report said. Fossil fuels are a volatile market with the price of oil, natural gas, and coal swinging sharply with changes in production and consumption. This price volatility often makes it tough to determine government revenue projections, which in turn makes funding strategic and national security a challenge. "U.S. dependence on fossil fuels undermines economic stability, which is critical to national security," according to the CNA report.[17]

If members of the U.S. military are taking seriously the threat that global warming and peak oil pose to our national security, maybe the rest of us should, too. Innovation will be key to solving our security issues. In fighting World War II, many brilliant scientists led by physicist Robert Oppenheimer worked on a project to develop the atomic bomb as part of the military campaign against fascism. They called their secret work "the Manhattan Project." We need something similar today, wrote Lieutenant Colonel John Amidon in an article published in *Joint Forces Quarterly*. He suggests "a type of Manhattan Project for energy" organized by the federal government that will reduce our dependence on fossil fuels. "In sum," Amidon said, "trying to drill our way out of this crisis will not address the real problem, which is soaring demand and the danger of military conflict over shrinking resources."[18]

All branches of the U.S. military are now taking action to significantly reduce their fossil-fuel use in operating their bases and equipment. The U.S. Army is going green with an initiative using Fort Irwin in southern California's hot and sandy Mojave Desert to test solar panels and wind turbine technology. The electricity created by these sources powers computers and other electronics used by soldiers, as well as plug-in vehicles used to shuttle troops on the base. The Army also has developed tents for troops that are covered with up to three inches of insulating foam and a sun-reflective coating that reduces up to 75 percent of air-conditioning energy generation. This reduces the Army's carbon footprint by 35 million pounds a year—about the amount of carbon dioxide produced by 3,500 cars. The U.S. Navy is also experimenting with clean-energy sources, including using the hot water of underground geothermal sources to produce 270 megawatts of electricity to completely power its Naval Air Weapons Station China Lake in the Mojave Desert. The Navy is performing advanced experimentation with ocean thermal energy technology that one day might sustain its naval bases, which currently use up 25 percent of its annual energy expenditure. The U.S. Air Force consumes by far the most fossil fuel of all the four military branches. Jet fuel burned to fly heavy-duty cargo planes such as the C-5 Galaxy and supersonic fighters equals about 71 percent of all the oil consumed by America's military. Innovations that are now being developed in wing design will help to significantly reduce fuel consumption without losing aircraft performance. These innovations can go toward the design of new energy-efficient commercial aircraft carrying civilian passengers. Military ground transportation might one day go all electric. In 2009, Raser Technologies demonstrated an extended-range electric vehicle (EREV) Hummer H3 for members of Congress. The SUV drives 40 miles on a charge and can go up to 300 miles using electricity generated by a small gasoline engine, averaging over 100 miles per gallon in city driving. VIA Motors, a company based in Utah, purchased the technology in 2010 to manufacture an electrified version of a popular pickup truck called a VTRUX. Just as Department of Defense programs led to the development of the Internet, cell phones, and other technological wonders now commonly found in our modern society, investment in energy programs for military use will help spin off new clean-energy industries that will potentially create jobs for millions of Americans. The large tracts of land under the management of the American military can also be leased to private firms seeking to build solar, geothermal, and wind-energy sites—thus stimulating more jobs and economic benefits. The U.S. Army, for example, controls more than 12 million acres (4.9 million hectares)—much of it far from commercial and residential neighbors. This land could be used to generate much of the clean power to free us from fossil fuels.[19]

AMERICA AND CHINA

The problems of shrinking oil supplies and global climate change will affect everyone on our planet, including the more than 1.3 billion citizens of the People's Republic of China. Their nation is fast growing into a powerful economic Goliath as its government industrializes its infrastructure and modernizes its society. The dramatic changes we are now seeing in that Asian nation will require it to consume an ever-increasing amount of oil to sustain its growth. We saw alarming evidence of this in January 2010, when China's oil demands jumped 28 percent compared with the same month period a year earlier, according to the International Energy Agency (IEA). The IEA predicts that by 2035, China's energy demand will climb by 75 percent. Unless other energy resources are developed in China, its growing petroleum requirements will cause world oil prices to escalate. Climate-change problems could also devastate China, causing social and political unrest as its citizens face starvation and engage in violent conflict for diminishing resources.

China is now shaping strategic partnerships with oil-rich nations with which America has tense and deteriorating relations. Venezuela, Iran, Sudan, and, the biggest prize of all, Saudi Arabia are all forming long-term trade relationships with China. Venezuelan President Chavez, for example, has made agreements with Chinese companies to explore that South American country for oil and natural gas deposits and build new refineries. In March 2010, Chinese oil company CNOOC (China National Offshore Oil Corporation) announced a $3.1 billion cash deal to acquire a 50 percent stake in Bridas Energy, an Argentine-based oil-exploration firm controlling fields with a proven reserve of 636 million barrels of oil in Chile, Bolivia, and Argentina. In December 2009, another Chinese oil company, PetroChina, received the blessing of the Canadian government to purchase shares worth $1.9 billion in two oil-sand projects in Alberta. As U.S. relations with Saudi Arabia grew edgy after 9/11, the Chinese saw a business opportunity and stepped in to develop strategic partnerships with the House of Saud. The Chinese have even offered to sell intercontinental ballistic missiles to the kingdom.[20]

By 2030, China is expected to import more foreign oil than the United States does.[21] That day might be the tipping point for global politics, as China and its oil-producing allies edge America out as a customer, especially if the Chinese currency is worth much more than the U.S. dollar after several decades of a growing trade deficit. Dr. Gal Luft, a noted energy expert, believes that China's developing addiction to imported oil explains why the nation is linking up with petroleum-producing countries with which America is now at odds. "Though some optimists think that China's pursuit of energy could present an opportunity to enhance cooperation, integration, and interdependence with the U.S., there are ample signs that China and the U.S. are already on a collision course over oil," Luft told a Senate Foreign Relations Committee in October 2005. He added: "This will have profound implications for the future and stability of the Middle East and for America's posture in the region."[22]

U.S.–Chinese relations are relatively solid now. That situation, however, could dramatically change as the competition for Middle East oil intensifies after peak oil problems grow more prominent. The U.S. trade deficit with China, which hit a record $268 billion at the end of 2008, will hurt our economy, especially as increasing oil prices cause larger U.S. debts to this and other nations. China in November 2009 owned $789 billion in U.S. Treasuries—which gave it the largest ownership (about one-third) of the outstanding U.S. government debt. These debts compounded with a weak American economy could undermine our national security if we find it difficult to fund our military and security operations. Our trade deficit also results in a loss of jobs for Americans as more production goes to low-paid Chinese workers.

A century after Teddy Roosevelt's Great White Fleet sailed the world, America's military today stands as the most powerful in human history. As global climate change and peak oil upset global politics, we'll see the spread of international conflict. We can prevent these conflicts by decreasing our dependence on foreign oil so that we won't one day face unbearable economic competition with a modernized China and other countries. Promoting a sustainable-energy society and creating energy efficiency across our nation are vital steps in developing our national security and foreign policy in future years. Peace is America's best protection. Just as Roosevelt's Great White Fleet proved to the planet that America was the *military* power of the twentieth century, achieving our energy freedom will prove that the United States will be the *peace* power of the twenty-first-century world.

CHAPTER 6

Energy and the Environment

O n March 27, 1868, a twenty-nine-year-old traveler reached San Francisco on the steamship *Nebraska*. Soon after his arrival, he asked a local carpenter for directions for the quickest way out of the city. The workman replied, "Where do you want to go?" The traveler responded, "Anywhere that is wild."[1] That brief conversation set the Scottish-born John Muir on a walk into the wilderness that would make him a leader in the movement to save America's environment from exploitation. During the first stage of his journey, he passed through the Eden-like Santa Clara Valley and admired flowers blooming in sheets of spring color across the hillsides. By mid-April, he reached the tiny farm village of Gilroy and asked for directions to the Sierras. Someone pointed him east toward Pacheco Pass, which cut through the Diablo Mountain Range. On or close to his birthday on April 21, Muir arrived at the pass's summit and gazed toward the rising sun, beholding a landscape that would inspire him for the rest of his days. As he gained his first sight of the Sierra Nevadas on the other side of California's great Central Valley, Muir christened these magnificent mountains "the Range of Light." It's a description still used to convey their geologic grandeur.[2]

If he could observe our twenty-first-century world, the most important environmentalist in American history would certainly be concerned about the impact that pollution from fossil fuels has had on our planet's natural environment. Muir would no doubt support the energy-freedom movement in its goals of promoting renewable green-energy sources because he would understand that clean energy helps protect wilderness. He would also be troubled by how the global climate changes now taking place will wreak havoc on the natural landscape he loved so much.

Many Americans share Muir's passion to protect the environment. But others see protecting the environment and our need for energy as contradictory or mutually exclusive goals. Too many of us seem to regard our natural world as a garbage dump for our fossil-fuel debris and not as a beautiful home we are obliged to take care of for ourselves and for the future Americans who follow us. We often tend to place financial profit over the protection of the delicate ecological systems that we and all other life on Earth are a part of. Nowhere can this be more clearly witnessed than in the production, distribution, and consumption of fossil fuels. If we continue to increase our use of hydrocarbon energy in the coming decades without wise safeguards for the environment, we will do even more damage to the land, water, and air resources our biosphere and our lives depend upon.

OIL AND THE ENVIRONMENT

Some individuals have strongly endorsed a plan to reduce America's reliance on foreign oil by opening up a portion of the Arctic National Wildlife Refuge (ANWR) to oil exploitation. They also are demanding the development of offshore drilling along more and more of the environmentally sensitive portions of the outer continental shelf. Environmental groups have protested these proposals, insisting that the potential hazards to the delicate ecological systems in these areas do not warrant such a controversial policy. Oil companies, on the other hand, insist that they have the technology to drill and distribute this petroleum without harming animal and plant life. If the recent past is an indicator, we must be wary of such claims. We saw in the spring and summer of 2010 how the Deepwater Horizon oil rig disaster, which killed eleven platform workers and released 4.9 million barrels of crude into the Gulf of Mexico's waters, did extreme damage to marine and wildlife habitats, as well as devastated local fishing and tourism industries.

Deepwater Horizon was owned by offshore drilling contractor Transocean Ltd., and leased by London-based oil firm BP. Contract employees from oil service firms Halliburton, Anadarko, and M-I Swaco also resided on the rig. On April 20, 2010, workers on the rig located 41 miles (66 km) off the southeast coast of Louisiana were drilling an exploratory well into the Macondo Prospect. At about 9:45 P.M., an eruption of mud, methane, and seawater shot up the drill column. The methane gas ignited, engulfing the platform in a firestorm of explosions. Workers unsuccessfully tried to activate the blowout preventer. The 115 crew members who survived the accident were forced by the fire sweeping the platform to abandon the massive structure. The rig burned for thirty-six hours and then sank about 5,000 feet (1,500 meters) to the seafloor on April 22, 2010. As the world watched via underwater video cameras, the oil continued spewing for three months. The oil slick spread across the Gulf waters, damaging sensitive ecological niches. More than 125 miles (201 km) of Louisiana shoreline were covered with the crude. Alabama, Mississippi, and Florida beaches also got hit. President Barack Obama visited the region several times to check on BP's clean-up efforts and actions done to stop the spill. BP chief executive officer Tony Hayward created a public relations gaffe for himself and his company when he seemed to trivialize the spill, calling the oil slick and the 400,000 gallons of dispersant chemicals sprayed on the petroleum to break it up just a drop in the ocean. "The Gulf of Mexico is a very big ocean," he said. "The volume of oil and dispersant we are putting into it is tiny in relation to the total water volume." A month after the disaster started, Hayward did more damage to BP's corporate image when he sailed in a race in a 52-foot yacht around England's Isle of Wight while plumes of petroleum continued spewing from the uncapped Gulf well.

On July 15, 2010, engineers shut off the oil spill with a temporary cap. After relief wells permanently closed the well, BP officials on September 19 confirmed that the Deepwater Horizon spill was "effectively dead." In October, BP estimated that its total cost of the spill was $11.2 billion. This included the response to the spill, containment, costs to the federal government, grants to the states impacted by the spill, and individual claims. But the costs to the environment cannot be put into a spreadsheet form.[3] Repeating a sad story seen in many major oil spills throughout the world, thousands of birds, fish, and sea mammals were killed by the oil disaster, considered the worst spill in U.S. history. The environmental lesson we Americans must take to heart is that one poorly run well among hundreds or even thousands of well-run wells can do devastating damage to a region's ecosystem, especially one as complex and sensitive to petroleum pollutants as our oceans. Oil companies can never guarantee a 100 percent perfect safety record, and financial greed and human nature's propensity for taking shortcuts increase the risk of more such accidents happening in the future. Time and a thorough investigation will eventually confirm what mistakes were made that caused the Deepwater Horizon catastrophe—and who made them. In October 2010, the National Commission on the BP Deepwater Horizon Oil Spill released a report that revealed Halliburton officials allegedly knew of the flaws in the cement mixture that rig workers used to seal the well before the blowout but had not taken steps to address the issue.

The federal government has a responsibility to guard our natural environment from damaging exploitation of its resources by industry. After the full range of causes of this accident are fully analyzed, we must take steps to protect America's coastal waters and land from another oil-spill devastation. One way to do this is to promote legislation that moves us forward toward becoming a clean-energy nation. We still need to see if Americans were stirred by the Gulf of Mexico disaster to take action to minimize our offshore oil drilling by pushing political leaders to enact renewable-energy policies. A similar spill in Santa Barbara, California, in 1969 resulted in a nationwide environmental movement that created the Environmental Protection Agency to try to safeguard our natural world from such devastation. It is hoped that Deepwater Horizon will provide us with a growing awareness about how our daily actions impact our living environment.

Overall, the vast majority of the world's crude reaches its destination without incident. But still, a small percentage that does find its way into nature can do a great deal of damage. One estimate figures that 250 million gallons (950 million liters) of petroleum is accidentally released into the environment every year from tankers and offshore oil rigs. Although most of the oil drilled annually in Alaska and on offshore rigs doesn't necessarily pollute the environment in those locations, some of it unfortunately does get released into the wild. Aging equipment and harsh wilderness conditions found in the Arctic latitudes create conditions for accidental spills. Corrosion of the three-decade-old Trans-Alaska Pipeline in 2006 created a break in the pipeline that leaked up to 267,000 gallons of petroleum onto the frozen tundra. It not only made headlines but also made oil prices hit a record high as petroleum company BP shut down its drilling facilities in Prudhoe Bay. BP also had to shut down many of its Alaskan oil wells, owing to leaking. These incidents aren't anomalies. The Alaska Department of Environmental Conservation estimated that an average of 504 oil spills occur each year on the North Slope as Prudhoe Bay petroleum passes through the pipe.[4]

The environment is still not safe from petroleum peril when Alaska's oil ends its journey through the 800 miles (1,287 km) of pipeline and reaches the docked shipping tankers that will transport it to the lower forty-eight states. This pollution danger was infamously proven in 1989, when the tanker *Exxon Valdez* struck a reef and ruptured its hull, resulting in 37,000 tons (10.9 million gallons) of oil spilling into the waters of Prince William Sound. The petroleum spread across the waves to cover the pristine coastal ecology. More than 250,000 seabirds, whose feathers had been covered in oil, perished as a result. About 2,800 sea otters had their fur saturated with crude and died either of hypothermia or from ingesting the toxic substance when they tried to lick it off. The oil spill hurt Alaska's fishing industry for many years by killing off billions of salmon and herring eggs.[5] Although it ranks relatively low on the list of the world's largest oil spills in the amount of petroleum discharged, because of the fragile ecology it devastated, the *Exxon Valdez* disaster caused one of the oil industry's worst environmental calamities.

Petroleum tankers have grown massive in size over the last half century, vastly increasing the potential impact they might have on the environment if an accident happens and spillage occurs. In 1945, the largest tankers carried 16,500 tons of oil. Today's supertankers can hold more than 550,000 tons,[6] and their immense size also makes them harder to maneuver if they face an emergency situation during shipping. In the post-9/11 age, when the United States must deal with the ever-present threat of terrorism, the large, lumbering tankers could be prime targets for an attack or a sabotage.

The Gulf of Mexico's tropical environment is particularly endangered by oil pollution because of the high concentration of offshore rigs in this region. Every year, many thousands of gallons of crude product get spilled or dumped into the waters there, spreading their toxic material such as mercury through the fishing regions. The Gulf region also often gets devastated by powerful hurricanes, creating a threat that will most certainly grow worse as climate change from our planet's warming increases the strength of these storms. In 2005, many oil rigs in the Gulf of Mexico failed to withstand the forces of Hurricane Katrina and Hurricane Rita. Katrina destroyed forty-six offshore platforms and caused 233,000 gallons of oil to spill. Hurricane Rita destroyed sixty-nine offshore platforms, resulting in 508,000 gallons of oil going into Gulf waters. Adding to the environmental pollution, when Katrina hit Louisiana landfall, it caused the release of 8 million gallons of oil and hazardous chemicals stored at refining plants.[7] These toxic substances were carried by floodwaters into the city of New Orleans and surrounding suburbs. They leached into the soil and buildings. If left untreated, the long-term exposure to them experienced by humans and animals can result in leukemia and other life-threatening illnesses.

The visual of massive oil spills in ocean waters is dramatic and makes eye-grabbing images for the media. But much of the petroleum that pollutes our natural environment also comes from less sensational sources. Every day, refined oils find their way into our natural world from relatively small deposits, such as leaks in people's vehicles or illegal dumping down municipal drains. Washed by rains, much of this petroleum seeps into creeks, rivers, lakes, and bays, or it percolates through the ground into aquifers used by communities and farms. Some of this hydrocarbon gets broken down and detoxified over time as bacteria nibble on it in a process ecologists call bioremediation.[8] One side effect of this microbial digestion, unfortunately, is that it contributes to global climate change by releasing tons of carbon dioxide into Earth's atmosphere every year.

COAL AND THE ENVIRONMENT

Oil, of course, is not the only fossil-fuel pollutant. Coal is even dirtier and does considerably more damage to the world's natural environment. With its immense reserves, the United States produces more coal than any other form of energy. Before the 1970s, most of the country's coal was taken out of the ground by workers who rode elevators into deep mine shafts 2,000 or more feet under Earth's surface. As American oil production peaked in the early 1970s, and the demand for coal-generated electric power grew in the 1970s and 1980s, the coal industry started the widespread use of surface mining and open-pit techniques. Explosives blow up the rock and soil covering the coal reserves. Bulldozers and other heavy equipment then push the "spoil" aside to reveal the energy riches underneath. This mining technique produces more coal at less economic cost, thus broadening the bottom line for many coal companies. The environment, however, pays a steep price for these profits. Fertile soil erodes into rivers to be carried far away. Rainwater mixes with the toxic substances from the mining process and seeps into the surrounding water supplies. Wind lofts powdery coal dust into the air and spreads it onto vegetation and into the lungs of people and animals for miles around.

Today, the United States has more than 600 coal-powered plants generating about 54 percent of our nation's power, according to the U.S. Energy Information Administration. China is fast catching up to us in fossil-fuel usage as it undergoes a historic industrialization that requires the nation to produce ever more electric power from coal to meet the daily needs of its people. Coal power is revving up China's economic engine, accounting for about 69 percent of the primary energy it produces.[9] Unfortunately, China's coal-powered electricity is not subject to the same standards of environmental protection that regulate American plants.

The lack of pollution control is the main reason China's major cities have some of the dirtiest air in the world. Soot from burned coal dusts everyone and everything, causing serious health problems. The power plants spew out sulfur dioxide, which causes acid rain, damaging the ecology not only in China but also in neighboring South Korea and Japan. And the toxic pollution from Chinese coal plants hurts America's own natural environment, too. The smoke particles take as short a time as ten days to drift across the Pacific Ocean on trade winds before dropping down on U.S. soil and into waterways. One study pointed out that about 20 percent of the mercury found in Oregon's Willamette River comes from Chinese coal and other overseas locations.[10]

As globalization increases in China and other developing nations, the production and consumption of coal for electricity will grow significantly, putting added burden on the environment. The worldwide demand for coal is expected to grow between 60 percent and 80 percent between 2002 and 2025, depending on economic growth levels.[11] Many of the new coal-burning plants in foreign nations will not include carbon dioxide and pollution control systems, thus dirtying our air even more and increasing the planet's overall warming. But coal production might spike yet higher in coming decades once oil production peaks and starts to decline. The reduction in oil supplies might prompt an increase in a technique called coal liquidification to produce a synthetic fuel substance similar to gasoline to power the world's vehicles. The process was invented by German scientists and used for Nazi military efforts during World War II. They turned coal into a liquid fuel by adding hydrogen, thus producing a liquid hydrocarbon energy source to fuel the Third Reich's fighter planes and tanks as Germany's traditional oil supplies ran low. In our modern world, the mass production of coal as a liquid fuel to replace petroleum would have an immense environmental cost. Not only is it economically expensive to produce but it also generates large amounts of carbon dioxide. The Union of Concerned Scientists estimates that the production and consumption of liquid coal fuel would result in the release of 80 percent more greenhouse gas than would be created by petroleum-based gasoline.[12]

CLIMATE CHANGE

Letting the effects of our planet's current global warming grow worse with ongoing emissions of greenhouse gases means we will see greater stresses on Earth's ecological systems. Scientists describe a potential steady acceleration of climate changes because certain positive feedback loops in the environment will cause the release of more carbon dioxide into the atmosphere and thus increase the overall global temperature.[13] Under normal circumstances, there are a number of integrated systems—environmental control gauges, if you will—holding our planet at a stable temperature. Unfortunately, humans have meddled with these systems by dumping the vast quantities of greenhouse gases from fossil fuels into the thin mantle of air that envelops our planet. We can now see the warning signs that our tampering with the climate is starting to change the delicate ecological balance, beginning with the steady melting of the world's glaciers and alarming reductions in the polar ice caps. These large ice areas serve much like giant mirrors, as their white surface reflects solar radiation back into space, thus helping to keep the planet's temperature at a comfortable level. Liquid water, however, has the opposite effect. Water absorbs the sun's heat, thereby adding more energy into the system, which gradually increases Earth's ambient temperature. The melting of glaciers and polar ice thus sets up a feedback loop as less incoming solar heat is radiated into space and more is absorbed by newly melted water. As the oceans grow warmer, the process speeds up because more ice melts faster with the increasing heat. In the Arctic Ocean, the polar ice quantities are declining almost every year. The fabled "Northwest Passage" connecting Europe and Asia might, by 2030, be a reality during summer months, when the Arctic is essentially an ice-free area.[14] The opening of the ice might also trigger territorial disputes in the coming decades among nations seeking to exploit the petroleum, natural gas, and mineral reserves known to exist below the seafloor under Arctic waters. Beginning in 2006, Canada, Denmark, Norway, Russia, and the United States have each sent expeditions to the Arctic to support claims for exclusive rights to potential resources on the extended continental shelf.

If it were to melt entirely, the Arctic polar region would have only a little effect on the world's ocean levels because its ice is less than 10 feet thick and it floats on top of the seawater.[15] Humanity has a much more serious crisis, however, brewing on the opposite side of the globe. There, the world faces potential widespread environmental catastrophe because the southern polar region is also showing signs of melting. Unlike the Arctic's sea ice, most of Antarctica's ice rests on continental land. Over many millennia, nature has stored here trillions of tons of frozen water—about 90 percent of Earth's ice— to reach as high as three miles (4.8 km). Scientists have witnessed the increasing breakup of the ice in Antarctica as the great melt accelerates. On January 31, 2002, a massive 1,250-square-mile (2,011-square-km) piece of sea-based ice began, over a span of thirty-five days, to break off from the continent and drift into the waters of the southern oceans. The U.S. Geological Survey in February 2010 published a science report stating that between the years 1947 and 2009, the ice shelves in the Antarctic Peninsula have been retreating—and dramatically more since the 1990s.[16] This disappearance of the floating ice attached to Antarctic landmass is an indicator of what might continue to happen in the coming decades to planet Earth's ice-bound continent. This situation becomes particularly frightening because the sea-based ice forms a rim around Antarctica's shores that serves as a kind of dam holding back the mass of land-based ice. If the sea-based ice sheets are reduced in size as warmer water melts them, a tipping point will be reached where the land-based ice will lose its buttress and begin to slide into the ocean. Such a situation could spell disaster for many low-lying islands and coastal population areas. Billions of tons of ice spilling into the sea will significantly raise ocean levels and flood low-lying regions around the world. This rising seawater could play havoc on delicate coastal ecosystems by eroding beaches and killing off many animals and plant species that could not migrate elsewhere or adapt fast enough. The rising water levels could also potentially contaminate freshwater aquifers, thus imperiling agriculture industries and coastal communities.

Like Antarctica, Greenland's ice is also stored on a landmass. Scientists have estimated that if all of Greenland's ice or a major section of Antarctic ice melted or broke off into the ocean, the resulting sea level rise could be as much as 23 feet (7 meters).[17] If this were to happen, many cities—including London, Beijing, San Francisco, New York, and Sydney—would be forced to build expensive civic-engineering projects to deal with the rising tide. U.S. coastal areas in Gulf of Mexico states such as Louisiana are now seeing their land levels fall owing to the commercial extraction of oil and natural gas, which causes the continental shelf to collapse like a deflating balloon. Mounting sea levels will only compound the problems of this subsidence, forcing Americans who live in these areas to choose between losing their land or spending billions of dollars building barriers to protect their property from the rage of rising waters.

Climate change could also kill off large expanses of vegetation and create another equally scary positive feedback loop that would dramatically accelerate an increase of temperatures across our planet and further damage ecosystems. As the plant life dies off, it releases carbon dioxide and methane gases into the atmosphere. For example, the delicate tundra and permafrost in the Arctic regions of Alaska, Canada, and Russia are now being hit hard by the effects of our planet's increasing heat energy. Many of the trees that have evolved to live in these frozen locations are now finding it impossible to remain standing because the tundra melts during unseasonably warm summers and causes their root anchors to give way. Thousands of acres of "drunken trees" around the Fairbanks, Alaska, area sway off center as if intoxicated and eventually die. The permafrost in Alaska, Canada, and Russia also holds vast quantities of methane hydrate in a frozen state called a clathrate. As the Arctic continues to thaw, vast quantities of this molecule will be released and converted into methane gas, a greenhouse gas that is twenty-five times more potent in retaining heat than carbon dioxide. If enough permafrost hydrates melted over several decades, the methane-caused heat spike in atmospheric temperature would set off yet another positive feedback loop that would result in an accelerating climate-change event that humans won't be able to stop.

Climate changes can devastate environments in more temperate latitudes, too. As the planet gradually heats up, we might regularly see vast regions of the United States—especially those in the Midwest and the Southwest—hit by mega drought conditions lasting for many years or decades. The snowpack in the Rockies and the Sierra Mountain Range will also diminish or disappear, reducing in turn the supply of water that sustains many of America's farms and communities in the West. Long-term parching heat without rain conditions would make much of our nation's heartland resemble the Dust Bowl era of the 1930s and cause hundreds of thousands of acres of forestland to die and burn in devastating wildfires. This ecological disaster would add to the amount of carbon dioxide in the atmosphere, thus aggravating runaway climate change even more.

THE OCEAN WORLD

Marine plant life will face a particularly harsh environmental challenge from climate change. Some scientists theorize that the warming of the world's oceans will severely harm the tiny phytoplankton organisms that live in them. As the temperature of the top ocean layers rises, these plants receive fewer nutrients, such as nitrogen and phosphorus, because heated water stops transportation of these substances from the bottom upward when it hits a ceiling 100 feet below the ocean surface. These microscopic plants—essentially one-celled algae—serve as the foundation of the ocean's food chain. Tiny sea animals called krill that resemble shrimp live off of the plankton, and krill is eaten by larger sea creatures, from the smallest fish to the largest whales. If phytoplankton quantity declines, our oceans will face the reduction or even extinction of many of the astonishing organisms that inhabit them, including a variety of fish species and shellfish that we enjoy eating. A damaged food supply is not the only problem. The reduction of phytoplankton could add to the rising temperature of the planet. As small as these algae are, they exist in colossal quantities and therefore consume substantial amounts of carbon dioxide in the natural process of photosynthesis. If they become greatly reduced, the oceans would have a significant reduction in their ability to sequester this greenhouse gas, thus potentially speeding up climate change by creating yet another positive feedback loop.[18]

Fossil-fuel emissions pour a tremendous amount of carbon dioxide into the world's seas. About one-third of the carbon dioxide that human beings have spewed into the atmosphere from consuming ancient hydrocarbon for the last 200 years has sunk into the churning waters of the oceans. Although this is a good situation in one sense, because it serves to put a brake on climate change's effects for the interim, this process might be a major global catastrophe in the long term. Carbon dioxide mixing with the ocean's waters chemically raises the ocean's acidic level.[19] The resulting carbonic acid conditions as the seawater's pH level drops will deteriorate the saturation of calcium carbonate in the water. Calcium carbonate is an essential ingredient for sea life because many sea creatures use it to build their shell structures. Colorful coral, for example, builds its skeletal frame out of the material, creating incredible gardenlike reefs that give a haven to fish and other ocean critters. In recent decades, coral gardens around the globe have begun "bleaching" as they die off, providing us with a sad sign that much of the life in our world's oceans faces imminent demise because of the acidic corrosion. A study published in the February 2010 issue of the journal *Nature Geoscience* warns that our planet's oceans are acidifying at a rate ten times faster than another dramatic drop of the pH levels that occurred 55.8 million years ago, when naturally occurring global warming was caused by a rapid rise of carbon dioxide and methane in the atmosphere. Known as the Paleocene-Eocene thermal maximum, that prehistoric chemistry catastrophe, when ocean waters became too corrosive for single-celled organisms to form calcium carbonate shells, led to a mass extinction of many marine species, with a major breakdown of the food chain.

The sea around us plays an important role in maintaining Earth's environment in another significant way by more evenly dispersing the planet's heat energy and thus creating a relatively mild-mannered climate balance for most life forms. Oceans make up about 70 percent of our planet's overall surface and reach a depth of 6.8 miles (11 kilometers) at the Mariana Trench in the South Pacific. The heat energy stored in seawater has a direct influence on Earth's weather patterns. The circulation of ocean currents as water moves from the warm tropical regions to the frigid northern latitudes and back is particularly important for weather creation. The Gulf Stream, for example, functions much like a liquid conveyor belt by transporting the sun's heat energy, which is absorbed in tropical Gulf of Mexico waters, up to the chilly North Atlantic regions. This balances the temperature books and keeps Europe from turning into a giant Popsicle and mid-Atlantic regions from suffering as a yearlong sauna. The melting of the ice in the Arctic and Greenland, however, might someday flip the off switch on the Gulf Stream. Using advanced computer systems, scientists have modeled what might happen if these ice sheets melt and the freshwater dilutes the salty water of the Arctic and North Atlantic oceans. They have theorized that because the water would be lighter without the salt mineral, the Gulf Stream, when it reaches northern regions, would stop sinking into the depth as it loses heat. Putting a standstill on this important heat conveyor belt would cause the people living in northern latitudes of Europe and North America to suffer record-breaking freezing temperatures throughout much of the year. Faced with this dramatic change in the environment, many animals, plants, and people that couldn't adapt quickly enough would perish from starvation or extreme cold.

The shutdown of the Gulf Stream would have serious consequences for Americans living in lower latitudes, too. The constant flow of its waters helps to channel equatorial heat away from the southeastern states. If this circulation stopped, the temperature of the water now trapped in these regions would rise owing to the sun's daily radiation on it. People in the Caribbean, Mexico, and the southern coastal areas of the United States would possibly witness a significant increase in the number of hurricanes or a greater intensity of these ocean-born storms. Extreme weather events such as Hurricane Katrina might become more common catastrophic occurrences. Perhaps we are already seeing the early signs of more raging weather that will come in this century. A 2005 study done by Massachusetts Institute of Technology researchers found that major storms in both the Pacific and the Atlantic regions have increased in duration and strength by more than 50 percent since 1970.[20] *Nature* published a paper in 2008 analyzing satellite data of tropical storms since 1981, from which it was determined that maximum wind speed in the strongest storms grew significantly over the period of time studied. The researchers concluded that warmer sea-surface temperatures caused the stronger storms. The heated ocean water and warmer air increased the evaporation rate, which provided more energy for these superstorms, thus making them more intense in their fury.

HUMAN POPULATION

Most Americans fail to grasp the important fact that fossil fuels have played a key role in the steep human population growth the world has witnessed over the last 200 years. It's no coincidence that the rising human consumption of oil, coal, and natural gas correlates closely with the explosion in the number of people who inhabit our planet. Looking at the big picture, we see that it took 250,000 years for the human race to reach the 1 billion mark around the year 1800, which is right when the industrial revolution was just starting to build momentum and modernize the Western world. More than a century later, in 1927, the world population was 2 billion people. By 1960, there were 3 billion of us, and by 1974, 4 billion. We hit the 5 billion milestone in 1987, and the 6 billion mark in 1998. We are now closing in on the 7 billion mark expected in the year 2011, according to the Population Reference Bureau's World Population Data Sheet for 2009. If the trend continues, there will be 9 billion of us taking up surface space on the planet by the year 2050.[21] Like it or not, our growing multitudes create tremendous strain on Earth's natural environment.

Fossil fuels give the human race an artificial advantage over the natural world's tendency to prevent a species from achieving such explosive population growth. Fossil fuels provide material to make fertilizers, pesticides, and herbicides that civilization's modern farms require. Agricultural equipment and the trucks, trains, and ships used for transporting food across worldwide distribution systems all run on fossil fuels. Fossil fuels provide us with heating and cooling systems for our homes, enabling most of us to survive extreme temperatures that in preindustrial ages would have killed off the physically weak of our species. They enable us to treat sewage and supply clean water to towns and cities, thus reducing the spread of disease. Fossil fuels have also blessed humanity with the widespread distribution of medicines such as antibiotics and the availability of state-of-the-art medical equipment. These health blessings dramatically increased the human population during the last century by raising the average human life span from less than thirty years in 1900 to sixty-seven years in 2006.[22]

Unfortunately, the fossil-fuel-induced proliferation of the human species comes with a huge environmental price. As we expand our population base at the same time that we are increasing global industrialization, we are forced to exploit more resources to sustain the modern lifestyle we have grown so accustomed to living. Hydrocarbons let us concentrate most of our species in immense urban areas that dot the globe. As our modern cities spread in suburban sprawl, land and waterways must be altered to provide for the needs of the mounting numbers of urban dwellers.

The success of *Homo sapiens* and our ability to grow in numbers, and thus alter Earth's ecology, puts in peril many other life forms on our planet. Numerous animal and plant species face the ever-mounting threat of extinction because people are encroaching upon their territories. Perhaps because many of us live in urban environments, we have a human tendency to forget that we must share our world with other organisms that have a right to live on Earth. We also tend to forget that we are part of a complex web of life. The more species that are cut out of this planetwide web, the less secure is our own survival. What is especially frightening is how climate change caused by humankind's use of fossil fuel is damaging that delicate interlocking of all life forms. Some scientists predict that changes to Earth's climate systems during the next 100 years will kindle a massive die-off of many plant and animal species that can't adapt or evolve fast enough to deal with the sudden alterations of their habitats. One study done at the University of Leeds in England warns that by the year 2050, "well over a million species" now on Earth will have their ecological niches altered so severely from climate change that they will be threatened with extinction. Because humans are accountable for the causes of this potential catastrophe, we have a primary responsibility to prevent it.

We must acknowledge that sudden mass die-offs of animal and plant life have happened on our planet in the past. About 250 million years ago during the Permian Age, Earth suffered a massive loss of 95 percent of its marine species and 70 percent of land animals and plants. No one is sure what exactly killed so much animal and plant life so suddenly, but one theory is that a sudden massive release of methane into the atmosphere might have caused the planet to heat up too quickly and thus created high stress on the biosphere. A similar event might be on the verge of happening in the future. In the twenty-first century, scientists studied the methane in permafrost submerged underwater in the East Siberian Arctic Shelf and found that 8 million tons of this gas is escaping into the atmosphere each year. Levels of methane in Arctic air are higher than they have ever been in at least 400,000 years, the researchers found. According to an article in the March 5, 2010, issue of *Science* magazine that featured this study, the undersea Arctic permafrost is showing signs it is destabilizing and might release even more methane.[23] This has the potential of altering our biosphere so much so quickly that many species would not be able to evolve fast enough to survive. A 1998 poll done by the American Museum of Natural History found that 70 percent of the 400 biologists surveyed believe that a similar mass extinction of life on Earth is now under way and will put at risk humanity's existence, too.[24] This threat is yet another call for the human race to reduce fossil-fuel emissions worldwide.

GOING NUCLEAR?

As the world's supply of fossil fuels starts to decline, Americans will debate more and more about whether we should build power plants that generate electricity using the energy of the radioactive element uranium. Nuclear power has a controversial history, but it could supply a significant portion of our nation's energy (it now provides 20 percent of America's electric power). Its advantages and shortcomings should be given serious consideration. France is often cited as the poster child of a successful national nuclear program, with government-controlled utility Electricité de France (EDF) producing nearly 80 percent of that European nation's electricity at its fifty-nine nuclear power plants. Electric power in France, however, costs more to produce than power in most of the United States, and electric utility cost is an important consideration, especially to American consumers. The French reactors use a single engineering design, minimizing potential technical problems. Moreover, France's nuclear-waste issue has also been well engineered, with the waste stored at various facilities such as a 350-acre (141.6-hectare) site in the province of Ardennes, rendering its entire nuclear system as safe and efficient as possible. If the United States decides to embark on a "go nuclear" program, France's approach is one to consider modeling.

Current U.S. policy offers subsidies for nuclear-fission power, but these subsidies have so far been insufficient to entice investors to put up the money needed to build new nuclear power plants. No new nuclear power plants have been built in the United States for the last thirty years, but this might change if our global climate crisis and the decline of oil supply spur a renaissance in energy from the atom. In February 2010, President Obama pledged more than $8 billion in conditional loan guarantees to build two nuclear reactors in Georgia. In addition, some well-known environmentalists, such as British environmental scientist James Lovelock, have strongly advocated increasing the world's use of atomic energy because they believe it is "environmentally friendly" for our planet.[25] They argue that replacing coal- and oil-powered electricity plants with nuclear reactors will significantly reduce carbon dioxide emissions. The nuclear-power industry itself is now pitching to the public the potential benefits of nuclear power as a "green" energy solution to global climate change. But before our nation starts taking steps to construct more nuclear power plants as an alternative energy source to fossil fuels, we must carefully weigh the environmental risks that the proliferation of fission-powered reactors poses for us.

Certainly, if looked at narrowly, the radioactive decay of uranium that releases energy at the heart of a nuclear reactor produces no carbon by-products. But if we think about the big picture, if we consider the entire process of generating nuclear energy from start to finish, we find that with current technologies, great quantities of fossil fuels are still required. Oil is used to mine the uranium ore from out of its geological deposits and ship it by truck and train to processing sites. Here, more fossil-fuel power is required to crush and mill the ore and to enrich it to form concentrated uranium pellets. Building the nuclear power plants themselves also requires the use of coal and oil—especially in producing the hundreds of thousands of tons of cement and steel needed to fortify the containment structures. (New technology is now being developed that might one day sequester carbon dioxide in a new form of cement, thus helping to solve this problem.) Nuclear energy also requires large amounts of water for cooling purposes, and water requires energy—presumably fossil-fuel energy—to process and transport.

An analysis report titled "Nuclear Power: The Energy Balance" was prepared for the Green parties of the European Parliament by Jan Willem Storm van Leeuwen and Philip Smith for the United Nations Climate Conference in 2000. Since then, they have updated their report several times and they warn that the nuclear-power industry's portrayal of nuclear energy as a solution to climate change might not be quite on the mark. The authors state in their detailed study that "the use of nuclear power causes, at the end of the road and under the most favorable conditions, approximately one-third as much carbon dioxide (CO_2) emission as gas-fired electricity production." They then warn us about the unsustainability of nuclear power. "The rich uranium ores required to achieve this reduction are, however, so limited that if the entire present world electricity demand were to be provided by nuclear power, these ores would be exhausted within nine years. Use of the remaining poorer ores in nuclear reactions would produce more CO_2 emissions than burning fossil fuels directly."[26]

After the process of extracting the uranium from the ore, millions of tons of mill tailings carrying radioactive debris are left as waste. In the past, this debris was often dumped in out-of-the-way places, such as on the tribal lands of Native Americans.[27] The discard became an environmental hazard that polluted water and soil and made the dump site a toxic wasteland. Exposure to radioactive tailings can cause significant health problems years later. The nuclear industry has a moral responsibility to bury this waste safely in deep underground locations where there is a minimum of environmental danger.

But the cost of this proper disposal process—estimated at four times the original mining process—puts a steep price tag on nuclear energy, making the economic challenges of nuclear power much more difficult.[28] This remediation activity also would emit more carbon dioxide into the air from the fossil fuels burned to operate the heavy equipment used in the digging and covering process.

The environmental menace from a nuclear reactor incident caused by equipment failure, human error, natural catastrophe, sabotage, or attack must be assessed as the United States contemplates building new nuclear power plants in the future. Although the U.S. nuclear-power interest groups tell the public that the power plant designs are, on the whole, safe under all circumstances, some skepticism is warranted. A terrorist attack could cause a Chernobyl-like catastrophe, and it is clear after the Fukushima disaster in Japan that natural events cannot always be foreseen. Calamities such as these could poison thousands of square miles of American soil for several generations. Depending on the extent of the damage, the environmental devastation from such a disaster could, depending on location, severely injure our nation's and the world's economy for many years. Environmental disaster might also come from a terrorist attack. A declassified U.S. National Academy of Sciences report prepared at the request of Congress and made public in April 2005 found that tighter security is required at many U.S. reactor sites. At special risk are the spent-fuel cooling pools. Located outside of the main reactor building sites, these water pools store the hundreds of tons of highly radioactive nuclear waste left over from years of energy production by the reactor. The study found that "under some conditions, a terrorist attack that partially or completely drained a spent-fuel pool could lead to a propagating zirconium cladding fire and the release of large quantities of radioactive materials to the environment."[29]

Another environmental worry that arises from nuclear power concerns the proper disposal of the used radioactive waste material. This waste can remain highly toxic for as long as 600 years for both strontium 90 and cesium 135, and 500,000 years for plutonium 239. This creates an ongoing disposal problem for many generations who follow us. More than 75,000 metric tons of spent-fuel waste have now been created by nuclear plants and defense-related activities in the United States, and its continued production will only accelerate if more such energy facilities are built. The federal government looked into the nuclear-waste disposal problem and decided to select a permanent central storage site for our nation's radioactive material. In 1987, Congress picked Yucca Mountain, a remote location in the Nevada desert about 93 miles (150 kilometers) northwest of Las Vegas, to store 70,000 metric tons of spent nuclear fuel and radioactive waste.[30] The choice of this out-of-the-way site, however, is controversial. Yucca Mountain is in a geologically complex zone with active earthquake faults in the vicinity of the mountain. One 5.6-magnitude earthquake on June 29, 1992, did at least $1 million in damage to the Department of Energy's (DOE's) facility built eight miles (12.8 km) from the mountain site.[31] A study commissioned by the DOE and jointly released in 2002 by the International Atomic Energy Agency and the Nuclear Energy Agency of the Organization for Economic Cooperation and Development (OECD) determined that the DOE's understanding of the "hydrogeologic performance" of the proposed nuclear repository was "low, unclear, and insufficient to support an assessment of realistic performance."[32] In short, the peer-reviewed report brought into question the maturity of the science used to determine whether or not Yucca Mountain was the environmentally right choice for America's nuclear-waste dump site.

In March 2010, the Energy Department withdrew the application to build a nuclear-waste depository at Yucca Mountain. The Obama administration established a panel to recommend other alternatives for dealing with the waste. But the issue is seized with political and practical problems. If a central storage facility for nuclear power plant waste material is ever built, the United States would need to transport, over many years, tens of thousands of tons of radioactive material thousands of miles across a multitude of state lines. In more than 50,000 shipments,[33] the waste would be hauled on diesel-powered trucks, barges, and railroad cars that would emit carbon dioxide into the atmosphere. These shipments would also make a tempting target for terrorists intent on causing mass devastation by irradiation of a region. Certainly, the shipping of the nuclear waste would cause great political controversy for the various communities along the route to the nuclear-waste storage facility, resulting in years of headaches for elected officials at both the state and the national level. We saw an example of this in Dannenberg, Germany, in autumn 2010, when more than 4,000 antinuclear activists clashed with riot police to try to stop the shipment by rail of 123 tons of nuclear waste from a French reprocessing plant. The demonstrators also sought to protest Chancellor Angela Merkel's plan to extend the use of Germany's seventeen nuclear power plants by twelve years beyond their initially planned use period.

As the nation rejuvenates its interest in nuclear energy, more advanced power-plant technologies are being suggested. One innovation being promoted in recent years is small modular reactors (SMRs), which would be about a third of the size of traditional nuclear power plants. These would be manufactured in factories and transported to a site where they would be literally plugged into an electric grid. The Obama administration has requested $39 million from Congress to advance this technology. Reprocessing waste by separating out the plutonium element and using it in breeder reactors is another possibility—one that might help the United States reduce the total mass of nuclear waste to dispose of. France uses "mixed oxide" (MOX) fuel in its nuclear plants. The trouble with reprocessing is the peril of proliferation—the plutonium could be used for building a nuclear bomb. The reprocessing is also extremely expensive, costing at least $20 billion to build a reprocessing plant. A third potential technology is the "traveling wave" nuclear-reactor concept first suggested in the 1950s. This nuclear-energy system is a slow-burn reactor in which uranium fuel is placed in a closed cylinder and a self-sustaining chain reactor is induced that breeds neutrons—perhaps for as long as 100 years. As for now, this traveling-wave technology remains unproven, although it received an impetus of interest in early 2010 when Microsoft founder Bill Gates put some of his money behind a private venture called TerraPower LLC, exploring ways to make it a reality. Other technologies in nuclear-reactor designs exist, such as the fast-neutron reactors that have the capability to reduce nuclear waste in the process of generating electricity. This technology has the potential of transforming nuclear energy into a safer and more cost-effective power source than conventional reactors. Fast-neutron reactor technology should be researched and, if proven safe for the public and clean for the environment, developed as appropriate to advance our nation's access to a non-fossil-fuel energy source. However, before we take steps in implementing any type of advanced nuclear-reactor technology, we also need to have a clear understanding of the true costs—financial, health, and environmental—associated with generating new forms of nuclear energy so we will make informed decisions.

Despite the environmental drawbacks of using current systems for generating nuclear power, technological advances are possible that could provide a truly green source of power from the atoms. Scientists around the world are doing research that might one day develop technology allowing nations to build nuclear power plants that use fusion reactors to produce electricity. Unlike today's fission reactors that require tons of enriched uranium to serve as the heat source, fusion-powered reactors would use the much cleaner energy contained in atoms of hydrogen. By means of a process similar to the one the sun uses to create nuclear energy at its core, a fusion-powered reactor would generate high pressure and temperatures sufficient to fuse the nuclei of hydrogen atoms together and release neutrons to create heat that would then be used to generate electricity. The United States is currently researching this potentially game-changing technology at the National Ignition Facility in Livermore, California, which has the world's largest and highest-energy laser; and also at New Mexico's Sandia National Laboratory, which has the Z Machine, the largest X-ray generator in the world. We have no guarantee, of course, that human beings will ever achieve the needed breakthrough in fusion-power technology for its safe use in commercial energy production. But if we can find a way to tap such a sustainable source of energy, it could provide a significant portion of electric power for our modern civilization. Some people say that such a breakthrough is possible by the year 2050. Others say that we'll never find the answer.[34] Time and human ingenuity may prove the naysayers wrong. Some remarkable scientific innovation in fusion-power reactor design that might develop in the next forty to fifty years would make this potential energy source more than just a pipe dream. In the end, whether it be fission or fusion, nuclear power must prove to be both safe for public health and the environment and cost-effective for consumers. As the price of producing and consuming fossil fuel increases and as nuclear technology improves, the power contained in atoms will look more attractive.

If American environmental hero John Muir were to stand at the summit of northern California's Pacheco Pass one morning here in our twenty-first-century world and look out upon his beloved Sierra Mountains, he'd see certain striking changes from his first view, back in 1868. Unless he lucked upon a rare clear day, the Range of Light would most likely be hidden from view by the layer of thick smog that often covers California's Central Valley. He'd be puzzled by the endless parade of cars as workers commute along the ribbon of an asphalt highway snaking through the mountain pass to nearby Silicon Valley. Certainly, he'd be amazed to find out about the rotating turbines of the Pacheco Pass Wind Farm on a nearby ridge. He'd be astonished to learn that the turning blades provide power for about 3,500 homes. If somehow he could witness today's America, Muir would take a keen interest in how significant the issue of energy is in relation to the ecological health of our planet. He would surely be concerned about the impact that fossil fuels have on the natural world. And he'd be curious about nuclear energy and how the power inside atoms might be a "green-energy" source. Muir would understand that energy and the environment are closely connected, and that would prompt him once again to serve America in a political activist role by pushing clean- and sustainable-energy sources for the preservation of the wilderness. Unfortunately, Muir can no longer save America's environment for future generations to enjoy. But *we* can.

CHAPTER 7

Energy and the Economy

Fossil fuels made the Roaring Twenties a champagne time in American history. Powered by hydrocarbon, our nation experienced a decade of massive production and consumption of goods, which helped to stimulate a boom in the U.S. economy. The large-scale automaking plants in Detroit, for example, churned out a seemingly endless stream of vehicles for the millions of U.S. citizens hungry for the freedom of the road. Factories manufactured appliances such as washing machines, vacuum cleaners, stoves, refrigerators, and other electric goods sold to legions of consumers on installment credit options. The economic expansion of the boisterous Jazz Age seemed as if it would continue forever, so many Americans grew giddy with dreams of Wall Street wealth and began investing heavily in stocks. Often, they speculated on margin, gambling with money they didn't actually possess.

Unfortunately for many, the exciting nationwide party ended with heartache when Black Tuesday hit America on October 29, 1929. As stocks plunged in value the economy nosedived with them, plummeting America and the rest of the world into the Great Depression of the 1930s. Our nation faced the worst financial slump in its history. Factory production, once heavily fueled by coal and oil energy, came to a shuddering stop as many Americans faced heavy debts and lack of employment.

Here in the twenty-first century, Americans can learn some valuable monetary lessons from the 1920s and the 1930s. We've built an economy on the shifting sands of fossil fuels, and this situation now imperils us to the dictates of the hydrocarbon market. Once the energy supply of oil and natural gas sources reaches its zenith and starts an ever-accelerating plunge toward depletion, the fossil-fuel-based production of manufactured goods throughout the world will also inescapably start a parallel free fall. Fossil fuels are the economic lifeblood of the American nation. The industrial sector accounts for 38 percent of all energy consumption,[1] and the vast majority of this energy comes from coal, oil, and natural gas. Investors and business institutions across the United States understand what this high dependence on hydrocarbon energy means to the economic strength of our nation. The basic laws of supply and demand regulate the rise and fall of the price of fossil fuels. This fact will cause our nation severe financial strain in the near and long term as the world deals with a growing population of people demanding a dwindling supply of oil and natural gas.

We got a preview during the 1970s, after oil prices spiked when our nation faced the threat of a reduced supply of crude because of the OPEC oil embargo. A domino effect resulted. As a consequence of the price volatility of oil, many American companies had to close their doors because they couldn't cope with the high energy costs. That resulted in many people losing their jobs. Increased unemployment meant that Americans couldn't purchase as many goods and pay for services, resulting in the spread of even more economic hardship across our nation. The unhappy outcome of the OPEC-induced oil price hike was a severe recession that reduced the quality of life for many Americans.[2]

Today, the entire world faces a nagging uncertainty about the supply of the crude oil that many people heavily depend upon for their economic security. When sooner or later the production of oil peaks, as it must, we will begin to see tsunami-size shock waves ripple through the global economy as the decline of petroleum products accelerates financial loss around the world. Perhaps we are now seeing the warning signs of this ominous situation as oil prices show a pattern of increasingly dramatic fluctuation. Crude-oil prices averaged $33.39 a barrel in 2000 (in 2007 dollars). In 2007, the annual average had almost doubled, to $64.92. The price passed the $100 a barrel mark for the first time in December 2007. It continued to go up and hit $147 in July 2008, rising more than 400 percent during a seven-year period. In 2010, the annual average price for a barrel of oil in the United States was about $76. Compare this price to that of 1998, when a glut of oil on the world's market put the price tag for a barrel of oil at an annual average of $15.35 (in 2007 dollars).[3] Those days of bargain-basement petroleum prices might now be only a memory as the economic laws of supply and demand start propelling price trends in a generally upward direction in the coming decades.

Cheap fossil-fuel energy helped stimulate America's astounding economic expansion of the 1990s—much as it did in the 1920s. With prices at the pump at such low levels during the last decade of the twentieth century, car manufacturers flooded the market with SUVs. The booming times encouraged millions of our citizens to follow the American dream and purchase "McMansion" homes for their families. These houses, of course, needed to be filled with items to make them comfortable for their new owners. That meant that Americans spent more of their disposable-income dollars at appliance shops, furniture stores, and home and garden centers, which in turn helped build businesses, created even more jobs, and further stimulated our economy. Unfortunately, economic booms can go bust. Throughout American history, we have seen the cycle of wealth generation go through dramatic swings. If the United States continues along with its business-as-usual energy strategy, we will face more and massive economic downturns in the future, as the world's production of petroleum plateaus and starts to decline.

The fiscal problems of peak oil that America and the rest of the world now face will only be compounded by climate changes brought about by the burning of fossil fuels. The consequences will be decreased productivity around the world as extreme weather events transform our planet's environment. Long periods of drought would reduce freshwater supplies for crops and manufacturing. These dry spells would also hit the tourist business in vacation-oriented regions of the United States. A reduction in mountain snowpack, for example, would impair the skiing industry. Shrinking lakes and streams would cause a sharp decline in the number of vacationers devoted to fishing or water recreation. If it's not a drought, it's a deluge. Hurricanes and other storms will grow in intensity, causing severe catastrophic financial loss across heavily populated regions along America's Gulf Coast and Atlantic Coast. Hurricane Katrina cost the U.S. economy an estimated $200 billion—more than 1 percent of the gross domestic product. If continued climate change results in greater severity of these massive storms, certain regions of the United States will have to cope with catastrophic bashing by the weather and face significant economic problems.

The effects of climate change could also hurt America's economic productivity. Employees could end up taking more sick days owing to hot weather and related problems of poor water sanitation and insect-carried illnesses. A decline in the quality and quantity of food caused by climate change could result in poorer health for many workers and their families. Rising health-care costs as more U.S. citizens become sick from climate-related illnesses would cut into paychecks and reduce the amount of money we can spend on other items. Property damage loss would also hurt the U.S. economy as we face an increase in intense storms and tornadoes in the East and Midwest and devastating wildfires in the West and Northwest caused by higher temperatures. The social disorder that might result from climate change as people grow desperate for food and water would create additional property damage if law enforcement cannot cope with a breakdown of public order. Production losses stemming from the dual crises of peak oil and climate change could cause a nasty long-term downturn in our national economy, resulting in less money in community coffers to pay for many basic public services such as police, fire, and hospital care.

CAP AND TRADE

If the money experts are right, climate change will bring a nasty blow to America's and the world's financial health if we fail to take action to diminish its effects by implementing smart energy and transportation policies. A 2008 study by economists Frank Ackerman and Liz Stanton estimated the total cost of climate change to Americans if current trends continue. They found that by the year 2100, global warming will have as much as a 3.6 percent impact on our nation's GDP.[4] There have been several highly respected studies on climate change's impact on the future of the global economy, but none made as much of a stir as the 700-page report prepared for the British government by Lord Nicholas Stern, who served as the chief economist for the World Bank between 2000 and 2003. Released in October 2006, "The Stern Review: The Economics of Climate Change" provides us with an eye-opening appraisal of the high financial stakes our planet's warming will have on all nations. A man not given to exaggeration, Stern said in his report that "climate change presents very serious global risks, and it demands an urgent global response." Stabilizing greenhouse gases will be costly, but the costs of continuing on with a business-as-usual attitude will be far more expensive in the long run, he said. He added that the financial toll will hit people even harder than the combined effects of World War I, World War II, and the Great Depression. "Our emissions affect the lives of others," Stern said. "When people do not pay for the consequences of their actions, we have market failure."[5]

Stern's report projected that the world could possibly avoid the worst impact by keeping our emissions at current levels at a financial cost of about 1 percent of the annual gross domestic product for the entire globe. In 2009, the world's GDP was more than $70 trillion, so 1 percent would equal about $700 billion. That's a lot of money, but it's a better deal than doing nothing at all. A lack of action in climate control will cost the world between 5 percent and 20 percent of its annual gross domestic product, Stern figured. If we don't aggressively deal with the problem now, the people of our planet will pay many trillions of dollars every year to deal with climate change's effects.

Stern's report also provided policymakers with a number of suggestions for how to pay for programs needed to stabilize greenhouse gas emissions to prevent a catastrophic global climate crisis. Among them are regulating the greenhouse gas output of industry. These plans would essentially punish businesses for their carbon emissions. But one of the more creative concepts involves financially rewarding the market for regulating itself. The "cap-and-trade" idea works much like the stock market by making pollution reduction a kind of commodity asset for businesses. A government entity sets a total mandatory emission cap—or permits—that polluters must purchase in order to emit CO_2. It is widely accepted that a public auction of CO_2 (or other greenhouse gas) emissions permits is the fairest way to dispense emissions allowances. There is some controversy, however, on how to best transition to auctioning all carbon permits versus initially granting some permits to traditional carbon emitters. Some businesses will find it possible to meet these fixed emissions allowances, and even *earn* permits by producing clean energy. They can then sell, for profit, their surplus permit allowances to companies that are unable to stay under the cap. Environmental groups or other organizations can also buy the allowances and "retire" them from the market, thus increasing the value of the allowances that are left because of the reduced supply. This carrot instead of stick approach provides a high financial incentive to the business market to come up with improved technologies for carbon emission reductions. These innovations can then be sold to other companies that will use them to increase their own profitability in carbon-emissions trading.[6]

The cap-and-trade system is a proven idea. It was developed by the U.S. Environmental Protection Agency (EPA) as a successful experiment to reduce acid rain caused by sulfur dioxide emissions from coal-burning plants that were destroying the forestlands of northeastern North America. The system requires several components to make it operate successfully. An enforcement agency—such as the federal government—administers the program and allocates or auctions off the permits. The regulating agency must have enough legal bite to make sure companies follow the rules. Cap and trade also requires an accurate way to measure and verify emission readings and a reporting process that is transparent enough to make sure the integrity of the measurements is preserved. Because carbon dioxide gases mix thoroughly into our planet's atmosphere and thus have a worldwide effect wherever their source might be, this greenhouse gas is ideal for a cap-and-trade system of emissions control as it creates a market with a level playing field.

Combined with the capping and trading of carbon emissions, we must also consider improving the aging condition of America's electric grid infrastructure, because its energy inefficiency contributes to the rise of climate-change challenges and thus also endangers our economy. Our nation's power plants—the majority of them running on coal—provide energy every second to a network of 157,000 miles (252,667 km) of high-voltage transmission lines that link to America's homes and businesses. According to the Department of Energy (DOE), the average thermal efficiency of the power plants on the grid is about 33 percent, not far from what it was fifty years ago. Because coal-powered plants produce so much carbon dioxide, improvements that would raise their thermal efficiency to 50 percent or more—as we might be able to do with advanced gasification technology[7]—would help to reduce greenhouse gas emissions considerably. The beauty of the cap and trade system is that it would give the owners of these plants a financial incentive to develop and install the technology to reach this level of energy efficiency. They would be rewarded for cleaning up their energy production processes. Considering the broader energy industry, cap and trade would also promote innovations, driven by public and private investment, to make low-carbon energy technologies cost less than fossil-fuel energy. If managed wisely, this will stimulate an upward spiral of economic growth for our nation.

The overloaded condition of America's electric grid also impacts our nation's global emissions because of power that is lost in the lines. Bottlenecks and inefficient management of energy passing through the transmission system both cause waste. This energy waste can equal as much as 9 percent of the electric power passing through the system.[8] The electricity transmission loss problem will get worse unless we take action to fix our grid with more energy-efficient power lines and substations. Unfortunately, the economic risk of installing electric transmission systems is discouraging utility companies from proceeding with new installations. Promoting a cap-and-trade system might be one way for these businesses to find a financial stimulus to increase the efficiency of their power distribution, thus cutting down on energy waste and enabling them to make a profit by selling off the permitted carbon allowances.

Our nation's economic strength is directly plugged into our electric grid system and depending on an aging and overcapacity system can be dangerous for our future financial health. As our population increases and we demand even more electricity to power our homes and businesses, we will experience increased congestion over existing lines. Blackouts and brownouts will become more frequent occurrences if we fail to make the needed improvements. These power outages will lead to lost productivity and severe damage to regional economic development. According to the DOE, power outages, as well as reduced quality of electric service, cost the American economy between $25 billion and $180 billion every year in productivity losses. If a large region gets hit by a power failure lasting several weeks, it would cost tens of billions of dollars. Economists have estimated that if a third of the American nation—about 100 million people—lost power for three months, it would result in a loss of $700 billion in productivity.[9] That kind of potential financial devastation to our nation makes our power grid a prime target of terrorists or enemy nations. If they could cut segments of our national electric network—by either a cyberattack or physical destruction of substations—they would create tremendous hardship to millions of Americans. Improving the integrity and efficiency of our national grid system will help to prevent such economic and social calamities. It will also reduce the amount of electricity lost in the transmission lines, which lets power plants decrease their coal consumption, thus saving them money and lowering their carbon dioxide emissions. A small improvement can add up to big energy savings. A 5 percent increase in America's electricity grid efficiency, for example, would cut the need to build ninety large coal-fueled electric plants in the future, according to Jon Wellinghoff, the chairman of the Federal Energy Regulatory Commission.[10]

Power disturbances will become more serious over the next two decades if we don't upgrade the quality of our national grid. According to the U.S. Energy Information Administration, the United States will require 281 gigawatts of additional generating capacity by the year 2025 to meet increased consumer electricity use. Producing this tremendous amount of energy would require construction of 937 new 300-megawatt power plants during the next fifteen years. Adding to the problem is that many aged U.S. power plants are coming to an end of their usefulness and will be shut down and decommissioned. Upgrading our nation's electric grid will be a Herculean task that will require $100 billion or more.[11] The project can perhaps be paid for, in part, through cap-and-trade incentives. If significant energy-efficiency improvements made to the grid could be counted as carbon allowances, then electric utilities would have a financial incentive to make such improvements. Regardless of how we pay for it, the money we invest in improving our aging grid system will be small indeed compared to the tremendous losses that will accrue to our economy and society if major sections of the power grid break down continually as customer demand for electricity increases over the coming decades.

Energy freedom as a goal may help persuade local, state, and national leaders to take action to improve our grid. One option is to make this complex electric network smarter by installing more information-technology components into the system that will monitor the power flow and provide distribution operators with the real-time data they need to better match electric supply with customer demand. This would vastly improve customer service and lower energy waste and production costs. Also, "smart meters" installed at homes and businesses would enable customers to better manage their electricity dollars by using power at nonpeak times. Technology is now available that will enable us to build decentralized electric grids to distribute power to customers in a narrowed location instead of the three large regions that currently transmit electric power. The construction of modern decentralized grids would help us to better manage a localized network of power plants that use sustainable fuel sources such as solar, wind, geothermal, hydropower, and biomass to produce electricity. Because electricity wouldn't need to travel far distances to reach customers, less energy would be wasted from transmission-line loss or bottlenecks. The smaller scale and diversity of the decentralized grid would also make it less likely to cause a cataclysmic economic collapse in the event of equipment failure or a terrorist attack. Developing decentralized grid systems also would make it easier for individual customers with solar or wind power systems to connect to the network and sell surplus power to other customers.[12]

GREEN-ENERGY ECONOMY

The incentive of financial profit will be one of the biggest drivers in enabling America to achieve energy freedom. Across the United States, business leaders and investors from both sides of the political fence are starting to see that not only is green energy good for the planet, it's also good for the bottom line. It's a cliché that "green is the color of money," but it's true and being proven every day across the United States. American companies are building energy efficiency and clean-energy strategies into their business plans not only because they believe it saves the environment—which it does—but also because it saves them money in the long run. It also increases the productivity of their workers, helps in job recruitment, and bolsters their public image as patriotic organizations that care about their community. None other than Walmart, the world's largest retailer, is going green by cutting waste and boosting the energy efficiency in its stores. In 2005, Walmart announced it would spend $500 million a year to hit ambitious green targets that include cutting energy use at its giant stores by 30 percent, eliminating solid waste from its stores by 25 percent, and doubling the fuel economy of its fleet of trucks in ten years. For each mile per gallon that Walmart's fleet of trucks gains in moving merchandise down America's highways, the company projects it will save more than $52 million annually.[13] The initiative hints at a new philosophy among big businesses toward the environment that more and more U.S. companies are incorporating into their mission. As Lee Scott, Walmart's CEO, told company employees in a speech describing the company's new energy-efficiency program: "As one of the largest companies in the world, with an expanding global presence, environmental problems are our problems."[14]

Wall Street also is paying special attention to the growing clean-energy revolution, realizing that as the movement grows, it will provide excellent returns that will make millions of dollars for investors. Investment houses understand that as oil prices increase in the coming decades, the market for renewable sources of energy will expand with the increasing government and economic incentives to develop exciting new innovations in clean-tech. The political climate will also change as climate change becomes a more pressing social issue for the world, pushing elected leaders to be more active in passing laws and promoting programs that expand the clean-energy market. So far, the signals to Wall Street have been mixed about whether the U.S. government really supports the clean-energy market. But once it is clear that we as a nation are truly committed to clean-energy freedom, the floodgates to investing in green technology will be opened wide. We are already seeing the hot interest in investments in clean-tech, a market segment that has been making headlines as the fastest-growing venture category for the last several years. In 2005, $469.7 million was poured into clean-technology companies; a year later it was $1.4 billion, and in 2007 it reached more than $2 billion.[15] In 2009, clean-tech venture capital investments totaled $5.6 billion.[16] Among the most gung-ho clean-energy investors is venture capitalist John Doerr, a Silicon Valley legend famous for making billions of dollars by getting in on the ground floor of success stories such as Amazon, Apple, Cisco Systems, and Google. He has been guiding his venture capital firm, Kleiner Perkins Caufield & Byers, to devote substantial investment capital ($700 million) to green innovations during a three-year period starting in 2008. Insisting that clean energy is "the mother of all markets,"[17] Doerr is particularly keen on placing his investment bet on solar thermal energy, photovoltaic technology, and innovative biofuels developments. In June 2010, Doerr and other well-known American business leaders, including Microsoft cofounder Bill Gates and General Electric chief executive Jeffrey Immelt, started the American Energy Innovation Council. According to the group's website, its members intend to encourage the investment of $16 billion a year in clean-energy innovations to "foster strong economic growth, create jobs in new industries, and reestablish America's energy technology leadership through robust, public investment in the development of world-changing energy technologies."

Not all companies will hit home runs out of the clean-energy ballpark, of course. Many start-ups will be investment duds that look promising at first but will fail to live up to their initial high expectations. We can use the information-technology industry as a model for how to possibly look at clean-tech investing. As computers, telecommunications systems, and the Internet evolved in the 1980s and 1990s, thousands of companies emerged that were built on innovative ideas and novel technologies based on the developing digital infrastructure. The heavy hitters that stood out—such stellar companies as Microsoft, Apple, Cisco, and Google—were the exceptions and not the rule. Still, people in the lesser-known companies did make money providing their products and services. We'll see the same thing happen as America moves toward achieving its energy freedom. It is too early to predict which companies will be the standouts, but there will be plenty of opportunity for all clean-tech start-ups to financially profit if they can come up with solid energy ideas and work hard to develop them.

Building up the clean-energy economy will be good for American workers. It will create hundreds of thousands of "green-collar jobs" in constructing, installing, maintaining, developing, and administering renewable energy and energy-efficiency products, as well as service jobs such as mass-transit operators and drivers. A study done by the Environmental Law and Policy Center found that if the United States set a renewable-energy profile of 22 percent by the year 2020, we could create 37,000 new jobs in wind energy alone in ten midwestern states.[18] Another study done by the Energy and Resources Group (part of the Goldman School of Public Policy at the University of California at Berkeley) found that the "renewable energy sector generates more jobs per megawatt of power installed, per unit of energy produced, and per dollar of investment, than the fossil-fuel-based energy sector." The study's analysis determined that more than 188,000 new jobs would be created by the year 2020 if America set itself a goal of consuming 20 percent of its energy from renewable sources, with 55 percent of that from wind energy.[19] A study released in June 2009 by the University of Massachusetts, Amherst, and the Center for American Progress analyzed the American Recovery and Reinvestment Act and the American Clean Energy and Security Act and found that these legislative measures could allow the United States to generate as much as $150 billion a year in clean-energy investments over the course of a decade. This investment money would create 2.5 million new jobs for Americans. "Our key finding is that clean-energy investments generate roughly three times more jobs than an equivalent amount of money spent on carbon-based fuels," the study's authors said.[20]

This work can't be outsourced to other nations either, meaning that the energy-independence movement will give our citizens more job and financial security and protect America's middle class, which 80 percent of us make up. Empowering our middle class with job security from energy freedom will shore up the economy by increasing our nationwide earning power with the creation of more jobs. By building up our clean-tech industries, we will create jobs for more of our citizens in factories and offices where they will earn good pay for honest labor while helping America end its dependence on fossil fuels. And it will also help spread the taxpayer burden and save us tax dollars in the long run. Developing a green-energy economy will also help make American workers healthier because of a decrease in environmental pollution, thus reducing the budget burden on healthcare programs.

TOWARD A GLOBAL ENERGY ECONOMY

Just as oil, coal, and natural gas provided the power for America's economic success during the last hundred years, fossil fuels are now propelling the move toward a globalized economy by making possible the technologies that are increasingly interconnecting the economies of the nations around our planet. Manufacturing, communication, information processing, and transportation are all necessary components of globalization. And in the industrial infrastructure that exists today, these components require massive amounts of energy from hydrocarbons to continue running. Whether Americans like it or not, the trend toward globalization is pushing our economy to be more closely tied to other nations—many of which will become increasingly competitive with the United States. And as globalization's impact increases, our own economy will rise and fall based on the energy supply and consumption in those other countries. A sudden shortage of fossil fuels in China, for instance, would cause manufacturing in some Asian industries to decline or even come to a stop—and that would in turn cause the prices of Chinese-made goods to spike sharply in U.S. stores as rising consumer demand meets shrinking supply.

Because the global economy is heading toward ever-tightening unification, it is important for Americans to realize that our economy is becoming absorbed into an increasingly complex and interconnected international economic system that we simply can't isolate ourselves from. The more complicated this system grows as nations become interdependent, the more the United States will face financial breakdown if the engines of the global economy begin to sputter because of a depletion of fossil fuels.

Globalization also plays a role in how we need to consider domestic oil drilling in the coming decades. When it comes to reducing our reliance on foreign oil, some of our elected officials argue the case for opening the Arctic National Wildlife Refuge (ANWR) in Alaska, as well as areas offshore, to oil exploitation. According to a 1998 U.S. Geological Survey (USGS) estimate, ANWR has between 4.4 billion and 11.8 billion barrels of crude under its frozen landscape.[21] The United States consumes about 7.6 billion barrels of oil a year, so ANWR could in theory provide us with up to four years of petroleum if we include our present import level in the equation.[22] Realistically, if ANWR were exploited at the maximum possible rate, it might be able to produce about 100,000 to 200,000 barrels of oil per day. The United States currently consumes approximately 21 million barrels of oil per day, so even at the best production rate, ANWR would supply only about 1 percent of our demand. Clearly, this would not have a very significant impact on the price of gasoline or our national energy security. The science of accurately predicting American oil reserve quantities in the Arctic can be difficult. For example, in October 2010, the USGS significantly revised its estimate of the National Petroleum Reserve in Alaska, an area northwest of ANWR, dropping its 2002 estimate of 10.6 billion barrels by about 90 percent to a new estimate of 896 million barrels.

The economic argument given by those who support broadening the policy on domestic oil drilling is that it will provide more gasoline on the market and thus give us breathing room to build up a renewable-energy infrastructure. In the early 1970s, the reality of our dependence on foreign oil became painfully obvious. During the oil shortages of that period, Saudi Arabia saw that the United States and Europe were taking a hard turn away from dependence on oil by requiring more efficient automobiles and developing new sources of energy. In response, the Saudis sharply increased oil production to drive prices down, thereby keeping us addicted. The tactic worked and cheap oil in the 1980s and 1990s further reduced the incentive to go green in meeting our energy needs. Today, we are replaying the same scenario. Prices have skyrocketed and all nations have reduced consumption. The Saudis in turn have increased production in an effort to lower prices and keep us addicted. However, Saudi Arabia is at peak production and won't be able to swing the market as it did in the 1970s. Politicians advocating the "quick fix" of ANWR will only hurt our economy by delaying us from preparing for the difficult time when easy oil is no longer plentiful for America.

We Americans need to learn the lessons from the Roaring Twenties and the Great Depression era that followed that thriving decade. Taking steps now to build a clean-energy infrastructure will help protect the U.S. economy from similarly dramatic financial turmoil that could take a heavy toll on our citizens' lives. Becoming a clean-energy nation will also help us better compete in a world economy moving toward sustainable-energy technologies. One day, we might be able to export our American-made clean-energy products and services and help other countries build their own green-energy economies— particularly developing nations that will need to leapfrog fossil-fuel use. We can also help the nations of the world strengthen their economies as oil becomes a scarcer resource, thus helping to stabilize them socially and politically. To prepare ourselves to minimize the potential financial crisis that will hit us and the rest of the world, we must make energy freedom a foundation of our future economic security.

CHAPTER 8

Energy and Transportation

On July 7, 1919, the U.S. Army began an experiment that would eventually lead to the dramatic transformation of America's transportation system. That day, eighty-one vehicles, ranging from motorcycles to heavy trucks, left the zero milestone marker in Washington, D.C., and started on a westward journey to California. This convoy intended to test the viability of long-distance ground travel across the American continent. The experiment would establish how fast and how effectively the U.S. armed forces could send troops and heavy equipment to the West Coast if that region might ever be invaded by foreign aggressors.

America's first transcontinental military convoy experiment included an intelligent U.S. Army lieutenant colonel who served as an official observer. The young officer noted that roads in America's eastern states were of relatively good quality for travel. Once the convoy passed the border of Illinois and made its way through the less populated western states, however, conditions became no better than in the pioneer days of the nineteenth century. Ruts and holes damaged truck axles. Vehicles became stuck in mud from rainstorms. Old bridges that spanned rivers and creeks almost collapsed under the weight of the heavy trucks. In Utah, the entire convoy was almost lost in quicksand. After sixty-two days and behind schedule, the convoy arrived at its final destination of San Francisco. The lieutenant colonel's official report estimated that at least 1,800 miles (2,900 kilometers) of the U.S. roads it traveled on would need to be significantly improved for purposes of speedy military transport. He recommended to his superiors that, for the purpose of national defense, the federal government build and maintain a national highway system, a concept that was initially rejected. In 1953, that Army officer became America's commander-in-chief. Influenced by his convoy excursion to California, as well as his favorable impression of Germany's Autobahn network of highways that he had observed during World War II, U.S. President Dwight D. Eisenhower pushed the passage of the Federal Highway Act of 1956 and the modernization of U.S. transportation by constructing our nation's Interstate Highway System. Americans now had a level of travel convenience never before known in history.

It is difficult for many of us living in the twenty-first century to imagine that only a hundred years ago, most people in the United States did not often travel more than a few miles from their homes. The primitive nature of transportation back then made long-distance travel impractical. A century ago, many Americans still lived in a horse-and-buggy world and relied on mule teams to haul goods to market on wagons. The gasoline-powered combustion engine, however, revolutionized U.S. society in a short period of time and made it convenient for those with wanderlust to journey to whatever destination they wanted, whenever they wanted to travel there. The car culture created in the decades of the twentieth century dramatically redefined us as a nation as it reshaped our landscape with intricate ribbons of roads connecting America's cities and towns. A romance developed between Americans and their automobiles, perhaps because these vehicles gave us the freedom of mobility that reinforces our inherent restless nature. Getting a driver's license in the United States is now a rite of passage signifying a young person is adult enough to responsibly handle a heavy vehicle that can reach high speeds. Cars are also status symbols.

Our nation's modern network of highways requires our society to keep a constant and dependable supply of petroleum for making gasoline and diesel fuel so that our cars can use these roads. Highways also stimulate the need for a supply of coal to produce the steel and other materials to build our automobiles. About two-thirds of the 21 million barrels of oil America uses each day is burned for energy in getting people and products from point A to point B. Much of it goes up into the air, with the average passenger car producing 9,600 pounds of emissions a year and the average light truck producing 14,400 pounds (if both types of vehicles are driven 12,000 miles [19,312 km] a year). In considering the entire transportation picture, increasing fuel efficiency across our national vehicle fleet of cars, trains, planes, and ships must play a prominent role in our national energy policy if we are to gain energy freedom. Our main focus, however, must be on improving the vehicles we personally drive. Two-thirds of the oil used in U.S. transportation is refined into gasoline for use in cars and light trucks, with the remaining third providing diesel fuel for commercial trucks, jet fuel for airplanes, and fuel oil to run tankers and large ships.[1]

There's a heavy price to pay in creating a culture that is so highly dependent on cars and the petroleum fuel required to keep all those motors running. "America is addicted to oil," as President Bush so famously said in his State of the Union speech in 2006, and much of this national petroleum fix comes from the fact that we as a people are hopelessly in love with our wheels. According to the Center for Transportation Excellence, the average American family spends 19 cents out of every earned dollar on transportation, the second highest expenditure after housing costs.[2] The cars we drive in turn help drive our national economy by producing jobs, either directly in manufacturing or sales, or indirectly by providing the goods and services to support our automobile-based society. So when the time comes that we are forced to face an ongoing reduction in the world's petroleum production, America's financial health could be severely damaged if it still continues to be heavily dependent on the production and use of oil-burning automobiles.

As a nation, we are highly inefficient in the ways that we use our cars for transportation. Compared to many other countries' vehicles, our vehicles have poor fuel economy. The U.S. fleet currently averages 22.4 miles per gallon. Compare that to Japan, which has a fleet achieving 50 miles per gallon, and Europe, where the average car gets 43 miles per gallon.[3] One of the reasons is that America's service stations have, in the last decades, sold gasoline at relatively inexpensive prices compared to the petrol sold in Europe and

Asia. Many U.S. drivers have been so sensitized to cheap gasoline that the $3 and $4 a gallon figures that have appeared on corner gas station price boards have induced a state of national sticker shock. Europeans would think these prices a bargain.

Despite the rising expense of driving, Americans will continue to buy motorized vehicles because our national way of life has evolved around them. In 1955, America's roads carried 65 million cars and trucks. In 2008, that figure was 250 million. By the midcentury point, nearly 400 million vehicles are projected to be pounding the pavement. Our roads, however, can't continue to sustain a growing number of vehicles because the mounting traffic is clogging the arteries of our extensive highway systems. Thirty-six percent of America's major urban highways face a serious congestion problem, according to an analysis done by the nonprofit research group TRIP, which studies national transportation issues. In one-third of American cities, drivers waste more than forty hours throughout the year stalled in traffic, according to the Center for Transportation Excellence. This total congestion wastes gasoline and diesel fuel, as well as reduces productivity, since the time people spend in traffic causes loss to our nation's businesses. Some argue that we need to build more highways to deal with the problem, but building up our public transportation systems might be a better solution. If the United States spent $100 billion over a ten-year period to improve its public transportation systems, it would increase American worker productivity by $521 billion, whereas spending the same amount on the construction of more highways would provide only $237 billion in increased job productivity.[4]

Our growing traffic-congestion problem has other costs as well. Our roads were not originally designed for the large number of vehicles that pass over them day in and day out, and now they are starting to crumble from this massive overuse. The rough conditions of our roads cost an average American motorist an additional $413 in car repair and maintenance costs, as well as increased fuel consumption. Wear and tear on vehicles costs drivers in the Los Angeles and San Francisco Bay areas as much as $750 a year.[5] Deteriorating highway conditions are also a national safety issue because they contribute to accidents. Car crashes add to our nation's fossil-fuel usage every day by causing miles of backups, wasting not just time but massive quantities of gasoline as drivers idle their engines waiting for the accident site to be cleared by safety officers.

One reason that Americans feel highly reluctant to part with their big cars is that many of us believe fuel-efficient vehicles are less safe than the gas-guzzlers. This perception has been perpetuated by the American automakers and their marketing agencies because selling SUVs and large trucks provides higher profit margins compared with sales of small cars. The Honda Motor Company did a study comparing the size, weight, and safety features in vehicles and concluded that to promote better fuel economy, factors such as design and technology are much more critical than size and weight.[6] A risk-analysis study done by researchers at the Lawrence Berkeley National Lab and the University of Michigan in 2002 confirmed that the quality of the vehicle is a "much more important safety factor" than vehicle weight. The study also found that, despite the conventional wisdom, SUVs "are no safer for their drivers than the average midsize or large car and not much safer than many of the most popular compact and subcompact car models."[7]

When it comes to the United States achieving its energy freedom, we can use advanced technologies in all our new cars—both large and small—to earn better mileage in the coming decades. In today's combustion-engine vehicles, 12 to 20 percent of the energy from gasoline in the average American car is converted into useful movement.[8] Most of it is wasted as engine heat or from friction loss and idling. We have many innovations available to make our vehicles more fuel efficient without causing car buyers to give up power and luxury. Engines, for example, can be designed with deactivation devices to shut off cylinders when idling or when little driving power is required. High-tech ignition systems can cut the engine and start it again automatically when idling at stoplights or in traffic. Vehicle chassis can be manufactured with lighter-weight carbon-fiber material instead of heavy steel. Aerodynamic design features can help reduce air drag, which eats away at fuel economy.

FUEL EFFICIENCY

In 1973, when the OPEC oil embargo hit America's economy, the United States made a series of improvements to its vehicle fleet and nearly doubled our national average mileage. We can double it again. We have the technology to do it in the next two decades without sacrificing comfort, safety, or performance. But we have for too long lacked the political vision to push ourselves toward a goal of making our vehicles more fuel efficient. Fortunately, this is starting to change. Our national leaders are beginning to accept the reality that our society's ongoing dependence on oil will bring us increasing economic, social, and national-defense risks. One sign of positive change came in December 2007, when Congress and President Bush passed the Energy Independence and Security Act, raising the national Corporate Average Fuel Economy (CAFE) standard to 35 miles per gallon by the year 2020—a decent 40 percent increase over the past standard of 27.5 miles per gallon. In May 2009, President Barack Obama announced a plan to upgrade CAFE standards to have passenger cars achieve 39 miles per gallon and trucks achieve 30 miles per gallon (for an average of 34.5 miles per gallon) by the year 2016.

As important as advancing more ambitious CAFE standards and building better vehicles will be in achieving our energy freedom, the United States can still do much more to improve the fuel efficiency in its overall transportation system. Getting better mileage in gasoline-powered cars is only one part of the solution. We must resist the temptation of looking for a "silver bullet" and instead focus on the "silver buckshot" option of creating a multitude of ways to reduce our transportation energy consumption. As global oil production peaks, we and the rest of the world will need to develop and promote a market for vehicles that run on nonpetroleum fuels. Vegetation-based fuels such as ethanol and biodiesel are already sold in some regions of the country, but they make up only a small percentage of the energy now used to run our vehicles. A big reason for this small market penetration is that we don't have a big enough financial incentive to drive research and development, as well as production and mass distribution, of biofuels. Just as it took many decades for America to develop the infrastructure of oil refineries and gasoline service stations that fuel our cars today, it also takes time to develop the infrastructure for biofuels. We are seeing progress, however, as global warming and the rising price of gasoline provide greater incentives for these nonpetroleum liquid fuels.

Electric cars offer another viable option in the future for getting the nation's transportation systems to reduce oil consumption. The first electric vehicle (EV) in the United States was built in 1891 by William Morrison of Des Moines, Iowa. By 1897, New York City residents saw electric taxis rolling down Broadway and other avenues. Cheap gasoline throughout the twentieth century, unfortunately, put a brake on American ingenuity in improving electric-car technology. In the twenty-first century, the hybrids that are becoming increasingly popular with American consumers give us a taste of things to come. Still, the market for purely electric vehicles is still in its infancy. To test demand, in 1996 General Motors came out with its experimental EV1 automobile, which was made famous in the 2006 documentary film *Who Killed the Electric Car?* Although the futuristic-looking automobile was a hit with many of the drivers who leased it, GM decided to take its pioneering model off the market because the advanced technology made its continued manufacture unprofitable at that time.[9] Now, as market forces change its corporate thinking, GM's engineers have developed a new electric-gasoline hybrid car called the Chevrolet Volt, which was launched into the U.S. market in October 2010 at a starting sticker price of $41,000. The future will show how long-established American automakers like GM will fare as they go up against maverick carmakers like California's Tesla Motors, which aim to establish themselves in this potentially lucrative market.

Cars run by electricity have never enjoyed large market penetration primarily because they have faced one major obstacle: Batteries could not be charged quickly enough or sustain a long enough charge to compete with the convenience of gasoline. Today, an important question with EVs is what to do with the electric car batteries once their usable life is over.[10] We must not allow these toxic components to damage the environment. These challenges will eventually be solved because researchers are now finding ways to improve electric car-battery technology as increasing competition for the growing market for these cars brings amazing new innovations. Critics have also cautioned that electric cars are not necessarily "clean" because they run on energy produced by coal-powered plants. Although there is weight to that argument as our energy infrastructure now stands, innovations in solar- and wind-power generation will in the future drive down their cost and enable EVs to rely on increasingly less energy from fossil-fuel sources. Progress is being made. Forward-looking cities such as San José, California, are now installing charging stations for electric car owners to plug in and power up their vehicle battery during their working hours. And the American Recovery and Reinvestment Act of 2009 contributed $2.4 billion to encourage American ingenuity in developing next-generation electric batteries and related technologies. If successful, this program will generate tens of thousands of new jobs as it stimulates expansion in the EV industry.

Cars with hydrogen-powered fuel cells will most likely take a lot longer than electric cars to come to your local dealership. There are major technological hurdles to overcome before America can establish the "hydrogen highway" infrastructure that will service these zero-emission cars. In 2004, California tried to jump-start the market for fuel-cell cars when Governor Arnold Schwarzenegger signed an executive order to establish a network of hydrogen-fueling stations. By early 2010, twenty-one stations were operating in the state and ten more stations were being planned to fuel a small fleet of fuel-cell vehicles, most of which were experimental models run by government agencies.[11] This pioneering effort in the Golden State is providing researchers with the knowledge to find ways to improve these cars and the fuel-distribution and storage systems they require. Cars that run on methane (or natural gas) from farm animal manure and other natural sources are another option for a potential future fuel market. Vehicles running on methane or compressed natural gas (CNG) are already in service in some American cities but will require a significant infrastructure investment for widespread usage.

As alluring as bringing technological innovations to market might sound in helping improve the energy efficiency of America's transportation system, we must also consider simpler and low-cost solutions that save fuel. One of the most effective ways to help the United States gain its energy freedom lies in getting many more of us to practice better driving behavior. One study found that aggressive driving habits, such as fast starts and breakneck braking, result in a 37 percent increase in fuel use. And as harsh as it might sound in a country of lead-footers, many more of our citizens can get into the habit of following the law and keeping the speedometer at the posted speed. Over a long trip, obeying those speed limit signs can result in an average fuel savings of 12 percent—not to mention the dollars saved from avoiding paying for tickets from traffic cops. Avoiding excessive idling can help cut as much as 19 percent of fuel consumption. Using the cruise control can save up to 7 percent in gasoline.[12] More Americans might be more inclined to follow better driving habits if they saw this simple fuel-saving method as a patriotic act.

Perhaps as foreign-oil dependence becomes a greater liability to our personal freedoms, more American workers will start using carpools and vanpools to get to their jobs. Between 10 million and 16 million people carpool to work regularly, and the number is expected to grow as gasoline becomes more costly. Still, most commuters drive to work alone. According to the U.S. Census Bureau, 88 percent of us get to work by car and 77 percent of those people drive solo.[13] Carpooling is an exceptionally easy way to cut fossil-fuel use in half during the daily commute. When carpoolers use high-occupancy vehicle (HOV) lanes, it takes more cars off the road, helping to alleviate congestion, and it cuts down on the amount of time people spend on the road. Employers are offering workers perks to promote ride sharing, such as special parking spaces, bonus money, and the loan of energy-efficient cars to take care of personal chores during lunch hours. Work-at-home options also help to reduce fuel consumption by cutting out commutes entirely. Not all jobs, of course, let employees avoid the daily road grind, but companies are finding that workers who can telecommute are highly productive and can save the company money. AT&T, for example, cut up to $150 million a year in overhead and other costs by letting workers labor at home-based offices.[14] Employees were also happier, especially those with family needs, and so are less likely to quit the company, thus reducing hiring costs. To save the expense of sending employees to distant meetings, a growing number of companies are also developing videoconferencing systems that quickly pay for themselves in travel-expense and time savings. This is an easy and relatively low-cost way for many corporations to help reduce America's fossil-fuel consumption and greenhouse gas emissions.

MASS TRANSIT

Most U.S. cities in the twentieth century evolved to satisfy the needs of our emerging car culture. Before 1950, many American citizens working in the urban jungle traveled to their jobs on trains, trolleys, and buses. The year 1946 saw the peak of American public transportation, with 23.4 billion passenger trips. In the post–World War II years, the widespread construction of asphalt highways and roads allowed more and more residents to drive many miles between their suburban neighborhoods and jobs. While Europe modernized its public transit systems, many American cities went in the opposite direction, taking out trolley and train tracks and cutting bus service, thus making mass transit an inconvenience and pushing up car use even more. Public transportation decreased steadily, hitting rock bottom in 1972, with 6.5 billion passenger trips. The energy crisis of the 1970s started the rise again, and higher gasoline prices will certainly accelerate the use of mass transit in the coming decades. According to the American Public Transportation Association, mass-transit systems save 1.4 billion gallons of gasoline a year—the equivalent of 300,000 cars a day getting a fill-up. If 10 percent of Americans used buses, trains, and trolleys, we could cut up to 40 percent of the foreign oil we use and reduce our carbon dioxide emissions by 25 percent. The use of mass transit can also release lots of cash for purchases other than gasoline and car care. Families who use public transportation systems instead of driving to their destinations can save up to $6,200 a year.[15]

The drawback to mass transit, however, is that for too many Americans it is inconvenient or not readily available. People in rural communities across the United States often have no frequently scheduled public transit systems. And workers in urban areas often drive to their job sites because their schedules don't allow them to use a transit system or they want the option of having their private car at hand in case of an emergency. Many of us also drive to work because it's a long-ingrained habit, or because we don't want to take the effort to learn the system of changing buses and trains. To service their growing numbers of passengers, mass-transit systems in many American metropolitan areas are now becoming easier to use. Schedules and connections are more convenient, and information technology lets passengers find bus and train schedules on their cell phones so that they can see how long it will take the next bus or train to arrive at their stop. A 2008 experiment done by the Bay Area Rapid Transit (BART) system in northern California proved successful in letting passengers pay for their fares and pass through station gates by using special attachments on their mobile phones.[16]

One frequent criticism of mass-transit systems is that they need to be highly subsidized because the fare box hardly pays for operating costs. Overall, American public transit systems get about one-third of their expenses paid by riders.[17] The rest of the funding comes from local, state, and federal governments. The trade-off, however, is that this subsidy money helps provide a service that reduces traffic congestion and thus makes workers more productive. It also reduces our dependence on foreign oil and cuts greenhouse gas emissions. Building and running mass-transit systems also helps create jobs, thus strengthening the tax base. It saves Americans money by helping to keep gasoline prices from rising even more because much fewer people are using private vehicles. Total public-transportation funding from the federal government for fiscal year 2009 was set at $10.3 billion, whereas annual oil subsidies and tax breaks are estimated at $4 billion.[18] If we were to spend that annual oil subsidy money on building up our U.S. public transportation systems and getting more Americans to use them, we could go far in cutting our need for petroleum from foreign sources.

As the problems of peak oil and climate change become more prevalent in the twenty-first century, America's cities will be forced to evolve to become greener and cleaner in their energy use. Public transit will no doubt increasingly play its role in this movement. But "smart-growth" programs in urban areas will also contribute to America's energy freedom. The idea for smart-growth cities came out of the energy crisis of the 1970s. Many cities in the United States concentrated substantial efforts on redeveloping their city centers and turning them into dynamic places for people to live and work. Now, a growing number of American cities are using the smart-growth paradigm to encourage the construction of high-density, multi-use buildings and public facilities in the downtown regions and around transportation hubs. Convenient public transit is designed to help residents reduce their car use. Good-quality sidewalks and bicycle paths encourage residents to walk or bike to work or school. Downtown residents also find that they don't have to drive too far to enjoy cultural events or entertainment because they have shops, restaurants, and theaters within easy walking or bus-riding distance. Smart growth is proving it can raise the quality of life in American communities; it creates more opportunities for interaction between people and makes people healthier because they get more exercise and breathe cleaner air. Another advantage is that smart growth helps to reduce taxes. Suburban sprawl can be costly for a city because it means that amenities such as new schools, roads, and sewer systems must be constructed. Smart growth works with the existing infrastructure and helps the local economy by making it appealing for more people to live in or visit the downtown area of a city.[19]

FREIGHT

The health of America's economy requires the transport of raw materials and manufactured goods throughout the country and to and from other regions of the world. Large diesel-fueled trucks rolling down our roads provide the bulk of this haulage, accounting for as much as 80 percent of U.S. goods moved. But with prices of diesel fuel rising alongside gasoline, the trucking industry is seeing its profit margins shrinking. At $4 a gallon for fuel, truck drivers are forced to spend between $600 and $700 to fill up the average tank of an eighteen-wheeler. That cuts into their livelihood and adds to the price of goods for customers. To survive in these tough times, truckers need to find ways to cut down on their vehicles' fuel consumption. One way is by simply reducing their speeds on the highway. National truck company Con-way Freight, for example, discovered it could cut 3 percent of its fuel costs by ordering drivers of its 8,400 trucks to travel at 62 miles per hour (100 km per hour) instead of the highway speed limit of 65 miles per hour. This decision also results in a yearly reduction of 72 million pounds of carbon dioxide emissions. Aerodynamic "wings" and airflow-control systems installed on trucks to reduce wind drag can cut up to 12 percent of their fossil-fuel costs. In 2009, FedEx retrofitted ninety-two of its older diesel-fueled delivery trucks to cleaner and more efficient hybrid technology. Advances in truck engines to make them burn diesel fuel more efficiently also show a potential economic benefit for the freight industry. One example is the Dual-Fuel combustion system from a company called Clean Air Power. The technology can drop carbon emissions by 25 percent by injecting natural gas into the diesel liquid as it burns, thus allowing the engine to consume fuel more efficiently. Freight companies such as FedEx are also experimenting with hybrid electric trucks to cut down on their fuel costs. Hybrids make an excellent choice for them because, in the delivery business, drivers are always stopping and starting their vehicles as they pick up and drop off packages. A fleet of 10,000 hybrid delivery trucks, for example, would save 7.2 million gallons of diesel fuel a year for FedEx, reducing America's oil consumption and saving the company money.[20]

For cargo transportation, freight trains provide, per tonnage mile, between six to twelve times the energy efficiency as trucks, and this figure is expected to improve further as new locomotives come on the market with computer controls that monitor consumption and adjust the fuel system for maximum energy economy. The railroad industry saw a 73 percent increase in its fuel efficiency between 1980 and 2002 as it found ways to cut diesel consumption even while it added freight tonnage.[21] A single train could take as many as several hundred trucks off the highway, thus reducing road congestion. According to the Association of American Railroads, if the United States switches only 10 percent of its truck freight to rail, the fuel savings would equal at least 1 billion gallons of diesel a year. Because of this outstanding fuel benefit, the transportation industry is developing plans for introducing more "intermodal" freight delivery. This system of linked hubs around the

United States works by having trucks load freight trains at one hub with cargo containers that are then carried by rail to a second hub. There, another truck is loaded with the cargo to take it to its final destination. A sophisticated computer system makes sure that the goods reach their right location on time. Intermodal systems are particularly useful for long-distance hauling because they offer faster delivery than reliance on trucks alone, thus saving shippers time as well as money. They also decrease traffic by getting more trucks off the road, thus helping ease wear and tear on U.S. highways.

Oceangoing cargo ships burn diesel fuel as they carry freight to and from other nations. As in other freight industries, rising fossil-fuel costs are slashing the shipping industry's profit margins and adding expense to the consumer items they transport. Wind power might be one innovative way to help reduce diesel consumption in these freighters. Don't expect ships to return to the days of the old square-riggers with tall masts and billowing sails. Instead, a high-tech towing kite called a SkySail is a modern innovation that might one day prove practical in giving cargo vessels an extra edge in fuel economy. Developed by a German company, the automated system uses a computer to control the steering and compensate for the ship's speed and bearing, and wind direction and velocity. Resembling a paraglider, the system can reduce a ship's annual fuel costs by 20 percent, according to data from a test voyage completed in 2008. The company says that fuel savings can theoretically be as much as 35 percent, depending on wind conditions.[22]

Airplanes carrying freight and passengers also need to find ways to cut down on their consumption of fossil fuels in order to stay competitive. The air-transport industry produces 2 percent of the world's carbon dioxide emissions, and jet fuel makes up one-third of the operating costs for airlines, according to the Air Transport Association. Every $1 rise in a barrel of oil costs the airline industry an additional $465 million in jet fuel expenses every year,[23] so cutting fuel costs is essential for airlines to stay in business. Several technological solutions are available, including more fuel-efficient engines and fuselage designs for future aircraft. An improved air traffic control system that enables airplanes to take more efficient routes could also minimize fuel burn at certain altitudes. The airline industry is also working on developing fuel from nonpetroleum sources. In September 2006, Sir Richard Branson, chairman of Virgin Group, announced that his company intends to spend as much as $3 billion over a ten-year period developing cleaner biofuel sources for airline and railroad companies. "It is in our hands whether our children and their children inherit the same world," he said, explaining why he made this significant financial commitment. "We must not be the generation responsible for irreversibly damaging the environment."[24] In February 2008, one of Branson's Virgin Atlantic Boeing 747-400 jumbo jets achieved a milestone for the airline industry by being the first commercial airplane to fly using biofuels during a flight from London to Amsterdam. The experiment burned a 20 percent mixture of coconut oil and Brazilian babassu nut oil in one of the airplane's four fuel tanks. Air New Zealand and KLM have also successfully tried burning biofuels in their jets. More testing still needs to be done before biofueled flights can carry passengers because biofuels are more likely than conventional jet fuel to freeze at high altitudes.

In the coming decades, America's efforts to develop better technology for fuel innovation can and will transform the transportation industry and help us achieve greater energy freedom. We are at the start of an exciting revolution that will create better ways to use energy to move people and products across the nation and around the world. Just as Eisenhower's transcontinental military convoy set out to cross a continent back in 1919—a trip that eventually led to the modernization of our nation's highway transportation system—we are also now setting out on a pioneering journey to find new ways to improve tomorrow's cars, trucks, trains, ships, and airplanes for energy freedom.

CHAPTER 9

Energy and Agriculture

On May 11, 1934, a monster began an attack on America's heartland. That day, a massive windstorm raged across the Great Plains and picked up the topsoil of millions of acres of farmland that had been turned into a virtual desert after three years of intense drought conditions. For two days, more than 300 million tons of dirt lifted into the dust storm to blot out the sun and turn noon into night. This calamity was the last blow for many hardworking farm families in the Midwest after years of futile struggle to make a living from the land. They packed up their jalopies and old trucks and began a mass migration westward with the hope they might find work that would help them survive their painful ordeal. Thousands of these hard-hit Americans came to California's San Joaquin Valley, where, if they were lucky enough to find a job, they picked fruits and vegetables for low wages. Some of these people stayed on in the region. They and their descendents saw the valley become one of the most productive agricultural regions in the United States.

California today produces as much as 13 percent of America's farm goods, and a vast quantity of this output comes from the eight counties making up the San Joaquin Valley. The energy of fossil fuels makes much of this agricultural bounty possible. But once fossil fuels start to run out, the farming industry in California and the rest of the United States could face a rapid decline in food quantity and quality. Our extraordinary dependence on fossil fuels to feed our growing population could be a recipe for disaster if we don't find alternatives to hydrocarbons to provide for our nutritional needs. If we fail to prepare for the day when we face the problems of global peak oil production, the San Joaquin Valley, as well as many other regions of America, could degenerate to desert-like conditions without the water and fertilizer needed to sustain the agriculture industry. Global warming may also compound the threat to our food security. Extreme weather conditions could, during this century, create dust storms as terrible as those monsters that howled through the Midwest in the 1930s. Many family farms would be wiped out, causing massive migration and social upheaval like that described in John Steinbeck's famous novel *The Grapes of Wrath*.

Americans too often take for granted that we can walk into our neighborhood supermarket and fill our shopping cart with a wide variety of grocery items delivered to us from distant locations around the country and even from around the world. Hydrocarbons enable hundreds of millions of people throughout the world to enjoy the blessings of the green revolution, a modernization of the agricultural industry started during the last century that has given farmers the technology to produce more than enough food to feed every person on our planet. Thanks to fossil fuels, in 2009 the United States exported $98.6 billion in agricultural products to other nations, helping to sustain their societies and reduce the threat of famine. The green revolution also has changed American society by requiring fewer workers for farm labor. Seventy years ago, with a total population of 127 million people, America had 6.8 million farmers producing our nation's food. Now only 1.9 million farmers provide our more than 300 million citizens with the bounty of the land.[1] This reduction in the agricultural labor force came about because fossil fuels provided farmers with the industrial means to harvest massive quantities of fruits, vegetables, nuts, grains, meat, and poultry products.

It takes significant amounts of fossil fuels to mass-produce all of this food using modern agricultural technologies. About 17 percent of America's fossil fuels are used in the production of agricultural products. When all factors are taken into consideration, it's estimated that one calorie of food on our dinner plate requires from ten to fifteen calories of energy in its production process. Distribution further adds fossil-fuel costs to food, with the average supermarket item having been transported a distance of 1,500 miles (2,414 km). There are many ways fossil fuels are used to produce our food. Petroleum is needed to operate heavy equipment such as tractors and combines that till the soil and harvest the crops. Gasoline- or diesel-powered vehicles are needed to transport laborers to various farm sites. Coal-generated electricity is used to operate the massive irrigation systems that pump water up from underground aquifers or transport it over long distances along pipes and canals. Petroleum is also used to manufacture herbicides and pesticides that keep in check the weeds and insects that might otherwise reduce the yield of a harvest. Fossil fuel is used extensively in the production of nitrogen fertilizer, a critical component for the green revolution. Using a method called the Haber-Bosch process, fertilizer manufacturers use natural gas to produce ammonia, a key ingredient in fertilizer. Producing this ammonia uses up about 5 percent of the world's natural gas production each year. This fossil fuel accounts for between 70 percent and 90 percent of the cost of the fertilizer production, so when the price of natural gas increases it also increases the cost of food products.[2]

Food and water, of course, are basic necessities for human beings to live healthy and productive lives. That fact means that our high dependence on fossil fuels puts everyone's well-being at high risk. Because modern agriculture consumes so much petroleum and natural gas, America's farming industry faces a looming crisis if we fail to prepare for the day when the world's production of these two fossil fuels begins an inevitable decline. Already, we're seeing the signs of this upcoming quandary. As the price of oil climbed above $140 a barrel (a price that we will see again and that may even seem modest as the future demand for fossil fuels outstrips demand) in the spring of 2008, Americans saw the cost of groceries at their local markets rise as well because farmers were forced to increase the price of food in order to pay their higher bills for producing it. Rising oil prices mean higher energy costs to irrigate farm fields and orchards, and a higher purchase price for supplies such as feed for livestock and herbicides, pesticides, and fertilizer. Factor in the increased fossil-fuel cost of bringing the food to market on semitrailer trucks, ships, airplanes, and railroad trains, and the tally at the supermarket checkout stand increases. Canneries, meat-processing plants, and other food-processing facilities also rely on fossil fuels for taking the raw agricultural ingredients and turning them into neatly packaged products for consumers. Storage facilities use a lot of energy for refrigeration or the freezing of meats, fish, and fruits and vegetables. Supermarkets also require a twenty-four-hour stream of electric power to keep perishable foods from spoiling. When we add all these various energy-consumption components up, it is easy to see how food prices will rise with the cost of fossil fuels. Escalating prices at the supermarket also have a ripple effect that hurts the American economy. Because food is so vital for basic biological survival, most people will hold off on purchasing nonessential items such as electronic equipment, furniture, and the latest fashion attire if their paychecks force them to choose between being nourished and satisfying the urge for luxury purchases.

By its very nature, farming is a tough business. Modern farming in America not only is physically demanding but also requires farmers to be experts in business, chemistry, farm equipment, water management, and government regulation. Added to this are the unpredictability of the weather and the precariousness of market conditions. But America's small family farms will fight for their existence in the coming years as we face the problem of peak oil. If our nation doesn't prepare for the unavoidable day of declining oil supplies, our struggling rural communities will be devastated with worsening financial problems. Many hundreds of thousands of American farming and ranching families—some going back several generations—will be forced to end their traditional way of making a living and sell their land to big agribusiness corporations with the economic resources to better deal with the challenges of peak oil. Other aspects of rural America will be overwhelmed by economic struggles, too, when the problems of a post-peak-oil society start to intensify. Tens of thousands of people in farming communities work in jobs where they process and package food, or provide the supplies and services needed for agricultural production. Sadly, the lives of many of these hardworking Americans will be severely disrupted.

GLOBAL CLIMATE CHANGE

The challenge of peak oil isn't the only fossil-fuel-related difficulty the United States and the rest of the world must manage in maintaining food production in the near and long-term future. America's agricultural industry will also be destabilized in coming years by the global climate crisis. Ironically, the green revolution has contributed to the problem of Earth's warming. It is estimated that modern agricultural techniques used around the world contribute about 14 percent of the greenhouse gas emissions into our planet's atmosphere. These emissions come from various sources, including the production of fertilizers, herbicides, and pesticides; the running of diesel engines in farm equipment; the tillage of soil, which releases carbon dioxide and methane into the atmosphere; livestock manure, from which methane vapors are released; and decomposing vegetable waste, from which greenhouse gases are produced. As much as 1.5 trillion pounds of carbon dioxide is released annually from U.S. farm production. Agriculture in other countries also increases greenhouse gases from deforestation practices undertaken to clear land for growing crops and raising livestock. Farmers in Africa, as well as the Amazon rain forest in South America, cut down and set fire to millions of trees each year, a process that releases carbon dioxide into our planet's atmosphere as they burn, thus adding to Earth's warming. The United Nations has estimated that about 32 million acres (13 million hectares) of trees are lost each year because of deforestation.[3]

Because agriculture is tied so closely to seasonal climate patterns, the extent that global warming alters those patterns will change how America and other nations feed people over the coming decades. Farmers have always been at the mercy of the weather, but the extreme weather events that scientists predict will result from climate changes will make it much harder for America's agricultural industry to keep up its harvest yield for the billions of humans in the world. Computer models project that global warming will in future decades cause a greater number of heat waves of more than 100 degrees Fahrenheit (38 degrees Celsius), lasting over a period of weeks, in certain regions of our country. As summers grow hotter, farmers in the midwestern and western states will need to deal with more intense sun heat leaching out moisture from topsoil.[4] They will be forced to increase their irrigation of crops, which in turn will require the burning of more fossil fuels to bring water to farm crops, thus adding more greenhouse gases to the atmosphere. Eventually, as global climate change creates severe drought conditions worldwide, there might not be enough water available for our nation's agricultural needs. Reduced annual snowpack in regions such as the Sierra and Rocky Mountain ranges will create intense water shortages requiring mandatory rationing. America might see an increasing amount of annual flooding as spring melts come much earlier in the year and overfill rivers and creeks, which will also impact the agricultural industry by wasting water and eroding soil. Mega-droughts, such as the one that wiped out the Great Plains states in the 1930s, might become common occurrences as global climate change's effects on our terrestrial climate begin to become more prevalent. Dry areas such as California and the American Southwest will need to develop extensive water systems, including construction of more canals, underground pipes, and storage reservoirs to stockpile and distribute this precious resource—not just for their agricultural industries but also for their growing numbers of citizens. Political squabbles between the states on the control and management of water might lead to conflict if climate conditions severely diminish the amount of rain and snow the clouds bring.

In human history, long-term droughts and massive flooding caused by pre–Industrial Age climate changes have devastated food production and reduced water resources throughout the world. This has resulted in social and political turbulence that brought the decline of once-mighty civilizations in ancient Egypt, China, and India, as well as the Mayan culture of ancient Mexico. In the twenty-first century, national and international conflict over water and food could arise in developing nations, especially those along the equatorial regions that will be most affected by drought induced by global climate change. One study done by Stanford University's Program on Food

Security and the Environment predicts that by the year 2030 Africa and South Asia will see a ruinous shrinkage of their staple foods such as maize, rice, and millet, as many years of drought from global warming bring desertification to their regions.[5] One-fifth of our planet's human population could starve if we cannot adapt our global agricultural system to deal with climate changes.

In certain areas of the United States, changes in our climate will also likely increase the number of extreme storms, such as hurricanes and El Niño–like rains. These events will cause the destruction of farm soil by erosion if drastic measures are not taken to prevent valuable land loss. Rising sea levels resulting from the melting of land-based ice in Greenland and Antarctica will also eat away at fertile land along coastal areas, thus impairing the world's food production. A one-meter rise in ocean water would cause millions of acres of farmland around the world to be flooded, especially in the Southeast Asian lowlands that are particularly vulnerable,[6] seriously hurting agricultural output in regions damaged by such a mounting tide. The rise in the world's ocean levels would also create an additional crisis for coastal area farmers all around the planet, as seawater seeps into freshwater aquifers and contaminates underground water reservoirs with salt minerals. If this happens, the salinized water will need to be heavily processed for use on crops, and this procedure will take a large amount of energy and will thus add even more cost to food production. Freezing weather can also hurt food production. If the Gulf Stream comes to a stop, as some climate experts fear it might if Greenland's melting ice pours enough freshwater into the salty North Atlantic, England and much of the northwestern European continent will face severe blizzard conditions or even a new ice age. If such catastrophic cold spells happen, farmers in these northern regions will find it nearly impossible to produce traditional crops as extended winters or even yearlong freezes bear down hard on their horticultural efforts.

Some scientific research suggests that the addition of carbon dioxide into Earth's atmosphere might in certain cases benefit grain crops grown in some agricultural locations. Some scientists suggest that the more abundant this greenhouse gas becomes, the more it will stimulate plant growth—perhaps by as much as 30 percent. This airborne fertilizer hypothesis has been endorsed by coal-industry lobbyists shielding their clients' interests in the release of millions of tons of carbon dioxide into the atmosphere every year. One study, however, draws a conclusion that as plants soak up more carbon dioxide as our industrial civilization's greenhouse gas emissions increase, their absorption of nitrogen and minerals from the soil will be significantly lowered. If this proves to be true, we might temporarily increase the quantity of grain we produce, but the nutritional value will be reduced because of the decline in protein value. The resulting lower food quality would cause public health to decline. Additional carbon dioxide would also cause weeds to grow more abundantly on farmland, resulting in the need for more expensive herbicides to be sprayed on cropland. Climate changes around our planet are projected to increase the number of pests such as rodents and voracious insects that if not properly managed would reduce the amount of food produced for human consumption. If warmer weather extends the spring and summer seasons, insects might double their reproductive cycle, thus forcing farmers to increase their use of pesticides. Insects such as certain beetles are killed off by winter freezes. An increased amount of warm weather throughout the year will mean that their population will have more time to reproduce and grow and thus do more damage to the planet's crops and forests. Rising temperatures will also increase humidity, resulting in more fungus growth on plant leaves and stalks. We can already see an example of this with the sudden-death syndrome that can wipe out soybean crops in some southern and midwestern states if not treated promptly.[7]

Global warming will harm food production in our world's oceans, as well as on its farms. Scientists have warned that the acidification of the seawaters as more carbon dioxide is absorbed into the oceans might cause vast areas of our water world to become inhospitable to many or most current forms of marine life. As the carbon dioxide converts into carbonic acid, it will make it harder for many marine organisms to chemically absorb calcium carbonate, which is a vital ingredient for making shells and skeletal structures. Marine biologists are already seeing this phenomenon happening as coral reefs around the world start to bleach. Reefs that once teemed with fish and other underwater organisms now are barren. An even greater threat to humans is the possibility that by the year 2100, the acidification of the oceans might substantially reduce the number of plankton in them.[8] These tiny organisms serve as the bedrock of the ocean food chain, so a dramatic drop in their population could cause a cascade effect on more complex organisms such as shellfish and fish. If this happens, the commercial fishing industry around the world would find it extremely difficult to make the catches required to help feed the world's population. As the sea around us becomes depleted of fish and other edible organisms, human beings will become more reliant on land-based food production for their survival.

RENEWABLE ENERGY FROM FARMS

Despite seemingly gloomy prospects for our food future, we do have solutions that will enable America's agricultural industry to financially profit by shifting from fossil-fuel-based farming to clean-energy farming. The clean-energy movement can help create a brand new green revolution that, instead of relying almost entirely on hydrocarbon fuels, can be based on our nation's renewable resources. Creating a clean-energy nation also holds the potential to create good jobs in rural communities across America by improving local economies. Workers will be needed to construct and maintain solar and wind power sources in these locations, as well as build and run plants that produce biofuels. The increased revenue from new employment can generate funding for new schools and other public buildings, as well as pay for public services in towns that take advantage of renewable-energy opportunities.

More and more agricultural businesses are exploring using renewable-energy technologies to run their operations. Harking back to the days when windmills were common throughout America's farmland, our nation's farmers are now installing wind generators to pump water or operate lights. Where conditions allow for turbine technology, farmers can also lease out land—such as on the edges of fields or hillside pastures—to companies that will install wind-powered generators hooked up to an electric power grid. Farms could make as much as $2,000 to $10,000 a year from each wind turbine. These energy producers have a relatively small footprint and would not significantly affect daily farming operations, allowing cattle and other livestock to graze around the towers. A U.S. Department of Energy initiative called Wind Powering America found that if the United States obtained 5 percent of its energy from the wind, our nation could annually produce up to $1.2 billion in new income for rural communities and create up to 80,000 permanent jobs by the year 2020.[9]

American farmers are starting to take advantage of the available solar resources by redesigning greenhouses to be more efficient at gathering and holding the sun's heat so that plants inside can thrive during cold seasons. This is done by installing double- or triple-pane glass on the greenhouse roof and constructing the building so that half of the walls are below ground level, thus providing greater insulation. Solar panels installed on barns and farmhouses can also help cut down on fossil fuels in daily farm operations. Photovoltaic (PV) cells are cheaper to install in remote rural areas compared with installing miles of electric power lines, so as the price of this solar technology steadily declines with manufacturing improvements, panels will become an excellent way to power more American farms. The PV cells will eventually become more cost-effective for pumping water in remote locations, too. And if farmers or ranchers have unused land that's suitable for large solar arrays, they might generate extra income by leasing out this piece of their property to a utility company or other business for the production of sun-powered electricity that can be distributed to a nearby community.

Another important way that farmers are helping push the energy-freedom movement is through more efficient use of America's water resources. Farms use a tremendous amount of water in irrigating their crops, and all that H_2O requires energy to clean and distribute it. Many U.S. farms are upgrading their irrigation systems to cut down on their use of water. For example, microirrigation or subsurface drip systems target water directly to the plants' roots instead of spraying it high into the air from above-ground sprinklers. Farmers can save up to 25 percent of their water-pumping costs by incorporating drip systems into their horticultural practices, which reduces evaporation and runoff loss.[10] Effective water-management techniques will save farmers money on herbicides, pesticides, and fertilizers, too, because they will need to use fewer of these products as they decrease the amount that gets washed away from standard irrigation practices.

As gasoline becomes more expensive with the decline of oil reserves, Americans will start to use more biofuels in their vehicles. This is another excellent farm-production opportunity for our nation's farmers, but we must go about implementing it intelligently. In recent years, the United States has seen an increase in corn-based ethanol production to help supplement petroleum-based gasoline. Although this biofuel has been an economic windfall for many of America's corn farmers, the grain is not as energy efficient in production and consumption as certain other types of vegetation. One study from the University of California at Berkeley estimated that as much as six units of fuel is needed to produce one unit of corn ethanol.[11] Corn production for ethanol also causes a decline of this crop for food consumption, which has, on occasion, raised prices for consumers while reducing the supply of corn sent to the hungry people of other nations. There are much better options than corn-based fuels for our cars. Among them is the humble prairie grass, which promises to be an exceptionally attractive alternative vegetation source for ethanol production in the future, according to a ten-year experimental study done by University of Minnesota scientists. Researchers David Tilman and Jason Hill found that "native prairie plants (which would not otherwise be used for food or anything else) . . . thrive on poor soils (rather than using up precious farmland)," and according to them, prairie plants "yield bioenergy at a very significant rate." An added benefit with growing these perennial energy-crop grasses is that they require very little irrigation, fertilizer, herbicides, or pesticides. Still another advantage to the mass production of native prairie grass is that this plant removes carbon dioxide from the air—at about 1.5 tons per acre of land, according to Tilman and Hill's research.[12] The grass's roots store carbon in the soil, thus over time helping to add fertility to uncultivable dirt so that the land can later be used for food production.

Perennial energy-crop development in the future should also include wood as a potential source of biomass energy. Fast-growing trees can be planted by farmers for harvest in rural and wilderness lands. These trees would require less maintenance and be cheaper and more sustainable than annual row crops such as corn or soybeans. In warmer, dryer areas, trees such as sycamore, cottonwood, and sweetgum would thrive. In cooler and wetter climates, poplar and willow trees would grow in abundance. After seven or eight years, these trees can be selectively harvested to maintain their root base so that they will grow back in a short-rotation cycle. The wood can then be converted into pellets to be burned to generate electricity or sold to warm homes in energy-efficient heaters. Not only could these trees help reduce America's carbon footprint and our dependence on fossil fuels, but they also would add to the natural beauty of America's landscape. Likewise, they would help prevent erosion and improve the organic quality of the soil in areas where the land has lost nutrients due to an overproduction of row crops over many years.

As the supply of natural gas declines and rising prices make fertilizers costlier for farmers, the United States must start looking at ways to condition the soil without the use of valuable fossil-fuel-based products. One promising method uses an ancient technique called *terra preta* farming, which was originally developed by inhabitants of the Amazon rain forest. In this technique, unwanted plant material is slowly burned so that much of it turns into a charred ash. This "black earth" debris is then mixed into the soil as an organic fertilizer. Studies have shown that it can triple crop yields compared to ordinary soil. It also helps sequester carbon and reduces erosion and the need for tilling the land, thus saving farmers money. An added benefit of the *terra preta* technique is that the heat released from the burning production of the ash material can be used to generate electric power.[13]

Many other opportunities abound for American farmers to supplement their income at the same time as they help their nation ease its dependence on fossil fuels and combat global climate change. One of the most exciting is turning manure into money for dairy and beef ranchers by converting the methane gas produced by cattle waste into an energy source. Instead of just allowing this greenhouse gas to float out into the atmosphere and add to the problems of climate change, the methane from the cow dung is collected and burned to generate electricity. California utility company Pacific Gas & Electric has developed a program that takes the waste from dairy ranches and uses it to generate electricity to power more than 150,000 households.[14] There's also a potential that, in the future, this animal-produced methane can be collected to run farm vehicles. Researchers at the University of Missouri in Columbia are looking into using discarded corncobs as a methane-storage system.[15] Shelled cobs are placed in special tanks and when methane is pumped in, the honeycomb-like structures of the corncobs' pores keep the gas from dispersing. It's American ingenuity like this that will make the agricultural industry more self-sufficient and also more productive and profitable.

Another source of biofuels might come from the food waste generated in farming and the factory processing of agricultural products. Several companies are working on energy production methods using carefully selected species of anaerobic bacteria that eat and digest the carbohydrate matter from plants grown on the farm.[16] The microorganisms are kept in holding tanks where they break down the carbohydrate molecules and release hydrogen gas, which can then be collected for use in fuel cells or burned directly to generate electricity in power plants. If this technology proves commercially feasible, it will help farmers and food-processing plants in several ways. It will provide extra income from the energy generated. It will cut down on the cost of disposing of waste material. And carbon material left over after the bacteria is through digesting the carbohydrates can be put back into the land as a soil conditioner, thus reducing the need for expensive synthetic fertilizer. German scientists at the Westfälische Wilhelms University in Münster in 2006 came up with another biofuel breakthrough system, called a micro-diesel, that uses genetically engineered bacteria to convert crops—including the plant's bulk material—into biodiesel fuel.[17] The researchers modified the *Escherichia coli* bug to make it digest the plant material more efficiently and thus produce a fatty acid substitute for diesel fuel.

Additional biofuel developments might allow farmers to one day help Americans pump fuel into their vehicles produced by one of nature's most ancient organisms. Scientists around the world are experimenting with humble algae to try to figure out how they might be commercially used to produce a type of biodiesel fuel. Biochemists at Utah State University are now working on a biofuels program that will essentially cook up this energy product in large holding ponds of green algae soup that can be located at many sites around the world. They estimate that one acre of the slimy organisms could manufacture as much as 10,000 gallons of oil that can be converted into fuel for vehicles. Algae farming could also potentially help reduce greenhouse gas emissions from coal-burning power plants. Scientists at the Massachusetts Institute of Technology (MIT) have experimented with a system to use algae to soak up carbon dioxide from these power plants—and make extra profit for these electricity-producing companies at the same time as they clean up the atmosphere. If the project proves viable on an industrial level, one day we might see algae growing in large ponds next to our nation's coal-powered plants, with the coal-emitted carbon dioxide bubbling through the water to promote the algae's organic growth. The algae could then be harvested on a daily basis and processed into an energy-rich vegetable oil that could be used to power diesel vehicles. The MIT researchers set up a small experimental system using the exhaust from a 20-megawatt power plant on the campus and discovered that the algae cleaned up to 40 percent of the carbon dioxide and 86 percent of the nitrous oxide. Higher levels of carbon cleaning could come from genetically modifying strains of algae to absorb even more of the greenhouse gas, the researchers suggested.[18]

Bringing clean- and renewable-energy technology to America's farms—as well as making our agricultural industries more energy efficient—requires large-scale funding to pay for the capital start-up expenses. To make it easier for rural communities to obtain this money, we need to encourage the development of state and local "co-op" management systems that spread the risks and increase the benefits for farm and ranch neighbors. Our nation is already seeing this movement bear fruit with the growing number of rural electric cooperatives pooling money into farm-based wind- and solar-power production, as well as into energy-efficiency programs. Many of these cooperatives are now benefitting from funding from the federal government's Rural Energy for America Program (REAP), which was created in the 2002 Farm Bill to reduce fossil-fuel energy use in agricultural operations. (REAP was originally given the rather unappealing name "Section 9006.") REAP proved so successful that in the 2008 Farm Bill, Congress increased funding for grants and guaranteed loans of up to $25 million per project. Since its inception, this federal program has helped fund more than 3,000 farm-energy projects, bringing benefits to America by cutting down on our fossil-fuel use while also increasing the revenues for farming and ranching communities.

The many clean-energy-producing ideas and innovations we are now seeing emerge from American minds might help bolster our nation's agricultural industry in the coming decades. If America's farms and ranches can in the near future put into practical use the major technological breakthroughs being developed from research into biofuels and solar and wind power, we will go a long way toward reducing our dependence on fossil fuels as we protect our food security. We can learn much from the tragedy of the 1930s, when the Great Plains of the American heartland became the Dust Bowl. If the climatologists are correct in their projected scenarios, the United States might see similar devastation from the weather and seasonal changes from global warming in decades to come. Steps taken now by the American agricultural industry will combat the impending crisis and simultaneously reap rewards for America's farming families and rural communities by giving them lucrative financial opportunities in the green fields of energy freedom.

CHAPTER 10

Energy and Public Health

Around noon on July 26, 1943, citizens of Los Angeles were suffering through a major heat wave when an acrid smoke mysteriously started to smother the downtown area. It reduced visibility to only a three-block distance and stung the eyes of people caught in the spreading cloud. Many of them soon found they suddenly had trouble breathing. Those affected by the fumes began to cramp up with nausea and started vomiting. At first, residents feared they were facing a gas attack from Nazi or Japanese enemy agents. Officials soon put the blame on the Southern California Gas Company, which operated a plant in the downtown area that made butadiene, a petroleum-based chemical used to manufacture synthetic rubber. After the factory was closed, however, the air crisis continued. With further investigation, experts later determined that the source of the smoke was the exhaust of train locomotives and truck diesel engines, as well as backyard trash-burning barrels scattered throughout the city. Blocked by the nearby mountains and an atmospheric inversion layer that hung over the city, the smoke particles were held in the Los Angeles basin as if contained in a box.

That summer day marked the first recognized instance when Los Angeles faced the extreme smog conditions that have now become a part of its urban ambience. As the pollution problem continued and caused respiratory and other health problems for citizens, officials set up a Bureau of Smoke Control within the city's health department. Laws and burning ordinances were passed as the smog continued to be a health threat. On October 14, 1947, the Los Angeles County Board of Supervisors established America's first air-pollution control district to regulate the burning of fossil fuels in that region and reduce the damage to public health.[1]

As demonstrated by L.A.'s infamous smog troubles, the pollution created by consuming fossil fuels can have a detrimental effect on our well-being. From small towns to big cities, communities throughout the United States must deal daily with quality-of-life problems associated with the harmful chemicals found in coal and petroleum pollution. Coal pollution especially can reduce the overall quality of our health. Although the 1970 Clean Air Act promoted increased pollution control in new coal-fired power plants, requiring them to reduce air pollution by 90 percent from levels before environmental regulation, coal power plants are the "largest contributor of hazardous air pollutants,"[2] and the airborne waste products they emit lower the level of public health conditions in many American cities located near them. Airborne particulates affect the physical condition of 116 million people in the United States, according to research done by the Environmental Defense Fund.[3] The air pollution released from burning coal in power plants and petroleum-based fuel in vehicles annually costs Americans $120 billion in healthcare costs, according to a study released by the National Academy of Sciences in October 2009.[4] Fossil-fuel-created air pollution doesn't even necessarily need to come from within our nation's borders to harm us. Winds circulating high in the atmosphere carry pollution particles over the oceans from coal-fired plants as far away as China, which eventually contaminate America's own air, land, and water.

According to the American Lung Association's "State of the Air: 2007 Fact Sheet," about one-third of Americans live in areas where unhealthy levels of ozone smog put them at risk for major health problems. Air pollution released from the smokestacks of coal plants causes as many as 30,000 premature deaths in the United States each year. A study done for the U.S. Environmental Protection Agency (EPA) by the Health Effects Institute in Cambridge, Massachusetts, determined that every year as many as 60,000 people in America's metropolitan areas die from damage to their bodies caused by breathing in fine particles of pollution generated from the burning of fossil fuels in vehicles and from other sources. Not only coal-powered electricity but also gasoline-driven vehicles cause high mortality rates. People who reside near a major road or highway are statistically more likely to die from cardiovascular diseases such as stroke and heart attack than people living where the air is cleaner. That's because ultrafine and toxic soot particles from burning coal or petroleum fuel can enter the body through the lungs. Coal energy also has severe health consequences. Miners who have spent years working in dirty conditions and breathing coal dust often suffer from a condition known as "black lung" disease. When silica and carbon particles become trapped in the tiny air sacs of a miner's lungs, this organ literally turns a dark black instead of remaining a healthy pink. The illness can result in emphysema, cancer, or severe heart conditions.[5]

Fossil-fuel pollutants also contribute to the growing number of asthma sufferers in America. Sulfur particles released from burning petroleum diesel can lead to respiratory problems such as asthma, as well as chronic and acute bronchitis. Asthma is the fastest-growing chronic disease in our nation, afflicting more than 22 million U.S. citizens, according to the American Lung Association. Children's lungs are especially vulnerable to smog-caused asthma because they are still in their biological development. Urban areas tend to have a concentration of vehicles producing airborne pollution that promotes respiratory problems, so youngsters in these areas often have a high rate of asthma. The problem can affect the future of many American kids who have their education continually interrupted because they are too sick to attend school. Parents also are forced to take days off from work and pay for medical care of their youngsters, creating added financial burden to families. The asthma problem is increasing in rural areas, too. California's San Joaquin Valley, one of America's most productive farming regions, had generally good air quality not that many decades ago. As the valley's population boomed, the increased vehicular traffic caused the region to begin to experience major smog problems. San Joaquin Valley now holds the dubious distinction of having the nation's highest asthma rate in children. According to the American Lung Association, one in six children in the region suffers from the respiratory challenges of asthmatic attacks, resulting in more than 800,000 absent days at schools annually and the loss of more than $26 million a year for the region's school districts.[6] The situation will only grow worse as climate change brings hotter days that cause pollen counts to rise and mold spores to multiply, thus intensifying breathing difficulties caused by asthma.

Climate change from global warming adds to air pollution's detrimental consequence in other ways, too. It increases the misery of people suffering from lung-related illness. Smog is created when nonmethane hydrocarbons and nitrogen oxides chemically react from the energy of sunlight and atmospheric heat, producing ground-level ozone, a toxic gas that can cause lung damage. As our planet starts to experience an increasing number of sizzling days, we'll also undergo an overall rise in the amount of smog produced in populated areas, which will result in more people suffering from lung disease. Hotter weather and additional carbon dioxide in the air will increase allergy suffering as well because more ragweed and other pollen-rich vegetation will release their spores.[7] About 40 million Americans suffer from hay fever, resulting in 3.8 million days lost at work and school in dealing with this health problem.[8] Energy-freedom initiatives promoting clean fuels will help us to increase our productivity by decreasing the detrimental effects of this condition.

CLIMATE CHANGE

Our health is directly tied to the planet's environmental stability, and that's why global warming is a serious public-safety threat that might result in hundreds of thousands of human lives being lost and many millions suffering from sickness. A 2005 study by the World Health Organization estimates that the yearly death rate from climate change is about 150,000 people, with an increase of 5 million illnesses a year. By the year 2030, these numbers could possibly double as global warming–related diseases such as diarrhea, malnutrition, and malaria grow more intense, according to the study.[9]

The cost to the quality of human life will be tragic. But there's an additional economic cost. Health problems caused by climate change will require billions of dollars to treat and comfort the ill. Industries can also suffer from lost productivity and absenteeism as more and more workers sicken and cannot show up to do their jobs at factories and offices. As an example of things to come, a study published in the May 2009 *American Journal of Tropical Medicine and Hygiene* found that dengue fever (which is spread by mosquitoes) cost eight South American and Asian countries a combined total of $1.8 billion annually in health care and a decline in worker productivity.[10]

Global warming now endangers people's safety and health in a number of other ways as our natural environment is transformed. Greenland holds nearly 10 percent of the world's frozen water, so if this Arctic island-nation's ice were to completely melt, the resulting seawater rise could reach as much as twenty-three feet around the world. The effect would be catastrophic because as many as 37 percent of all the people on the planet live within 60 miles (about 100 kilometers) of a coastline.[11] Population-dense locations— including such low-lying regions as the Florida Peninsula, Egypt's Nile Delta region, and India's Ganges-Brahmaputra Delta region—would face enormous social upheaval as worldwide flooding drowned hundreds of thousands of coastal acres. Over a period of several decades, hundreds of millions of people might abandon their homes to move to refugee camps located on higher ground. These environmental exiles would be forced to live in dense concentrations at their new locations, creating the perfect con-ditions for the widespread distribution of dangerous pathogens. If modern medicine and proper sanitation fail to stop the spread of disease, pandem-ics could increase in frequency. History shows us that the risks are real. Only ninety years ago, the world saw between 40 and 50 million people die from influenza in a six-month period during one particularly brutal global pandemic in 1918 and 1919. About 500,000 of those people were Americans.[12]

Changes in global weather patterns could bring about an increasing intensity of cyclones, hurricanes, typhoons, and tornadoes that would re-sult in many thousands of people getting hurt or killed. These extreme weather events will also imperil the lives of millions of people by eroding good harvest land and demolishing regional livelihoods. Flooding from major storms will especially cause great harm to public safety and health, as heavy rains relentlessly pound various regions. In December 1999, for example, 30,000 people living in a "shantytown" in Caracas, Venezuela, died after rain soaked the region and set off a massive mudslide that covered their tightly packed community. And more than 1,800 people perished from drowning in floodwaters or the physical trauma from flying debris, structure collapse, or stress when the intense winds and rains of Hurricane Katrina raged through Louisiana and Mississippi in 2005.[13] With the possibility that climate change will transform our planet's weather patterns in the coming decades, deadly hurricanes with the strength of Katrina or even worse will occur more frequently.

The alarm is now sounding, and we must wisely heed this clear warning of what extreme temperatures in our future might hold in store for us in managing America's public health. The world has witnessed the truth of this fact in several well-reported incidences: In July 1995, more than 700 residents of Chicago died when unseasonably hot weather hit the city for several days. In Europe in 2003, between 21,000 and 35,000 people were killed by the effects of a heat wave that broiled the continent in August; and in July 2006, a blistering heat wave hit many parts of North America and caused the deaths of about 225 people.[14] Hot weather also causes a population to use more electricity to run air-conditioning units. If America's unstable electric grid is not upgraded, or if we cannot produce electric energy to meet growing demand, scorching days could in the future trigger brownouts or even widespread blackouts as millions of people crank up the power to cool their homes and businesses. These power failures could result in potentially more deaths and illnesses if people with low tolerance can't deal with the extreme temperatures.

Increased heat also means more production of ground-level ozone, a pollutant that can, as previously discussed, damage lung tissue and raise the chances of pulmonary congestion. In America's western regions, the increase in blazing summer days will stress human health from problems such as heat stroke and heart conditions, as well as the air-related problems that come with an increase in ozone when the mercury soars. The upsurge in raging wildfires caused by the hotter weather will also endanger the public if the flames spread to homes and communities. The smoke caused by these infernos will drift over populations and cause thousands of people to suffer grave respiratory symptoms. If the climate changes bring about extreme freezing temperatures in winter months, America's medical professionals will see growing numbers of victims hit by hypothermia when Arctic cold fronts descend upon northern latitudes. The threat to human health will grow even worse as peak oil forces us to cut our burning of fossil fuels to heat our homes and businesses during blizzards or severe cold snaps.

Climate change could have other deadly consequences. Flooding from more intense storms and rising sea levels as the world's ice melts can contaminate our water supplies—a situation that will be especially problematic in poorer nations that don't have the financial means to protect the quality of their water resources. Long periods of droughts in other places will reduce the availability of water in regions that cannot import it from other locations. The result will be increased hardship for millions around the globe who will get severely sick and possibly die from the tainted water or the scarcity of this liquid so vital for life. The warming of our planet's oceans will over time change delicate marine ecosystems so that we'll see an increase in algal blooms on the surfaces of our seas, lakes, and ponds, thus serving as nurseries for the *Vibrio cholera* bacteria that cause cholera. Warmer waters will also result in more incidents of shellfish poisoning, thus reducing the food supply for many people throughout the world or sickening them if the toxic seafood is eaten.[15]

In the United States and around the world, ecological changes on our planet caused by the transformation of its climate might endanger public health by promoting the spread of infectious bacteria and viruses transmitted by a mounting number of insects and vermin. These germ carriers will be able to more easily survive and breed thanks to warmer weather conditions. Many cities in the Americas, Africa, and Asia were built at higher mountain elevations that in the past enabled them to keep safe from certain diseases because the cooler climate prevented the carriers of disease from surviving in those locations. In the future, as we face warming conditions that bring hotter days to these formerly cooler zones, many of these high-elevation communities will start to confront the growing problem of insects and rodents that carry harmful microbes. Mosquitoes, fleas, tsetse flies, ticks, rats, and mice might all bring their packages of pestilence to new locations inhabited by humans. We are now just starting to see these carriers make new homes in many areas around the world that cooler weather once kept off limits—including here in America. As they settle into these territories, they expose many more millions of people to sicknesses, such as the West Nile virus, malaria, cholera, and Lyme disease. A 2007 study done by the International Panel on Climate Change (IPCC) forecasts that the global risk of malaria carried by mosquitoes will especially grow severe, increasing from 220 million victims to 400 million during the next hundred years. Malaria won't just affect Africa, where it has traditionally been a devastating public health problem. People in Asia and Australia might also suffer from the disease as well, the IPCC report warns.[16]

As we saw in Chapter 9, our food production could decline as climate change brings droughts, blizzards, and severe storms that hurt crop yields worldwide. Droughts stress plants, thus helping to promote the outbreak of aphids and white flies, which can decrease crop yields and finish off farm vegetation already wilting because of the lack of water. Malnutrition from a lack of nutritious food could stunt the growth and mental alacrity of many young children. Inadequate nourishment also decreases the body's immunity to diseases, increasing the chances that people will more easily contract infectious diseases. The problems of peak oil and the waning of petroleum and natural gas supplies further compound the climate-change challenge of producing adequate nourishment to maintain public health. Hundreds of millions of people—including many in the United States—might face malnourishment and famine if we don't find a solution to sustaining our agricultural output.

Poorer nations will be especially impaired because they don't have the economic resources to handle mass starvation and the health problems that come with food shortages. These problems compound political and social tensions, leading to violence as people fear for their continued survival. With the tragic human crisis in Darfur, we are only now getting a glimpse of what awaits as persistent drought increases competition for food and water. Food production in the world's oceans could also suffer from climate change as the increased acidification of seawater comes with rising levels of carbon dioxide. Fish make up as much as 20 percent of animal protein for human beings, and sea-based fisheries provide the bulk of this supply. As fish populations shrink owing to the decrease of plankton, populations that depend heavily on marine-produced protein will starve if they can't find nourishment from other sources.[17]

America must come to grips with the threat that climate change's health consequences will grow more detrimental as environmental conditions become more intense. These real dangers give the U.S. government a powerful incentive to start addressing the question of how we must manage the quality of our national health system to care for Americans made sick from climate-change-related causes.

FOSSIL FUEL AND MEDICINE

The rise in health problems from climate change comes at a time when many more people find that their lives depend on the modern medical supplies and equipment made and powered by fossil fuels. Adding to the problem in the coming decades is the fact that Americans born in the twenty years following World War II are now starting to require more medical attention as they age and face a growing number of health problems. "The baby boomers, a demographic cohort twice the size of the preceding generation, are beginning to retire and will annually consume twice as many medical resources as they do today," says Dan Bednarz, Ph.D., former associate director at the Center for Public Health Practice at the University of Pittsburgh Graduate School of Public Health.[18] He has written and spoken extensively about medicine and the global petroleum supply, strongly advocating that the American medical profession deal with the public health risks related to peak oil. His warning is not yet being heeded, unfortunately, putting people's lives at risk as the quality of medical care declines in the years following the peak in oil production.

Peak oil might be a turning point in public health because our medical care industry is so dependent on petroleum. Fossil fuels have enabled many people to enjoy excellent health over the last century. Much of our world population of 7 billion people is also living longer. Life expectancy world-wide has doubled, thanks in large measure to improvements in nutrition and sanitation that have been possible because of the energy that comes from petroleum, natural gas, and coal. Petroleum-based chemicals also help pharmaceutical companies manufacture a wide variety of medicines, including antibiotics, sedatives, antihistamines, and analgesics. Oil is used to produce pain relievers such as aspirin, as well as sterilizing products such as rubbing alcohol and ethylene oxide. Petroleum is used in the manufacture of a variety of plastic medical components, including heart valves, hearing aids, and prostheses such as artificial arms and legs. Radiological dyes and X-ray films require petroleum for their production. Fossil fuel is also required to make the plastics for disposal products used daily in hospitals, such as syringes, blood bags, intravenous tubing, catheters, bandages, oxygen masks, and many other necessities that help keep patients alive and comfortable. As oil costs soar, the price of these products will also go up, adding to the already high expense of medical care.[19]

Our world's amazing high-tech medical gadgets also require fossil fuels in their manufacturing process. As the medical practice becomes more reliant on these machines, it also becomes more dependent on the power that makes them run. Heart defibrillators, scanning machines, X-ray machines, heart monitors, breathing machines, and other devices all require electricity to keep them operating. Large modern hospitals depend on fossil fuels to run the refrigerators that store organs, blood, and temperature-sensitive medicine. Energy is needed to operate heating systems and air-conditioning units that help medical centers control indoor temperature for the comfort and safety of the patients and employees. Electricity runs the lighting in surgery rooms, keeps emergency-room monitoring equipment functioning, and powers medical computers and communication systems. Hospitals are required by government regulations to keep a stock of natural gas or diesel fuel at hand to run emergency generators in case of a power outage. Gasoline and diesel are also used in the medical industry for transportation purposes. These fuels run emergency vehicles such as fire trucks, ambulances, and life-flight helicopters that save many lives each year. Airplanes carry medicine, blood, and donated organs to locations hit by natural catastrophes such as earthquakes or hurricanes. On a less dramatic level, fuel is required to transport visiting nurses to their patients, health inspectors to restaurants, and pest-control personnel to job sites.

Modern medicine's dependence on fossil fuels is a double-edged sword. We can now enjoy the blessings of health at levels far higher than at any other time in human history. But as we deal with greater climate-change problems and the peak oil concerns of our fossil-fuel dependency, we will also find that we've created a healthcare system that won't be easy to sustain as our energy challenges continue to grow more complex. Our healthcare system is already overburdened, and peak oil will only exacerbate the problems of meeting the growing demand for quality health care. The medical profession will need to adapt to the situation by conserving supplies and managing energy usage more frugally. Peak oil is a direct threat to public health in other ways. As the world deals with an increasing lack of petroleum, many nations might choose to consume more coal energy, thus only adding to the health problems of air pollution and climate change. Shortages of essential resources such as water and food because of climate change and declining fossil fuels will also cause desperate people to erupt in violent conflict in cities and towns. If law-enforcement personnel can't deal with this crisis because peak oil reduces their job efficiency, many people will be injured in riots or criminal acts. Police, paramedics, and emergency-room staff will themselves face stress-related health problems from being injured or overworked during these social flare-ups.

❧

Historically for more than 100 years, America has rightfully spent many billions of dollars annually to guard against aggressive threats to our country.

Combating terrorism, modernizing our armed forces, and reinvesting in our economy have commanded significant public attention and resources. We should also bear in mind that global warming and peak oil likewise pose significant threats to our physical well-being. These threats must be given a level of attention equal to the danger they pose to our citizens. We learned from the Los Angeles smog "attack" in 1943 how polluting our air can negatively impact our health. The same can be said for polluting our water and land. Medical science shows that the toxic effects of fossil fuels can wreak havoc on our health and reduce the quality of life for many of our fellow American citizens. Becoming a clean-energy nation will help us achieve the goal of protecting our public health.

CHAPTER 11

Energy and Education

During the early years of the cold war era, the United States fell behind in an important race with its most dangerous adversary. On October 4, 1957, the Soviet Union successfully launched its globelike *Sputnik* satellite into an elliptical orbit around our planet. Using just a radio beacon's beeping to signal its position as it reached heights of 583 miles (939 kilometers), the world's first artificial moon changed the course of human history. When Americans first learned about *Sputnik,* many felt alarmed that the Soviets now had the rocket power and technology to send satellites high into orbit, and the ability to bomb our cities with nuclear warheads. We also felt humiliated that our great country had been beaten by a communist system of government in the politically motivated contest to cross first into the frontier of the stars.

If we look back half a century, however, the embarrassment of coming in second behind the Soviet Union at the start of the space race proved to be a blessing for America. It forced us to accept the painful truth that we had to radically improve our educational system if we wanted to successfully compete with foreign countries. *Sputnik* woke us up to the fact that we needed to make American students smarter in all academic fields, but especially in science and mathematics—the cornerstone subjects for all technological innovations. A year after *Sputnik's* launch, Congress passed the National Defense Education Act, which infused our nation's public and private schools with

$1 billion (more than $7 billion in today's dollars). That law helped alleviate the blow to our national prestige by enhancing U.S. brainpower. It allowed us to gain the lead from the Soviet Union not only in space science, culminating in manned trips to the moon a decade later, but in almost all other areas of technology and engineering.

Now the United States is engaged in an even greater pursuit than the conquest of space. This ambitious endeavor is one that requires us to use much more of our nation's brainpower than was needed to strive for the stars. The current challenges of supplying our future energy needs—as well as dealing with environmental and social problems pertaining to impending climate change—require us to come up with revolutionary new energy innovations in the coming decades. To achieve these technological advances means we need to make sure our citizens are well educated for careers in biotechnology, agricultural science, clean-tech, innovative carbon-sequestration systems, green architecture, green-product design, government energy policy, and many other important science-based areas relating to the better use of our energy resources. Education is the greatest gift that America can bestow on its citizens. It ensures the economic success of future generations—especially through clean-energy research and development.

If history serves as an indicator, many of the exciting ideas for future energy inventions and engineering feats will come from America's young people, who have the courage to be creative and to think beyond what others might deem the perimeters of possibility. Consider that in recent decades many of the great achievements in the high-tech realm bloomed from the minds of American innovators—entrepreneurs such as Microsoft's Bill Gates and Paul Allen, Apple's Steve Jobs and Steve Wozniak, and Google's Sergey Brin and Larry Page—all of whom were still in their twenties when they dreamed up their visionary ideas that transformed our modern world. These innovators would not have been able to achieve their accomplishments, however, without first receiving a solid education. Their classroom experiences fueled their brains with the knowledge, imagination, and intellectual discipline that enabled them to build upon the technologies of previous innovators. Increasingly in the coming decades, education must play a crucial role in providing the youth of the United States with the skills they need to help our nation win its energy freedom.

Unfortunately, our nation's schools as a whole are currently not in a condition to properly prepare massive numbers of U.S. students with the high-quality cerebral power they'll need for this vital pursuit. If not addressed, the state of America's present educational system will turn into the biggest stumbling block preventing our nation from achieving a sustainable-energy society. It is no secret that the United States has fallen behind many other countries in providing our nation's young people with the excellent education they need to survive and thrive in future years. Most Americans realize that our deficient school systems, if left to continue in their present state, will over time endanger our nation's economic and military competitiveness around the globe. The inadequate education we now offer the next generation will hold back our nation from attaining the groundbreaking technical ideas we must have to achieve energy freedom. Without brain-power, we as a nation will not go far along the road to creating a sustainable-energy future.

Improving education in America is crucial to making sure we have the scientists, researchers, and engineers who will provide us with the energy-efficiency advances we must gain in transportation, agriculture, national defense, manufacturing, communications, high-tech information processing, building construction, and other fundamental areas. Quality schools can provide us with the brainpower we need to create exciting breakthrough innovations in biotechnology, nanotechnology, robotics, and other advanced tools necessary for ramping up America's sustainable-energy industry. We also need to improve the caliber of our educational system to build a green-collar workforce of men and women who have the competent technical skills required to construct and service a sustainable-energy industry and infrastructure for the United States. If we cannot provide the good schooling American students must have to build an energy-independent future, at some point in the twenty-first century we will sadly face the fact that America won't be able to successfully compete with other nations that were far more vigilant in providing an excellent education to their citizens.

MATH AND SCIENCE

Scientists, mathematicians, and engineers are sounding the call for better academic instruction for America's students to deal with the energy problems in the coming decades. In its 2006 report "Rising Above the Gathering Storm: Energizing and Employing America for a Brighter Future," the National Academy of Sciences (NAS) shined a spotlight on the threat the American way of life faces if our nation fails to reverse the prevailing downward trend in the quality of education we offer our young people. The study points out that our nation will face an ongoing decline of its global economic strength if we can't compete against nations with better school systems—especially those nations that give their citizens a solid foundation in science and mathematics, the two subjects most needed for building advanced energy technologies. "Economic studies conducted even before the information technology revolution have shown that as much as 85 percent of measured growth in U.S. income per capita was due to technological change," the NAS report points out.[1] If current American educational trends continue and we can't raise our educational standards significantly higher, many U.S. companies—including those in industries vital to gaining our energy freedom—will be unable to hire enough American citizens with the necessary expertise in math and the various branches of science and engineering.

Because quality education leads to technological progress, and advanced technologies will lead to the expansion in the clean-energy independence movement, America's educational weaknesses imperil our future. We are already starting to see the warning signs of how the erosion of America's schools hurts our young people's academic performance in comparison with that of other nations. One alarming indicator of how poorly our students compare on an international level is highlighted from results of the Program for International Student Assessment (PISA) survey. This study is conducted every three years by the Organization for Economic Cooperation and Development (OECD), an intergovernmental agency that uses the survey's information to improve the educational systems of its members. The PISA survey tests fifteen-year-old students to measure the differences in science and mathematics literacy among their peers in all the nations that participate. In 2006, science was emphasized by the triennial test. American students scored lower on science knowledge than did their peers in sixteen of the twenty-nine OECD-member nations, according to the survey. The 2003 PISA survey emphasized mathematics skills and showed that the United States ranked a dismal twenty-fourth out of the twenty-nine OECD-member nations. In the 2009 PISA survey, American students ranked twenty-third in science and thirty-first in math among their peers in sixty-five nations that participated in the testing program.[2]

People who become interested in working in careers involving math, chemistry, physics, engineering, and biology—subjects vital for building energy-independent technologies—almost always do so in their early school years. And often it is because as young students they had at least one excellent teacher who instilled in them a genuine passion for one or more of these academic subjects. One of the problems with the American educational system is society's perception of schooling. Many of our young people are not inspired to do the hard work it takes to excel in engineering and the sciences. We need to transform the social environment into one that honors educators and students who work hard for academic achievement. The problem with many schools in America today is that they are simply not providing the environments that can inspire students from kindergarten to twelfth grade to excel in the math and scientific fields. Fiscal cuts in state education budgets aggravate the social and classroom environments, making it difficult for many school districts to attract and retain well-qualified math and science teachers. Many potential educators who have earned mathematics and science degrees choose better-paying industry jobs as engineers and scientists over education.

In an attempt to address the decline of our nation's schools, President Bush signed the No Child Left Behind Act (NCLB) on January 8, 2002. This federal legislation intended to put U.S. public schools on the course to providing a higher quality of education to America's young people and emphasized standardized testing to determine which schools were performing poorly. Many of those schools would face the threat of having their federal funding cut if their classes failed. The results of NCLB have been mixed at best. The law aspires to create more accountability among schools and teachers for student academic performance and raise the quality of teaching. But one of the problems many teachers and administrators have been forced to deal with from this national education law is that it forces them to "teach to the test" and develop a curriculum that ensures students pass the mandated exams measuring their English and math skills. So the law has caused many American schools to cut down on the amount of science education they provide their students in order to focus more classroom time on core English skills and basic math to pass the NCLB-required proficiency exams.[3] Because each state sets its own standards, there is no consistent national methodology for testing children across the United States. Thus, there's a potential risk that states might water down their educational quality standards in order to make their schools appear "proficient." Another problem with NCLB is that not all schools are created equal. Many states have districts with wide variability in socioeconomic conditions, as well as in English language skills, because many children do not learn English as a first language. These differences have a major effect on learning performance and often make it harder for some schools—particularly those in financially struggling districts—to provide the level of education needed to pass the proficiency tests. Poor urban schools may have greater problems meeting the standards because they find it harder to hire the better teachers and supply school-age youngsters with good classroom resources and a quality learning environment.

CREATING BETTER SCHOOLS

Americans need to better understand how the current state of our educational systems is building a barrier to our nation's achieving clean-energy freedom and its promise of long-term prosperity. Turning U.S. schools from "dropout factories" into world-class learning institutions will require better management of our educational resources—starting with making sure an increasing number of educators have the best tools and up-to-date knowledge to properly instruct their students. Significantly more resources, including money, will be needed to fix education in America. But it would be a mistake to assume that it's all about the money. It will not work to simply pour dollars into our educational systems and hope better teaching might result. The NAS report offers several solutions to deal with the challenge of improving America's schools to better prepare students for a much more competitive world than the one their parents knew. Among the suggestions is the creation of a program that will supplement the skills of kindergarten through twelfth-grade teachers in offering pupils better instruction in math and science.

Because the United States faces an increase in retirement of its teaching workforce in the next ten years, the NAS advocates that our nation recruit about 10,000 new science and math teachers each year to fill the growing gap of instructors.[4] And we are taking steps in this direction. In August 2007, President Bush signed a bill passed by Congress to both strengthen America's education in the sciences and increase research to sustain our technological innovations. The America Creating Opportunities to Meaningfully Promote Excellence in Technology, Education, and Science Act (America COMPETES) sets up programs to give teachers in elementary and middle schools the tools they need to improve student math and science skills. America COMPETES also contains an initiative designed to encourage over the next eight years as many as 30,000 science and math professionals to teach in America's schools.

Other opportunities abound for the United States to improve its school system and, in so doing, open the doors to an energy-independent society. One is to make sure that kids early on—preferably at a preschool level—start learning the classroom skills that will enable them to better grasp information, as well as develop their critical-thinking skills. All children, of course, have different learning abilities. If youngsters fall too far behind in their studies—particularly in complex areas such as mathematics and science, which require building a solid knowledge base before advancing to more complex levels—they will grow frustrated and most likely never catch up unless the matter is quickly corrected.

Various programs are being initiated throughout the United States that bring volunteers into schools to give students extra help. One of the most notable is the RE-SEED (Retirees Enhancing Science Education through Experiments and Demonstrations) program established in 1991 to assist middle-school math and science teachers. RE-SEED brings retired engineers and scientists into science and math classrooms at least once a week during the school year to give tutoring help to youngsters having difficulty grasping academic information. The volunteers frequently bring in scientific experiments to demonstrate the principles of physics, chemistry, or biology. They share their passion for their field of expertise and, because they have career experience, provide students with real-world knowledge. As mentors, the volunteers who take a one-on-one interest in students also can inspire them to consider going into jobs in science or engineering. Another successful program called NEED (National Energy Education Development) specifically focuses on helping kindergarten through twelfth-grade teachers develop energy-education programs for their classrooms. In partnership with the U.S. Energy Information Administration, NEED provides the curriculum and the materials that teachers require to help youngsters learn the complex science behind energy issues. Creating real-world connections, the program links teachers with businesses and community organizations that bring experts to their classrooms to use hands-on activities to make energy science come alive for the students.

TRAINING AND GREEN-COLLAR JOBS

Providing better education to Americans in the quest for energy freedom will also help stimulate our nation's economy in countless ways, including revving up the growth of green-collar jobs. The world stands now at the beginning of a clean-tech industry boom that will generate millions of new jobs around the globe. If the United States is going to successfully achieve a sustainable-energy infrastructure, our country needs to build a large workforce trained in clean-energy technology skills. Workers will be needed to make America's buildings and vehicles far more energy efficient than they currently are.

Engineers must have the know-how to work with innovative technological designs and construction techniques to build a solid national infrastructure for harvesting and distributing power from the sun, wind, biomass, water, and geothermal sources. Factories throughout the United States will require trained green-collar workers to manufacture products in mass quantities for the expanding renewable-energy market. An army of construction workers must also be trained to install these products, and technicians must have the expert knowledge to service complex renewable-energy equipment.

The United States is only just starting to take baby steps toward providing the necessary training to bring green-collar workers up to speed. Whether they are right out of high school or seeking new career opportunities after years in other types of employment, a growing number of Americans are now attending universities, community colleges, and vocational schools with the intention of getting the specialized knowledge they will need to find employment in green-energy jobs. These people can be assured that many of the jobs in the sustainable-energy industry cannot be outsourced. And, in contrast with many bygone industries, the domestic green-collar working opportunities will last a long time after our nation gets into gear for energy freedom.

Although high-quality classroom learning is essential for our nation's sustainable-energy future, practical working knowledge is also fundamental for citizens developing green-collar careers. The Innovations in Civic Participation group, for example, advocates the creation of more American clean-energy independence skill building through a national initiative for American citizens. The group's Energy Conservation Corps program, which is inspired by the Civilian Conservation Corps of the 1930s, would provide an opportunity to "expand green-collar job opportunity for the working class and poor, expand green service opportunities for all citizens to combat climate change, and demonstrate the promise of a clean energy future."[5] America can also perhaps develop its energy freedom with a program modeled on the Peace Corps that President John F. Kennedy initiated in 1961. An "Energy Peace Corps" program can potentially bring trained volunteers to various underprivileged neighborhoods in the United States and help them become more efficient in their energy use over a period of a year. The volunteers can accomplish this task by improving the energy efficiency of low-income homes or installing solar panels or energy-saving or energy-harvesting technologies to provide power for a community. The volunteers can also install solar equipment on the roofs of public schools, and thus help school districts reduce their energy costs and use the savings to spend on teachers, books, and computer equipment. Perhaps this program can be expanded to unite American volunteers with citizens from other countries to aid impoverished villages in developing nations, helping them leapfrog into a sustainable-energy economy.

The U.S. government could also stimulate growth of the green-collar job market by rewarding its military veterans for their years of service to this country by providing them with free or low-cost training for careers in the sustainable-energy industry. One model would be the Servicemen's Readjustment Act of 1944—better known as the Montgomery GI Bill—which helped military personnel returning from World War II ease back into civilian life by paying for college educations they otherwise might not have been able to afford. In the postwar years, the GI Bill helped to boost our national economy by building up a solid middle class and increasing home ownership of former military personnel. The program proved so successful that a version of it continues today, helping U.S. veterans to enhance their education and career opportunities. Recently, veterans have received a smaller educational benefit than did our nation's veterans after World War II, so in 2008, a new GI Bill called the GI Bill for the 21st Century was passed that increases veteran educational benefits so that they are more on par with the benefits received after World War II. Perhaps this will help the United States increase the workforce we will need to gain our independence from fossil fuels. Over time, the GI Bill for the 21st Century will be adapted to provide greater incentives for American military vets to go green in their job-training pursuits. One inducement might include giving qualified veterans who finish their sustainable-energy job training guaranteed low-interest mortgages to buy energy-efficient homes.

The growth of green-collar jobs will enhance the quality of America's overall society by helping many of our financially struggling citizens find their way out of a life on the edge of destitution. The Energy Independence and Security Act, which became law in December 2007, addresses this opportunity to lessen the plight of America's poor. It includes the Green Jobs Act, designed to provide funding of up to $125 million to train as many as 30,000 job seekers a year for work in clean-energy areas such as solar-panel installation and weatherization projects.[6] Some of the money is specifically targeted to the Pathways Out of Poverty program to prepare low-income workers in acquiring green-energy job skills. If this scheme proves successful, it can serve as a model for national, state, and local governments to create similar programs that will increase training for low-income American citizens. At-risk youths and impoverished minorities who receive training for well-paying green-collar jobs might soon find their lives taking a turn for the better as they help provide the United States with a labor force to achieve energy freedom.

There will be some concern about the resources needed to invest in green-collar training for American citizens. When we consider the big picture, however, these government-funded green-skills programs will generate more wealth in the long run. Putting more Americans into good-paying clean-tech jobs not only will cut down on the dollars spent for government-assistance programs but will also help create vast new economic sectors, building up our national tax base of employed citizens and U.S.-based businesses. Providing green-collar job training for the purpose of gaining our energy freedom will also save the United States many billions of dollars as it reduces our dependence on foreign oil.

ENERGY LITERACY

Obviously, improving American schools to ignite a sustainable-energy industry is of prime importance in how we gain our overall energy freedom during the coming decades. But increasing the general knowledge the American public has about the various issues of energy production and consumption will also play an important role in this endeavor. The quantity and quality of information about energy that reaches the public has a tremendous impact on how we make our decisions about our fuel future. Our nation's energy literacy thus becomes a crucial part of the education component in achieving energy freedom. When it comes to our collective knowledge base on energy issues, we Americans have room for improvement.

A national survey done by the Roper Center for Public Opinion Research studied how knowledgeable Americans are about energy and environmental issues. The findings were published in 2005 in the "Environmental Literacy in America" report released by the National Environmental Education and Training Foundation (NEETF). The survey showed that a large majority of Americans have major misconceptions about how power is produced and believe outdated facts about our nation's energy needs. Only 12 percent of our citizens can pass a test on basic knowledge of energy in the United States. Seventy-three percent of the people surveyed did not know what energy resources contribute to electric power generation in the United States, with 55 percent believing that nonpolluting sources such as hydropower and solar power produce the vast majority of America's electricity. Only 27 percent of those surveyed were aware that "burning coal and other flammable material" provides the majority of America's electricity production. The NEETF report also showed that 83 percent of Americans are uninformed about what our nation's nuclear-energy industry does with spent uranium fuel once it is taken out of the reactor core. About 34 percent of the people surveyed held the mistaken belief that this radioactive waste is kept in an underground storage area somewhere in the West, while only 17 percent of the people surveyed knew that the United States presently stores the spent fuel on-site at the various nuclear power plants waiting until a permanent means of disposing of the radioactive waste is found.[7]

The degree of sophistication and knowledge we Americans have about energy influences many aspects of our daily lives, including what kind of vehicles we drive and the kinds of energy-consumption habits we follow at home and at work. We allow ignorance at our own peril. With so much at stake in dealing with the problems of peak oil and major climate change in the twenty-first century, we cannot afford to continue to indulge our national energy illiteracy. The widespread lack of knowledge persisting throughout our population distorts the national dialogue we need to be having if we are to successfully deal with the declining supply of fossil fuels. It also bears heavily on the decision-making process in choosing our path to energy freedom in the coming years. Lawmakers and businesspeople who don't have a basic understanding of the science of various energy sources will be less likely to make informed decisions. Unwise state and national energy policy choices will harm hundreds of millions of people.

On the other hand, people who do have a good grasp of energy—particularly its effect on the environment—are more likely to practice better stewardship habits to reduce their fossil-fuel consumption. Energy knowledge and environmental literacy persuade people to save electric power and fuel at home and in their vehicles, regularly practice recycling habits, and take conservation steps such as reducing their regular water use. The better informed the American people can become about energy and its powerful influence on their lives and their communities, the more politically and socially active many of our citizens will be in taking steps to help the United States gain its energy freedom. Improved public awareness of fuel facts can also create a new attitude in American society that will inspire a nationwide confidence that we can achieve our energy goals.

The media can play a substantial role in educating the public about important matters relating to energy issues. Public-information outlets have a tremendous responsibility when it comes to shaping the knowledge base and opinions of a wide audience. Television news, radio talk shows, print magazines, and newspapers are starting to do a much better job in enlightening the American people about energy-freedom issues than they have in the past. In recent years, thanks to the influence of leaders such as Al Gore, the media have increased their coverage of the climate-change challenges the world now faces. As more people understand the problem, they have put more pressure on politicians to take action. In many ways—especially as higher gasoline prices hit pocketbooks—the American media are also starting to make energy independence a much bigger part of their news content, giving wider coverage to energy issues. Whether reporting the threat to the United States from the world's oil production peaking or describing potential economic prospects for Americans from the growth of green-collar jobs, newspapers, radio, TV, and Internet journalists are providing enhanced coverage of our energy challenges and opportunities, enabling a better-informed public and policymakers to engage in a more effective debate on our nation's fuel future.

Looking back at the lesson of *Sputnik,* twenty-first-century America would be wise to reform its educational system and give its citizens a solid foundation for developing the understanding we will need for achieving energy freedom. We have a long way to go in making our schools better and enhancing math and science curriculums before we can graduate the next generation of researchers, engineers, and technicians who will develop our sustainable-energy infrastructure. We can do much more to improve the general knowledge about energy that ordinary Americans possess, thus helping us make better social and political decisions about managing our energy resources. Following the Soviets' launch of their history-making satellite in 1957, America took assertive action to improve our schools to win the space race. That action made us more productive, more technologically advanced, and more affluent as a nation. It also led to a communication and information revolution that has vastly improved the lives of our citizens. We must again take assertive action to build a brain trust for energy freedom. If we fail to do so, we will fall forever behind other nations. If we succeed, we will open the doors for our children to step into the brighter tomorrow of a clean-energy nation.

AMERICA'S ENERGY FUTURE

The whole wide world is standing at the crossroads waiting for the sun to rise, waiting for a brand-new day. And in this section on America's energy future, we'll find out how we can bring about that brand-new day by exploring how all of humanity can benefit from creating a twenty-first-century civilization built on a foundation of clean- and renewable-energy sources and a more energy-efficient social structure. Chapter 12 examines how two regions of northern California are taking steps to improve their economies with various sustainable-energy projects and programs. Chapter 13 broadens our view by considering how the United States can be inspired by the progress other nations have made in moving toward energy independence. Chapter 14 tackles the issue of securing America's energy future to protect our defense, our economy, our public health, and our food supply. In Chapter 15, we'll look at the power of leadership, using the American Clean Energy and Security Act of 2009 as a learning experience for future legislation endeavors. Finally, in Chapter 16, the book closes with a message about how we can find inspiration from the past that can motivate modern Americans to progress forward toward a better energy future.

CHAPTER 12

Energy and Two Valleys

C alifornia has always been a place where people take big chances. This willingness for risk taking harks back to the heady gold-rush days, an adventurous period of midnineteenth-century American history when people from around the world readily endured great hardships traveling to the Golden State for the promise of quick riches. In the 1970s, 1980s, and 1990s, Silicon Valley opened up a new gold rush, the high-tech explosion. Again, people came from around the globe to participate in the exciting new creation of wealth, and many of them found bigger fortunes than they ever could have made in the original gold-rush bonanza. Today, the daring to take a chance with new energy technology is moving to the forefront of people's imagination. The massive windfalls that California's citizens will potentially receive from this growing movement could well prove to be even more lucrative than any quest for California gold or high tech.

When it comes to seeing real progress in energy innovation, we should look at two specific locations in California. Although we can never be certain where exactly any innovative development might eventually lead, California's Silicon Valley and the San Joaquin Valley can be credited with at least generating optimism for a better energy future. And unlike the forty-niners of old, today's risk takers don't need to rely on hope and hunches of where gold might be found. Instead, they know that developing new technologies and implementing more efficient management of our energy resources will unquestionably lead to economic bounty. Let's take a closer look at the growing industries and energy infrastructures that California's two famous valley regions are developing for their future. No doubt, they can provide some inspiring ideas that will goad other urban and agricultural regions of our nation to go for the gold when it comes to building energy freedom in the coming decades.

SILICON VALLEY

Surrounding the southern portion of the San Francisco Bay, Silicon Valley has been the world's hotbed for high-tech ideas since post–World War II days. This region has built its amazing prosperity from companies working on the processing and distribution of digital information. Its computer and telecom industry has made multimillionaires and billionaires of many businesspeople. Now the region is focusing its attention on the planet's energy needs, developing many groundbreaking technologies and initiating local government programs that will allow people to harvest greater quantities of fuel from sustainable sources.

City of San José

With about 1 million residents, San José is the juggernaut of Silicon Valley municipalities. And in 2007, Mayor Chuck Reed set the city on a path to becoming what he called the World Center of Clean-Tech Innovation. Reed gave the city a fifteen-year target to reduce its per-capita fossil-fuel consumption by 50 percent by integrating more energy efficiency and renewable sources of power into its overall infrastructure. To achieve this ambitious "green vision" goal, Reed proposed that during the next two decades, San José change its utility requirements to receive 100 percent of its electrical power from renewable sources, use 100 percent of its landfill waste for energy production, and recycle or reuse 100 percent of the city's wastewater (about 100 million gallons daily). He also called for the city to make all of the vehicles in its public fleet run on renewable fuels and to build or retrofit at least 50 million square feet of its buildings to make them greener. Under Reed's plan, the city will replace all of its streetlights with zero-emission lighting systems. In addition, it will plant 100,000 trees in its parks and streets to help cool the urban landscape during hot days and absorb carbon dioxide. Reed has projected that this clean and green transformation of the city will create at least 25,000 new jobs for its citizens, thus helping to pay for itself with the vitalization of the local economy.[1]

Google Inc.

With its unofficial motto "Don't be evil," the search-engine firm Google is a strong advocate of clean energy and has been carbon neutral since 2007 by using energy efficiency and renewable-energy technology. The company's philosophy has inspired projects to promote the use of renewable power sources in its daily operations. One of the most prominent examples is the installation of 9,212 solar panels on the rooftops of buildings at Google's Mountain View headquarters. At the time they were installed, Google had the largest corporate solar installation in the world.[2] Company founders Sergey Brin and Larry Page also started Google.org, a hybrid philanthropic venture that addresses climate change and energy challenges, as well as issues of global health and poverty. One of the philanthropy's first projects was the conversion of a fleet of hybrids into plug-in hybrids to demonstrate the potential of electric-car technology. (Hybrid vehicles have moderate-size batteries to store energy from braking and use that energy to make the vehicle operation more efficient, particularly when the cars start rolling. Plug-in hybrids have larger batteries that are charged by plugging into exterior electric sources such as utility power, and once fully charged, they can operate for 20 to 40 miles (32 to 64 km) on battery power alone, but they have gasoline or other internal combustion engines that kick in for longer trips when the battery power is exhausted.) Google.org is also making investments in breakthrough technologies and advocating for public policies that will help develop utility-scale renewable energy that is cheaper than coal. Among these is the "Bloom Box" that employs solid oxide fuel-cell technology running on natural gas or biogas to generate electricity at about 10 cents a kilowatt-hour. Google.org is also developing an internal research and development department to explore solar thermal, high-altitude wind, and enhanced geothermal technologies.

Google.org plans to spend hundreds of millions of dollars to create one giga-watt of electricity (enough to power about 750,000 homes) from sustainable sources over the next several years.[3]

Calera

A Stanford study researching how ocean corals produce calcium carbonate from carbon dioxide led to what might one day be a practical clean-tech system to minimize the greenhouse gas produced by coal and natural gas power plants. The Los Gatos–based company Calera (Spanish for "limekiln") Corporation is now developing this technology in which seawater is sprayed into carbon dioxide emissions. The water converts the carbon dioxide into calcium carbonate, which can be turned into concretelike pellets. This material can be later used for constructing buildings or highways. If Calera's technology proves viable and affordable, it could help reduce the carbon spewed into our planet's atmosphere from our energy facilities and lock it safely and usefully in an ordinary building material.[4]

Adobe Systems Incorporated

Headquartered in downtown San José, this software maker has turned into a corporate role model for energy efficiency. In 2006, the company received three platinum Leadership in Energy and Environment Design (LEED) awards from the U.S. Green Building Council—the highest honor for the three ecofriendly towers that house employees. The three buildings make up nearly 1 million square feet of office space, with an additional 940,000 square feet for a parking garage. Adobe earned the certification by spending $1.2 million to retrofit its edifices to reach higher efficiency in energy use, water conservation, indoor air quality, and waste reduction. It also received rebates of $389,000 from California utility company Pacific Gas & Electric for its upgrades. The efforts pay off, with annual savings of more than $1 million in energy and water costs. The company reduced its electric energy usage by 35 percent and its natural gas use by 41 percent. One of the significant improvements that made the savings possible was the installation of low-wattage lighting systems and real-time electric meters that allow Adobe managers to identify inefficient uses of power, such as heating and air-conditioning units that are not working properly.[5]

Electric Cars

Silicon Valley's engineers hope to create the technologies and energy infrastructure that will enable Americans to transition from fossil-fuel vehicles to electric cars. Among the most groundbreaking firms in the American electric car constellation is Tesla Motors. With high hopes of pioneering the commercial market for high-performance electric cars, the motto of this start-up based in Palo Alto is "Burn rubber, not gasoline." Tesla engineers developed an advanced battery based on lithium-ion technology, which makes these energy-storage devices lightweight and durable and provides a range of about 220 miles (354 km) between charges. The car's motor weighs about 70 pounds and is designed to be 85 to 95 percent efficient in converting electrical power into mechanical energy. The company's first vehicle is the Tesla Roadster, which was released to the public in early 2008. This electric sports car can accelerate from 0 to 60 miles per hour in less than four seconds and tops out at 125 miles per hour (201 kilometers per hour). The car company claims it requires only 2 cents' worth of electricity for each mile. In spring 2010, Tesla joined Toyota in a $50 million partnership to build an electric sedan with a range of 300 miles (483 km) at the former New United Motor Manufacturing (NUMMI) plant in the Silicon Valley city of Fremont.

A key to the widespread use of electric cars is having an electric energy infrastructure that will make these vehicles as easy to fuel as petrol-powered cars and thus reduce worries by drivers of their vehicles of the batteries' running out of charge while on the road. Better Place is a Palo Alto firm launched in 2007 with a plan to produce electric cars that allow drivers to pull up to a "battery-swap" station and exchange depleted battery packs for ones that are fully recharged. The stations will make the switch in under a minute, using electric-powered forklifts. Campbell-based firm Coulomb Technologies also aims to build the electric-car infrastructure by manufacturing special charging stations for these vehicles. In 2010, Coulomb unveiled its $37 million ChargePoint America program, by which it will install over

4,600 charging stations in nine metropolitan areas in the United States. A Department of Energy grant of $15 million is paying for a portion of this project in order to create jobs for Americans.[6]

SolarTech

The Silicon Valley Leadership Group is a nonprofit organization that brings together various businesses, government agencies, and other organizations to deal with issues of energy, transportation, education, and housing in Silicon Valley. It initiated the SolarTech consortium to make Silicon Valley "a world epicenter" for solar-energy research and development, and it plans to create a Solar Center for Excellence that will provide technical and educational resources for sun-powered technologies. The center will serve as a catalyst to make the solar-power industry as vital to Silicon Valley's economic life as the region's world-famous high-tech, biotech, and life sciences businesses. If its goals are met, SolarTech will bring down the cost of solar-generated electric power to make it much more competitive with fossil fuels. One research focus is producing less expensive but more efficient photovoltaic (PV) technology. SolarTech will also focus on solving the challenges that have blocked widespread acceptance of solar energy, including the administrative and financing barriers. It will work to develop better installation and performance standards for solar energy, as well as explore ways to improve connections to utility lines and streamline the process for obtaining rebates, building permits, and financing for solar-panel upgrades. The center will also seek ways to improve education and training of a solar-energy workforce, including giving industry professionals training and certification in the field of solar-energy technology.[7]

Silicon Valley's Solar Power Industry

Technology to harvest the sun's power is projected to be the next lucrative high-tech growth area, and Silicon Valley is poised to take advantage of solar energy's business opportunities. Governor Arnold Schwarzenegger's Million Solar Roof initiative has catalyzed the region's solar-based start-up companies, as well as established firms that are reframing their corporate mission to produce solar-energy products. Among the valley's older companies turning to the sun to boost profits is Applied Materials. Founded in 1967 and headquartered in Santa Clara, it originally established itself by providing products and services for chip-making factories. Because many solar panels use silicon—the same essential ingredient used to make computer chips—Applied recognized the potential massive growth of the burgeoning market and now provides factory equipment for companies to manufacture flat-panel solar displays and solar PV cells. Another Silicon Valley firm, SunPower, based in San José, is working on developing innovations to make solar-energy panels for homes and businesses more efficient and affordable. Its solar products are considered some of the most efficient in the industry, but rival company Nanosolar, established in 2001 and based in San José, might soon catch up. Instead of using traditional silicon to make its product, Nanosolar produces a thin, flexible solar cell made with a copper alloy. This material reduces manufacturing costs. Nanosolar is building what it says will be the world's largest solar-cell factory in a San José industrial district. When fully constructed, the factory will have a capacity to manufacture 430 megawatts of solar cells a year, significantly surpassing previous U.S. production rates. Santa Clara–based Miasolé also manufactures thin-film PV cells that weigh up to 90 percent less than traditional glass-plate solar cells and can be "incorporated into building materials like membrane roofing," according to company statements. Also based in Santa Clara, photovoltaic company Solaicx is focused on what its website calls "very high volume materials handling" with a product that the company believes will result in lower prices for customers. San José solar company Solexant makes an ultrathin-film PV product that uses printable nanomaterial technology to produce high-efficiency solar cells at low cost for commercial use.[8]

A San José–based company called Republic Cloverleaf Solar will use Silicon Valley as a testing ground for infill PV power systems installed along major highways. The company plans to partner with the California Department of Transportation to place 64,000 PV panels at seven interchanges along U.S. Highway 101 in southern Santa Clara County. Projected to be completed in January 2012, these panels will generate 15 megawatts of solar power combined, enough to supply electric power to 3,000 single-family homes. If the pilot project proves successful, it can be used as a model for states across America to raise revenue as they generate electricity from the sun on thousands of acres of unused highway-bound land.[9]

Sustainable Silicon Valley

This nonprofit organization was started in 2001 as a California Environmental Protection Agency project to help Silicon Valley organizations network on major environmental and energy issues. Funded by grants from various foundations, the organization develops partnerships with various companies, businesses, city governments, and other public and private organizations to reduce energy use from fossil-fuel sources. Members include Cisco Systems, Intel, Advanced Micro Devices, Hewlett-Packard, NASA Ames Research Center, the San Francisco International Airport, and Santa Clara University. It encourages cost-effective energy-efficiency efforts in various energy-intensive industries, including transportation, freshwater processing and delivery, and manufacturing. To educate its members, Sustainable Silicon Valley hosts a series of forums and networking opportunities for sharing innovative ideas that have been proven to work in reducing carbon dioxide emissions. Among its other goals is promoting wide community participation in achieving carbon dioxide reductions so that Silicon Valley can create a healthy environment and a vibrant economy for citizens in the future. It does not impose standards on its partners but instead encourages members to decide for themselves what fuel-efficiency methods will make the most sense, both financially and technologically, for their own specific organization.[10]

Energy-Efficient Data Centers

Silicon Valley's worldwide fame rests on the computer innovations created in the region that helps drive the global economy. Many of the modern data-storage centers throughout the world use a tremendous amount of energy in their twenty-four-hour-a-day, seven-day-a-week operations. One study commissioned by Advanced Micro Devices (AMD) found that consumption of energy from servers and the various electric-powered equipment used in data centers in the United States equaled the production of electricity from five 1,000-megawatt nuclear or coal power plants. The consumption worldwide equaled that of fourteen power plants.[11] These servers produce a lot of heat, so the facilities where they are stored must be constantly air-conditioned to maintain suitable service. That cooling necessity adds an additional expense to their operation. Seeing the potential for revenue as the energy movement grows, many Silicon Valley high-tech companies are focused on making their hardware more power efficient. It not only helps the environment but it also helps save money in utility expenses for consumers and businesses. For example, engineers at chip makers Intel and AMD are in a race to find ways to reduce the energy consumption of their products while increasing their processing capabilities. Making computers more energy efficient by as much as 30 to 50 percent can save consumers and businesses substantial money in power costs. Meanwhile, Silicon Valley computer companies Hewlett-Packard, Cisco, IBM, Google, eBay, Intel, Microsoft, Symantec, and NetApp, among others, joined together in an industry consortium called Green Grid (www.thegreen grid.org) to establish metrics and standards that will lead to new processes and innovations that can be included in the designs of their products to reduce power consumption and cooling demands for server systems. This organization has received the support of the EPA.[12]

SAN JOAQUIN VALLEY

Directly east of Silicon Valley, on the other side of the Diablo Mountain Range, lies central California's San Joaquin Valley, a rich agricultural area that supplies much of America's fruits and vegetables. This neighboring valley is also undergoing a transformation of its economy and society as it embraces emerging sustainable fuel technologies and develops exciting new energy projects for its cities and farm towns. The San Joaquin Valley contains substantial resources that will one day make it a national center for production of renewable energy. As the examples that follow demonstrate, the inland valley has wind power, vast solar resources, and potentially the nation's largest biofuels opportunities. In addition, because of high summer temperatures and water shortages, many innovators are taking steps to become extremely efficient with heating, ventilation, and air-conditioning loads and water usage. If these trends continue, the valley will be a leading exporter of both energy and energy technology.

Altamont Pass Wind Farm

Drivers along Interstate 580 that cuts through the Altamont Pass (connecting San Joaquin Valley to Silicon Valley) can see one of the world's earliest wind farms set along the rolling hills south of the Diablo Range. It was built in the 1980s, when the energy crisis caused many Californian entrepreneurs to look at developing renewable forms of power. The Altamont Pass location was chosen because it provides a natural channel for wind to travel as the Central Valley's hot, low-pressure inland temperatures pull in the relatively cooler, high-pressure marine air from the coast. The wind flow, however, is not always reliable because of occasional high-pressure conditions inland that essentially stop the movement of air. Altamont Pass has 5,200 wind turbines and is one of the world's pioneering centers for wind-energy research. Much of what was learned at this location helped to refine wind turbine technology and enabled later-built wind farms to operate much more efficiently. The site is still a testing ground for the next generation of wind turbines.[13]

National Ignition Facility

In sight of some of the Altamont Pass's wind turbines is a scientific wonder of the twenty-first century. America might one day break the technological hurdles toward achieving commercial fusion-nuclear energy, thanks to research now being undertaken at the Lawrence Livermore National Laboratory's National Ignition Facility (NIF) located in the Diablo Mountain Range between Silicon Valley and San Joaquin Valley. Built at a cost of just over $1 billion, NIF houses 192 giant lasers in a ten-story building covering the space of three football fields. These lasers will focus 2 million joules of ultraviolet energy on a hydrogen-filled, pea-sized capsule at the center of a target chamber. Scientists hope that this burst of energy will instantly heat and compress the hydrogen fuel and thereby produce a fusion reaction that will unleash much more energy than was used to start the nuclear reaction.[14]

ACE Train Project

Many Silicon Valley workers live in the San Joaquin Valley, where land is cheaper, making homes much more affordable to buy than in the San Francisco Bay area. Every workday, those who drive face a highly congested work commute through the Altamont Pass, which connects the two regions. As Silicon Valley boomed in the 1990s, thousands more people made the trek along Interstate 580 in the early mornings and late afternoons, wasting not only time but also gasoline as they waited in traffic. To help alleviate the massive traffic tie-ups, regional leaders created the Altamont Commuter Express (ACE) train project to connect San José in the Silicon Valley and the San Joaquin Valley's city of Stockton. The nationally praised commuter service was originally pushed by the San Joaquin Council of Governments, the Building Industry Association of the Delta, and the Stockton Chamber of Commerce. ACE was developed by the San Joaquin Regional Rail Commission, which initiated agreements between Alameda and Santa Clara counties to implement the plan. Train service began on October 19, 1998, and over the last decade it has grown increasingly popular, with four trains now running daily in each direction. The trains use an 86-mile-long (138.4-km-long) route owned by Union Pacific and they stop at various communities between the two terminal points. Funding to develop the ACE system and continue its operation came from a half-cent sales tax for transportation.[15]

Vintage Farms

Some people believe "poop power" might help the United States free itself from the fossil fuels. The millions of tons of manure produced each year by America's cows might one day be a common source of energy, thanks to experiments now being conducted at San Joaquin Valley dairies such as Vintage Farms located west of Fresno. The dairy is among the first in the United

States to make extra money collecting the methane produced by decomposing cow dung and injecting it into a natural gas pipeline that transmits it to a Pacific Gas & Electric Company power plant. The utility company burns the high-quality methane to generate electricity. The system reduces the amount of greenhouse gas that the dairy farm emits into the atmosphere, thus minimizing its impact on climate change. Vintage Farms' 2,600 cows excrete 130 tons of manure every day, enough to produce biogas-based electric power for 1,300 San Joaquin Valley homes. The system has worked so effectively that David Albers, owner of Vintage Farms, started a business called BioEnergy Solutions to help other ranchers collect methane from manure to sell to utility companies.[16]

25x'25 Initiative

People in the San Joaquin Valley see the social and economic potential for developing renewable-energy sources for the region's rural towns and urban communities. That's why many of them support an initiative to obtain 25 percent of their energy from renewable sources by the year 2025. Called the National 25x'25 Initiative, this growing coalition of environmental, business, energy, labor, civic, and government organizations will encourage the development of new energy technologies that will bring economic vitality to rural America. A study done by the University of Tennessee projects that if the initiative is successful in creating a better energy future for farm communities, it will boost rural economies across America by about $700 billion a year and create 5 million more jobs in the process. California's Central Valley region is being touted as an important test bed for this nationwide program to determine ways that farmers and ranchers can benefit from wind and solar power and biofuels. In 2007, the San Joaquin Valley Clean Energy Organization (SJVCEO) committed itself to the 25x'25 Initiative and started taking proactive steps to develop the region's renewable-energy potential and thus enable it to serve as a model for other rural regions of America.[17]

Fresno Solar-Energy Farm

As one of the most sun-drenched locations in North America, the San Joaquin Valley has a huge potential to harvest massive amounts of solar energy and convert it into electricity. With this in mind, a San Francisco–based company called Cleantech America is working with the Kings River Conservation District (KRCD) to build one of California's largest PV solar-production facilities, which will be located near Fresno. When completed, it will cover a square mile and provide up to 80 megawatts of emission-free power for the city and surrounding towns. A much-anticipated benefit will be the overall improvement of air quality in the region by cutting the production of about 100 million pounds of carbon dioxide—about the amount produced by 20,000 cars. The new solar plant will also help the local economy by producing thousands of jobs in constructing and maintaining it.[18]

Visalia

The more than 100,000 residents of the city of Visalia feel optimistic about the potential benefits of energy efficiency and renewable resources. To reduce America's dependence on foreign oil and improve regional air quality, city leaders have been at the forefront of programs promoting energy efficiency in Visalia's daily operations. The city has converted many of its waste-disposal trucks and transit buses to compressed natural gas, encouraged the addition of energy-efficiency features into the architecture of newly built facilities, and installed PV panels at the local airport. It is also actively seeking ways to encourage more residents to use renewable-energy sources, including ethanol, solar, wind, and biological-based fuels from garbage waste and animal manure. In 2007, one local business, Kawneer Company Inc., which manufactures aluminum doors and window frames, installed more than 4,300 thin-film PV panels on the roof of its 200,000-square-foot building, thus gaining 588,000 watts from the sun to meet up to 80 percent of its electricity needs.[19]

Urban and rural communities across America can use the progress made by trendsetting places like Silicon Valley and the San Joaquin Valley to inspire their own energy-independence initiatives. Now that we've looked at what energy projects are being done on a regional basis in California, let's go the global direction and see what entire nations are achieving in building a better fuel future. We'll now look at the energy of the world.

CHAPTER 13

Energy and the World

On June 6, 1884, a passenger ship arrived in New York Harbor carrying a twenty-eight-year-old Serbian scientist dreaming of making a new life in the New World. Nikola Tesla soon found work in Thomas Edison's invention factory, redesigning electric motors and generators to make them more energy efficient. The immigrant's innovations provided Edison with several patents that proved quite profitable. After a short time, however, the two volatile geniuses had a falling out. Edison refused to concede to Tesla that alternating current (AC) had significant benefits over direct current (DC) as a method for carrying electricity through transmission wires. Tesla soon left Edison and, after a brief time working as a ditchdigger, started a rival company focused on developing the technology for commercial use of AC power.[1] His inventions dramatically changed how America and the rest of the world now use electricity, and they helped create new businesses that made the United States an industrial powerhouse.

The metaphor of a melting pot often describes America's unique characteristic of mixing the cultures of other countries to reshape our nation. Millions of ambitious legal immigrants—people with the same dreams as Tesla—have crossed oceans and rivers to make new lives for themselves here in the United States. These waves of people have been a driving force for America, bringing to our borders the energy of the world's creativity. Time after time throughout our history, we have seen how the streams of people from diverse cultures passing through our portals have blessed our nation with the fruits of their drive and vision, resulting in hundreds of thousands of profitable inventions and innovations. Legal immigrants make the United States a stronger nation by building up new businesses and creating hundreds of thousands of jobs. They help drive our economy, which in turn promotes our national defense.

With advances in communications technology and the rise of globalization, however, the arrival of immigrants to American soil is not as necessary for our nation to take advantage of the emergence of visionary ideas from across the seas. In developing our fuel freedom during the coming years, we can find inspiring new energy ideas by looking beyond our borders. We can gain great inspiration by studying how other nations are facing their own energy challenges and pursuing various energy-related projects. In the innovative spirit of Nikola Tesla, let us now look at exciting energy opportunities coming from the world's neighborhood of nations. Their ideas can serve as a springboard to energy innovation here in the United States.

ASIA

The financially booming Asian region is building up a strong dependence on fossil fuels as it revs the engines of modern industry. The ongoing economic expansion of China and India especially will make these two countries major competitors with the United States for the world's petroleum reserves. China is the world's second largest consumer of oil behind the United States. China's carbon dioxide emissions will also rise even more quickly as more coal-burning power plants are built to supply the demand. The world's number one emitter of carbon dioxide from fossil fuels and other human activities, China produces more than 21 percent of the global output of this greenhouse gas. (In comparison, the United States comes in second by producing about 20 percent of the global total of carbon dioxide from human activity.[2]) Clearly, expanding the use of renewable fuel sources and increasing energy efficiency are vital to this booming Asian nation's future if it is going to sustain its economic growth.

Adding to its mounting fossil-fuel challenges, China's local environment faces the threat of severe damage as the nation's burgeoning population of consumers uses coal and oil in ever-growing quantities. In its cities, China's rivers and air are filth-laden with pollution from fossil fuels and related industrial activities, causing millions of Chinese people to suffer serious health consequences. To help lessen this dire predicament, the Chinese government passed a law in 2005 mandating that China increase its energy production from clean, renewable sources from 3 percent in 2003 to at least 10 percent by the year 2020. As the Chinese trade their human-powered bicycles for combustion-engine automobiles, the Asian nation also faces the quandary of finding enough petroleum fuel in the future to power its cars. Increasing fuel efficiency is thus an imperative, a major reason Chinese carmakers such as the Chery Automobile Company, BYD, and Geely are focusing on building hybrid, hydrogen fuel cell, and electric vehicles aimed at helping the Asian nation achieve this goal.[3]

The green spirit is sweeping China in other ways as the nation undergoes its own energy transformation—particularly in finding ways to harvest the sun's power. More than 30 million homes and businesses in the nation have installed rooftop solar panels that heat water for showers and dish washing. Many investors in China see not only environmental and social benefits but also tremendous financial profits in providing clean energy for these teeming masses. Among them is Shi Zhengrong, one of the wealthiest men in China, worth $2.9 billion in 2008, according to *Forbes* magazine.[4] He believes clean and renewable power will be the primary growth industry for Asia in the twenty-first century. Zhengrong's company, Suntech Power Holdings, makes silicon-based solar cells. He aims to improve technology to help bring down the cost of manufacturing these energy products so that eventually millions of Chinese and other people around the world will be able to afford them. Competition with Suntech Power could also stimulate growth in the U.S. solar-energy industry by forcing American companies to come up with more advanced sun-powered innovations as the world market expands.

Like China, the nation of India is looking to solar power to help it reduce its dependence on fossil fuels. India's National Solar Mission aspires to generate 20 gigawatts by the year 2020, about the equivalent of one-eighth of the nation's installed power base in 2009. Japan is also concentrating on building up its solar industry to supply the energy needs of its citizens in the near and long term. Electronics company Sharp Corporation, one of the world's largest manufacturers of solar products, got its start in this energy market in 1963, by providing solar cells for a lighthouse powered by the sun's rays at Yakohama Port. Since then, as the Japanese have built up their solar industry, the cost of producing electricity from this sustainable source has dropped by about two-thirds. Solar power will continue to get less expensive as research results in better technology for more efficient mass production of panels that will lower the costs and, in turn, raise the demand.

Because Japan's island geography contains little fossil-fuel reserves, the Japanese have been forced to develop technical solutions to reduce their consumption of coal, oil, and natural-gas imports. That's one reason the Japanese are well known for manufacturing energy-efficient vehicles and transportation systems. Most Americans are familiar with the popular Prius, Toyota's cutting-edge hybrid car that runs on both electricity and gasoline and helps save fuel by recharging a storage battery system when a driver hits the brakes. Some of Japan's modern trains also use an advanced braking system to generate electricity that can be stored in an advanced battery system. This system can cut energy use and carbon dioxide emissions by as much as 60 percent.[5] With an eye toward even greater fossil-fuel frugality, the Central Japan Railway Company has been testing advanced levitation systems for high-speed trains. Using powerful magnets to create an opposing electromagnetic force, the train's engine and cars are lifted slightly into the air and kept above the tracks as they are propelled along their route by the force of a linear magnetic motor.[6] Compared to traditional rail trains, this levitation method would cut fuel consumption by reducing the amount of energy lost to the forces of friction.

THE MIDDLE EAST

Among the most exciting energy projects in the Middle East is an initiative to one day harvest solar and wind energy in the Arabian Peninsula and North

African desert regions and to sell the surplus electricity to European nations. The electricity would be carried north to European customers by a network of modern high-voltage DC power lines and could potentially provide up to 25 percent of the continent's power needs by the year 2050. Called the Trans-Mediterranean Renewable Energy Cooperation (TREC), this developing project is considered by many scientists to be technically feasible if efficient transmission technology can achieve energy losses of just 10 to 15 percent as the electricity travels from desert regions to Europe.[7] But the controversial project will need considerable financial support, as well as political backing among Middle Eastern, African, and European nations. Still, as the challenges associated with fossil fuels increase during the coming decades, the potential benefits of having Sahara and Arabian desert–based solar and wind power plants provide electricity to a lucrative European market might give TREC enough economic leverage to make it a reality.

Israel is also highly motivated to develop its clean-energy infrastructure. Historically, almost all of Israel's energy has come from imported coal and crude oil, putting it at economic jeopardy from embargoes. But in recent years, Israel has devoted tremendous effort to achieving developments in solar-collector devices for heating water and other uses. Today, Israeli households have one of the highest deployment rates in the world for solar water heaters. The nation is also finding innovative ways to harvest the sun's energy through solar ponds and parabolic mirror technology.

EUROPE

Europeans developed a robust habit for energy conservation after World War II when citizens throughout Europe and Britain were forced to face limited fuel resources as they rebuilt their lives in the postwar decades. Europeans also understand the devastating impact from the climate perils of global warming, an additional reason so many of them want their officials to provide assertive leadership in developing renewable-energy infrastructures.

The European Union (EU) laid out an ambitious strategy, known as the "20/20/20 targets," to cut carbon dioxide emissions by at least 20 percent (from

1990 levels) by the year 2020. It proposes to do this through improvements of 20 percent in energy efficiency and by raising the use of renewable power by 20 percent among its member nations. Economists project that the plan could cost the EU about $88 billion annually, which is about 0.5 percent of its gross domestic product.[8] The plan is controversial, however, because industries that use high quantities of coal and oil fear that they will lose their market share to nations that are less stringent about carbon emissions. The European Commission, the executive branch of the EU, has proposed ways to speed the acceptance of energy technologies to cut carbon emissions. Among the ideas suggested is the creation of a European Energy Research Alliance that will work to bring together universities and research institutions across Europe to focus on achieving technological breakthroughs in renewable-energy development. Another proposal is the creation of the European Industrial Initiatives program that will lead companies throughout Europe to combine forces in developing innovations to bring down the costs and improve energy generation from sources such as the wind, the sun, and biofuels.

Individually, many of Europe's nations are making ambitious strides toward gaining their energy freedom. Denmark burns its garbage in waste-to-energy incinerator power plants to provide heat and electricity for many of its 5.5 million people. The plants benefit the environment by reducing the use of landfills and by eliminating greenhouse gas emissions from decomposing trash. Germany and the Netherlands are also building similar garbage-incineration power plants. The island of Iceland, with just over 300,000 people, is targeting cutting its greenhouse gas emissions by 50 to 70 percent by the year 2050, and one way it plans to achieve this goal is by becoming the world's first economy based on hydrogen. The nation is blessed with natural power sources from its numerous waterfalls and geothermal springs, which generate about 70 percent of the electricity for its population. Iceland will phase into a clean-energy economy by using incentives to build up a fleet of cars, buses, and fishing boats run by fuel cells powered by hydrogen produced from its renewably sourced electricity. Another Nordic country also ranks with Iceland among the most ambitious European nations for energy freedom. Sweden aims to get its 9 million people to obtain 49 percent of their electricity from clean-fuel sources by the year 2020. Almost 40 percent of Sweden's energy today comes from clean-energy sources, most notably hydropower, but it is building geothermal, wind, and solar power plants as well to meet its future needs. France has pioneered the technology of solar furnaces, or towers holding an array of mirrors that reflect concentrated sunlight onto a focal point that heats up to as much as 4,500 degrees Fahrenheit (2,500 degrees Celsius).[9] In 1969, the nation constructed the world's largest solar furnace in the city of Odeillo, in the French Pyrenees. The sixty-three mirrors of this parabolic reflector produce 1,000 kilowatts of power that is used to fuel a furnace that manufactures steel from iron ore.

Wind power is becoming a prominent source of sustainable energy for Europeans, making up a combined installed capacity of 74,676 megawatts in 2009 to provide for the EU's electricity needs. The European Wind Energy Association seeks an industry goal of providing 180 gigawatts of electricity by the year 2020—enough for about 107 million households. Germany is the undisputed European leader in wind developments, with an installed wind-power capacity of 25,777 megawatts (25.7 gigawatts) in 2007. But Spain, the land of La Mancha's famed windmills, has also been developing its own wind industry in recent years with about 19,149 megawatts (19.1 gigawatts) of wind-power capacity in 2009. Denmark is proving to be a European pioneer in deployment of large-scale wind-energy farms as it installs wind turbines in the shallow seas off its coasts. In 2003, the Danes built one of the world's largest offshore wind farms near Lolland. The Nysted Wind Farm's seventy-two turbines can produce as much as 166 megawatts of power. Denmark's wind-energy industry expects that as much as 50 percent of the country's electricity needs will be met by wind power by the year 2025, and most of this electricity will come from offshore wind farms.[10]

The United Kingdom also has big clean-energy ambitions, with the government in 2000 setting a goal of 10 percent of the nation's electric power produced by renewable energy by the year 2010. It failed to meet this ambitious objective, getting only to 2.3 percent, according to the National Audit Office. Wind power will play a significant role in its endeavor to go green. In

2005, Britain began planning a wind farm in the Thames River estuary 12 miles (19.3 km) off the coast of Kent, where 341 towering turbines would produce 1,000 megawatts of electricity—enough to power 25 percent of London's population. An even grander wind farm is being considered for the Bristol Channel, in western England. If built, an estimated 370 turbines standing nearly 500 feet (150 meters) tall above the sea would generate 1,500 megawatts for more than 1 million homes. Blessed with so much coastline, the British are also experimenting with innovative technology that uses wave power to generate electricity. Although they have achieved only mixed results, because many of the machines have been damaged by the battering forces of storms, the Brits persevere with testing this technology. One pilot system constructed in 2003 at Lynmouth, North Devon, in the Bristol Channel, receives a virtually continuous supply of strong currents that can propel underwater turbines. The experimental plant can generate up to 300 kilowatts of electricity. The British are also experimenting with an "underwater kite" system that uses a 100-meter-long cable to tether a 1-meter-long turbine to the ocean floor. A tidal-current turbine using this technology can theoretically produce 500 kilowatts of power. The beloved lochs of Scotland might also provide a viable way to use water power to bring energy freedom to Britain. One interesting project that was built there in 1966 is the Cruachan pumped-storage power station at Loch Awe in Argyll, which produces up to 440 megawatts of electricity during peak demand times. When electricity consumption is low, surplus energy is used to power four pumping facilities that haul the water kept in a reservoir buried 3,280 feet (1,000 meters) underground back up to be stored in Loch Awe. The water can then be reused to generate electricity during the next cycle of power need.[11]

London has taken steps to increase the energy efficiency of its transportation system by reducing the traffic gridlock within its boundaries. In 2003, the city's government made a controversial move to reduce traffic by requiring private cars to pay a congestion charge to drive through the city's center. The fee of £10 equals about US $15 (2010). Faced with this fee, more people began using London's excellent public transportation system of buses and the famous Underground train system. To reduce the amount of air pollution, the city is also converting its bus fleet to run on cleaner fuels, including natural gas and hydrogen fuel cells.[12]

NORTH AMERICA

With a population of nearly 34 million, Canada stands at the forefront of North American energy freedom in its development of a variety of renewable-energy projects designed to reduce its use of fossil fuels. One of the more interesting developments now being undertaken by our neighbor to the north is the growing commercial use of geothermal energy to cool or heat buildings and generate electricity. An area in British Columbia called South Meager is a potential site for a geothermal project that uses heat up to 240 degrees Celsius to produce as much as 100 megawatts of electricity—enough to power 80,000 homes. In Toronto, a private company called Enwave uses the cold temperature of the water in Lake Ontario to cool as many as 140 office buildings in the downtown region of the city. Called "deep lake water cooling," the project cost $128 million to build. The system pumps the chilled water through a network of underground pipes leading from the bottom of the lake to the buildings to cut electricity use from air-conditioning by up to 75 percent.[13] The water can also be used domestically for drinking.

The ocean is another bountiful energy reservoir where Canadians are literally making waves in technological innovations. The Ocean Renewable Energy Group is working with industries and universities to enhance technologies that capture power from subsurface marine currents and from the waves that the prevailing winds blow toward shore. The Annapolis Royal plant is one Canadian project capturing tidal energy from Nova Scotia's Bay of Fundy and turning it into electric power. An ongoing experiment in ocean power extraction since 1984, it is the first and largest such ocean-energy facility in North America. This plant uses as much as 14,418 cubic feet per second of water going through sluices 100 feet (30.5 meters) underwater to produce up to 20 megawatts of electricity from the ocean's tidal currents—or an annual energy production of 50 gigawatt-hours.[14] (Watts, kilowatts, megawatts, and gigawatts are measures of electric power that does work—such as turning on lights or running motors. Watt-hours, kilowatt-hours, megawatt-hours, and gigawatt-hours are measures of energy, which is power available or used over time. So one kilowatt-hour is one kilowatt of power used for one hour. Electricity is paid for in energy units.)

Like Canada, Mexico has been actively building an assortment of innovative energy programs as it faces uncertainties for its 112 million people when its oil production starts to decline. Mexico has been working closely with partners such as the Global Environmental Facility and the U.S.'s Sandia National Laboratories on a $31 million project called the Renewable Energy for Agriculture program. This project installs wind-power and photovoltaic systems that generate power to pump water, thus making life better for farmers and ranchers who live and work far from any electric grid. These energy technologies have been implemented at more than 200 sites throughout Mexico, resulting in many agricultural communities achieving energy-efficient farming practices.[15] The program has also saved farmers thousands of dollars in cattle feed, as modern solar-powered water pumps replace outdated irrigation systems traditionally driven by horses, oxen, and even human laborers.

LATIN AMERICA

With rising costs for oil and shortages of energy supplies hurting their economies, several Latin American nations have introduced laws that encourage sustainable sources of power and increased energy efficiency. Guatemala and Chile have formed initiatives to provide financial benefits such as tax breaks for the construction of sustainable-energy facilities. One small-scale project in Nicaragua shows a big potential for encouraging renewable-energy production for poor economies. The nonprofit organization Green Empowerment helped 220 farming families of San Jose de Bocay construct a 260-kilowatt microhydropower plant that uses energy created by the flow of small local streams to run a rice-hulling machine. The hulls are then burned as biomass to operate a rice dryer.

South America's widespread network of rivers has long served as a renewable-energy resource by generating electricity at hydropower plants. But the continent's people have grown worried that drought conditions caused by global warming might substantially reduce the powerful flow of these waterways. This concern has prompted South American nations to strive for diversification of energy by encouraging the growth of alternative power from wind, solar, geothermal, and biomass sources. Green Empowerment together with another nongovernmental organization, Fundación Nutura, now work with indigenous people in the Amazon region to install solar panels that can be used to power two-way radios and charge battery-powered woodworking tools that help craftsmen to build wood furniture, thus generating income.[16]

Brazil has become the South American superstar of energy freedom in recent years, producing almost 45 percent of its fuel from sustainable sources for its 192 million people. Most notable is its high consumption of ethanol made from sugarcane crops. Called the Saudi Arabia of biofuels, the nation of Brazil runs about 75 percent of its fleet of cars on pure ethanol or a gasoline blend called "gasohol" to significantly reduce its need to import oil. Brazilians have a choice of more than 35,000 service stations that offer drivers both gasoline and ethanol. (The United States lags far behind, with only 2,389 stations in September 2010 offering E85 fuel, which is a blend of 85 percent ethanol and 15 percent gasoline.) Researchers are also working on finding technological breakthroughs that will use bagasse (or cane waste) from Brazilian farms to power huge steam boilers that will generate the electricity needed to refine ethanol.[17] The refineries will also be able to sell a surplus of electricity to the national power grid.

SOUTH PACIFIC

The nations of the South Pacific have unique opportunities for developing their energy freedom. Australia particularly has become a hotbed for renewable-energy entrepreneurship. One example is the Australian government's $75 million Solar Cities program, which has set up urban trials of solar-energy projects in five communities located in various geographical sections on the continent. The city of Adelaide in the state of South Australia became the program's first solar city, receiving funding of about $15 million for sun-powered technology. Up to 1,700 photovoltaic panels were installed on residences and commercial facilities, generating as much as 2 megawatts of electricity. Other energy improvements for Adelaide include the installation of 7,000 smart meters that let consumers check their energy consumption and make changes in usage to save power and money. The projected benefits for the city include a 9-megawatt reduction in peak electricity demand and savings of 28 gigawatt-hours of energy each year, reducing the city's overall electricity costs by an annual $5 million. The town of Alice Springs, in the heart of Australia, is taking part in the Solar Cities trial as well. Receiving about $16 million in government funding for various energy improvements, the town has installed solar panels at various public facilities such as the airport, swimming pool, and sewage treatment plant, and has set up 1,000 solar water systems in homes. The installation of photovoltaic systems at 225 homes and five commercial sites is expected to generate up to 1.3 megawatts of electricity. Energy audits of up to 850 sites will help businesses and residences find resourceful ways to increase efficiency and cut down on energy use, reducing the energy bills of participants by up to 20 percent. The installation of 400 smart meters on homes and businesses in Alice Springs will further help customers reduce the energy they use at times of peak power demand.[18]

Besides the continent of Australia, islands scattered across the South Pacific are also finding ways to gain their energy freedom. The region of Micronesia, for example, must import its gasoline and petroleum at high prices to run cars, boats, and diesel-fueled electric generators. Preparing for the day when it won't be able to economically compete with larger nations for fossil fuels, Micronesia is now considering technologies that will enable it to harvest natural energy from the sun, wind, and ocean waves. It sees the potential of these resources to provide electric power on limited distributed systems, thus sustaining the energy needs of towns and villages without relying on a vast grid of electricity transmission lines. Creatively looking at one biofuel source unique to their nations, South Pacific islanders see coconut oil as a significant source of liquid energy.[19] Long a part of Pacific culture, the energy-rich oil is relatively easy to produce and affordable for most uses. Virgin coconut oil can be used as an energy source in unmodified diesel engines in cars and generators.

AFRICA

Many African nations have energy challenges that cause social and economic hardships. The continent ranks as the world's highest consumer of biomass energy, with two-thirds of its energy coming from firewood, animal dung, charcoal, and farm waste. The burning of this biomass, unfortunately, has grim consequences on the health of many African people. Women and children particularly suffer from respiratory illnesses resulting from the fuel's smoke. Developing nations in Africa also must deal with the destructive effect that the climate change caused by global warming is having on their economies and natural environment. West Africa has the world's second largest rain forest after the Amazon, and the thick vegetation of this region serves as an important natural system for carbon capture from the atmosphere. The combined impact of climate change and people burning this vegetation, both for fuel and to create farmland, could drastically increase desertification (the spreading of deserts) on the African continent, thus compounding the effects of global warming by reducing the region's ability to capture carbon.

These economic and environmental challenges have prompted African nations to head toward other renewable-energy sources besides biomass, including wind, hydropower, and especially solar. Among the more exciting projects is one in Kenya, which since 1986 has been building a decentralized electric system by installing a series of 20,000 photovoltaic systems in towns and villages.[20] The Republic of Namibia has also undertaken a similar project to help farmers by setting up photovoltaic panels in 100 homes in rural regions far from electric power lines. The South African government is seeking to promote a clean-energy industry by investing $49.3 million on research leading to more efficient and affordable fuel cells. These devices will use platinum catalysts, a metal that is plentiful in South Africa. The African nation is also experimenting with ocean-wave energy generators.

The sun-drenched Sahara region has great potential to provide Africa with electricity in the coming years. Algeria alone, for example, has enough solar potential to supply about four times the electric power needed by the entire world. As we've seen with the developments in the Middle East, much of this power can be exported for potential sale to European nations. But there is still plenty of electricity to be distributed to other nations of Africa, thus helping them to modernize and build industries that will help them to find economic and social stability.

Who knows from what parts of the globe the next great energy innovations will come. Perhaps somewhere in the world, in a humble home garage or in an advanced university laboratory, there exists some clean-energy genius—a wizard of science much like the brilliant physicist Nikola Tesla. And perhaps right now, that person is doing research on advanced energy technology that has the potential to provide new energy innovations that will reduce global energy consumption and have a positive impact on the future of humanity. Whether innovators live in Asia, Europe, the Middle East, Latin America, Canada, the South Pacific, Africa, or right here in the United States, all of humanity will benefit from revolutionary ideas that hold the promise to bring to our civilization more efficient production and use of its energy resources. By keeping an open mind to new ideas discovered in all regions of the world and by helping to develop these innovations to benefit all people, we Americans will enjoy enormous financial and environmental rewards by taking the lead in the global clean-energy movement. All humanity will benefit by fostering the development of any and all energy opportunities that make the world a safer and more prosperous place and shield from harm our planet's biosphere, which we and all other species depend upon for life.

CHAPTER 14

Securing America's Energy Future

Modernizing America as a clean-energy nation during the coming decades will give us a challenge as great in scope as any other major project in human history. We can achieve this technological and social transformation only if we work in partnership with each other. Our success in previous national ventures that enhanced us as a people can compel us to move forward together along a path to a greener and cleaner fuel future.

Consider the construction during the 1860s of the first transcontinental railroad, the iron path spanning the North American continent that created a sharp rise in the expansion of the American West. That project was pushed into political reality by President Abraham Lincoln, who saw the enormous economic and social value in having a mass-transportation system that could carry passengers and cargo from coast to coast in a matter of days instead of months. The construction of the Panama Canal, completed in 1914 after a decade's work, likewise sparked a revolution for America's commerce and national defense. Driven by President Theodore Roosevelt's leadership, the finished engineering project provided a shortcut between two oceans that saved ships time and fuel by avoiding the grueling journey around South America. The Interstate Highway System started in the 1950s revolutionized American society by providing our citizens with paved roads to journey long distances quickly and easily across the country. Pressed into construction by President Dwight D. Eisenhower, the superhighways now traversing forty-eight of our states unify our cities and towns in a network of strengthened economic and social bonds. Our nation's most ambitious space adventure in the twentieth century was the Apollo Program, which sent humans on a series of nine journeys to the moon in the 1960s and 1970s. With his vision for Apollo, President John F. Kennedy helped unite humanity for one brief shining moment on exciting celestial voyages to explore Earth's sister world.

These four feats were engineering marvels for their times. They share several key qualities that can encourage us to move forward on our own journey toward becoming a clean-energy nation. Their creation required pushing the envelope of technological innovation. They spurred enormous financial opportunity and business productivity for American citizens by generating new jobs and creating new industries. They all served psychologically as symbols of our national vigor and unity, and thus forged stronger the bonds that held our union. Their creation still inspires people to dare achieve remarkable undertakings with positive global impact. Most important, they were all conceived and achieved, in some aspect, by the necessity of strengthening our national security.

Framing our energy freedom in terms of enhancing our national security will bring into sharp focus a vital benefit of energy freedom and help inspire Americans to make the revolutionary progress necessary to succeed in this endeavor. Americans no longer want to suffer the threat of social, economic, and political manipulation from foreign nations that enjoy immense petroleum reserves. More and more of our citizens are awakening to this threat to our national security. The momentum of this growing awareness will ultimately help create effective legislation that will build a clean-energy infrastructure and generate new industries across our country.

The preservation of our national security will serve as the key to opening the door to political progress for accomplishing this ambitious undertaking. Just as we did in achieving the great engineering triumphs of our past, our nation will need to invest the necessary funding in new technology and infrastructure improvements leading to a clean-energy nation. As we observed in past projects, there will be apprehension about the short-term expense. But in the long run, an aggressive but well-managed energy-freedom program will pay for itself by saving taxpayers and businesses billions of dollars in annual energy costs. More important, over time, it will give birth to new energy businesses and clean-tech industries that will create a completely new economic sector with vast numbers of new jobs for Americans. The clean-energy revolution will also help reduce our need for foreign oil and thus trim our financial and military expenditures in protecting petroleum interests in the Persian Gulf and elsewhere. Our national security will grow even stronger as we morph into a clean-energy nation.

THE COMMON DEFENSE

Securing our nation's defense should become one of the principal reasons propelling us to transform America's energy policy to achieve our fuel freedom. A key component in the preamble to our Constitution mandates our government "to provide for the common defense." Affirming this constitutional obligation, the United States today stands well positioned as the world's supreme military power. To uphold the constitutional mandate to protect and uphold our nation's defenses, that military power should now be a part of the effort to make America a clean-energy nation.

Hydrocarbon fuels historically played a crucial role in making America the military power it is today. But as we become more and more dependent on foreign oil as our own reserves decline, this source of energy is quickly becoming our national Achilles' heel. It makes us all vulnerable to the dictates of foreign tyrants who do not have America's best interests at heart. Many of our military leaders have warned us that our national security is jeopardized by the climate changes caused by our use of fossil fuels. They also alert us to the uncomfortable truth that we do not have much time to take proactive steps to mitigate the double-punch impacts of climate change and peak oil.

A major part of managing our national security is working to lower the risk of wars and conflicts with adversaries by taking effective action to minimize the potential of international political tension. In the next forty years, the nations of the world will compete more and more for decreasing resources of water, energy, and food. This competition will grow more intense as the human population expands to over 9 billion souls. We must heed the warnings of impending global conflict. Such human tragedies as the genocide in the African nations of Sudan and Rwanda are stark examples of how environmental pressures can, in substantial part, impact a society. These potential conflicts could imperil our own national security by pulling us into costly wars in the coming decades if we fail to take action now to manage the impact of declining life-sustaining resources.

Just as they did in achieving the triumphs of the Panama Canal, the Interstate Highway System, and the Apollo Program, our nation's military leaders can provide much of the organizational and supervision talent to strengthen America's national security by transforming us into a clean-energy nation. Many of the men and women who have served in uniform—especially those veterans who developed advanced engineering skills in the armed forces—can play a major role in bringing energy technologies developed by the military and government research centers to the private sector. Thinking of winning our energy freedom as a national-security issue will enable the United States to use the talent, expertise, and organizational tools of the Department of Defense in attacking this massive undertaking. The military can and does work closely with the Energy Department. Together, these two organizations are capable of setting up an Apollo-like program to significantly improve energy efficiency and clean-fuel products throughout our nation. Opportunities abound for the military and the Energy Department to work with every other department and public agency on both federal and state levels. Advanced research in our national laboratories, as well as innovations discovered in our university and private-sector labs, will promote the development of state-of-the-art fuel technologies. These will create brand-new businesses and hundreds of thousands of jobs here in the United States as they transform us into a clean-energy nation.

SECURING OUR ECONOMY

If we wish to uphold America's national security over the coming decades, we will need to possess the financial strength that comes from a vigorous economy. The leaders in charge of our nation's corporations, financial institutions, and industries thus play a fundamental role in providing the fiscal power and business expertise to guide America to transform into a clean-energy nation. We learned during World War II how vital it was to have business and industry involved in building the weapons and tools needed to defend ourselves and other nations against the tyranny of fascism. America now requires similar efforts from today's business and industry leaders to implement the actions essential to ending our economy's overwhelming dependence on hydrocarbon fuel. The payoff is a more stable economy not controlled by the whims of the fossil-fuel market. Banks, venture-capital firms, and stock investment houses can and are helping stimulate this economic development by supporting the clean-energy revolution, thus igniting significant financial growth and healthy monetary returns for the burgeoning renewable-energy industry. The growing demand for clean energy and energy-efficiency products if properly incentivized will reinvigorate our economy by encouraging the increased production of renewable-energy equipment by American manufacturers. It can also spawn a labor and service industry that would provide many of our men and women with good-paying jobs mounting and maintaining clean-tech systems. The ripple effect would generate many more jobs for American workers in other industries, too. Achieving energy freedom will help build a robust economy and a broader tax base for the United States that will empower us to invest in our nation's transformation from a fossil-fuel society to a clean-tech society.

As the movement toward energy freedom gains momentum, U.S. businesses will realize a better bottom line as they improve their energy efficiency. American companies, large and small, will save significant sums of money in operation costs after they perform a major modernization overhaul of their energy systems to cut fuel usage. Today, many of our corporations burn a tremendous amount of fossil fuels to run their heating and lighting systems and other operating equipment, such as computers and copiers. The economics of energy efficiency, along with targeted incentives, could compel them to take action. America's companies will benefit from hiring professional consultants to carry out a thorough audit of their energy use. The gathered data can then be used to implement changes that eliminate waste and make American offices run more productively, employing both energy auditors and installation technicians.

Today, America's factories and manufacturing sites use a tremendous amount of energy, especially fossil-fuel energy, to churn out their goods. One study shows that more than 30 percent of all energy in the United States is used for manufacturing purposes. America's high dependence on fossil fuels puts many of the nation's 14 million factory workers at risk of losing their jobs if foreign sources of oil are suddenly cut off. With the expansion of the energy-freedom movement, however, America's laborers will achieve greater job security. By modernizing their facilities for greater fuel efficiency, more factories can stay competitive with overseas manufacturers. For example, antiquated technology such as inefficient motors that run utility lifts and conveyor belts consume much more energy than high-efficiency motors. Although factories face an initial investment outlay to install efficient systems, the fuel savings can slash up to 60 percent of annual energy costs, according to the findings of the same study.[1] The modernized plants also experience significant gains in productivity that help pay for the retrofitted equipment. Many large American manufacturers can also gain financial savings by partnering with state and federal government energy agencies to introduce more fuel-efficient systems into their production methods. Prompted by energy savings and tax credits, new business buildings and manufacturing sites can install energy-efficient innovations and renewable-energy systems such as solar panels and wind turbines that over time pay off handsomely in substantial energy savings.

The massive waste in fossil-fuel energy burned when transporting passengers and distributing goods and cargo has long had a hefty impact on our economy. Among the most noteworthy actions for achieving our energy freedom, our nation's transportation-industry leaders can team with federal and university laboratories to greatly expand research and development programs that will significantly increase fuel efficiency in American automobiles and trucks. Our nation's carmakers and truck manufacturers can show healthy profit margins by producing high-performance vehicles with more efficient engines, with improved aerodynamic designs that reduce drag, and that are made with lighter and stronger materials such as carbon fiber and light steel—features that make a vehicle more fuel efficient without sacrificing performance. Our nation can also make significant investments in research that produces lighter, more compact, and longer-lasting battery systems that can be charged quickly. Such high-density battery systems will prove to be the decisive component in commercializing the electric-car industry and stimulating the American auto industry with its advanced technology. U.S. automakers will move forward and produce clean-tech cars and trucks as the consumer market for these vehicles rapidly expands. Similar energy-saving advances can be incorporated into airplane, train, and ship transportation technologies. These and other energy-enhancement programs will assist our entire nation in achieving the momentum we need to get a good running start down the road to energy freedom. In the process, it will make our economy stronger and more secure.

SECURING OUR PUBLIC HEALTH AND FOOD SUPPLY

Just as our building a strong national security rests on ensuring that America has a healthy and vibrant economy to pay the billions of dollars for maintaining our military and other defense organizations, so does America's economic state depend on protecting the physical health of our population. Our nation's economy is powered by millions of employees who must stay in a physical state enabling them to deal with their daily job requirements. If too many of our citizens were to become sick, it would hurt our nation's productivity and thus cause our economy to decline. Our transformation into a clean-energy nation can help secure the well-being of our nation's workers by reducing the air, water, and soil pollution caused by producing and consuming fossil fuels. The benefits we will gain as our society shifts to cleaner and greener transportation will also make our workers healthier, thus adding to the stability and strength of our economy and national security.

The effects of climate change pose grave danger to America's public health. The extreme weather impact of droughts and blizzards, and also the spread of diseases by insects and rodents, can stress our physical bodies. But climate change will also negatively bear on the health of people in other nations, thus impacting their economies and destabilizing their societies. "An ounce of prevention is worth a pound of cure," the axiom goes. The truism is especially suitable when it comes to securing our public health. Transforming ourselves now into a clean-energy nation will help us prevent the illnesses that will force us to pay high costs to treat and cure later.

The quantity and quality of our national food production play a significant role in maintaining our public health. Our citizens will not be strong and healthy to work at their jobs if there is not enough nourishing food for them to eat. An inadequate supply of nutrition for our growing population will, in turn, hurt our national economy and national security. We have plenty to eat now, but our nation's food supply can be jeopardized when the fossil-fuel supply used to produce crops and livestock on our nation's farms hits a peak and starts a decline. The environmental shocks of climate change from global warming can also severely damage our nation's ability to produce enough sustenance for our people. Modernizing America's farms and ranches to use cleaner and greener energy should play a part in creating a national energy and climate policy that is devoted to supporting our defense objectives. To achieve this, state governments are working more closely with the U.S. Department of Agriculture to encourage America's farming and ranching communities to develop and adopt more energy-efficient methods of food production.

Many American farming and ranching families are struggling to survive against the rising prices of fuel, fertilizers, and pesticides. With the growth of clean-energy technologies, however, more efficient and sustainable agriculture methods are being developed as the United States makes a steady transition to going green. One possible action state and federal agricultural leaders can take is to encourage the farm industry to start using carbon-based fertilizer derived from the by-product of algal biodiesel production. Adding this new generation of green fertilizers to their fields will save farmers labor and money because it requires less tractor tilling than conventional petroleum-based fertilizers. This carbon fertilizer may make once arid land bloom. Millions of revitalized acres across the globe will absorb atmospheric carbon dioxide and help ease our planet's climate-change challenges.

Protecting and conserving our freshwater resources from fossil-fuel pollutants is also vital to securing our nation's public health and food supply. Improving the distribution of our nation's water resources will provide additional help in our winning the fight for energy freedom. Currently, the United States consumes about 4 percent of its electricity to distribute and treat water and wastewater, and much of this water is used by our nation's farmland to produce crops. State and federal agricultural researchers should continue to develop improved techniques to use less water and energy in growing fruit and produce and in raising livestock. Americans can help our nation's farms and mitigate climate change during the coming decades by making the move toward using more liquid biofuels, such as biodiesel and prairie-grass ethanol, in our vehicles. In the spirit of being green, we should especially be fuel frugal when using water to grow environmentally friendly crops such as sorghum and switchgrass for motor fuel. This trend toward Earth-friendly biofuels may very well prove to be an economic boon for our nation's rural communities by creating more jobs and widespread prosperity.

State governments can also incentivize farmers and ranchers to partner with utility companies to bring solar- and wind-energy technology innovations to rural regions. Much of the agricultural and ranch land across our nation has significant acreage suitable for installations of solar-panel arrays and wind turbines. These clean-tech opportunities can provide farmers and ranchers with a supplement to their income by allowing them to sell extra electric power to utility companies for distribution into decentralized electrical grids for regional transmission. The federal government can include grants and improvement loans for America's farmers and ranchers to encourage them to take steps to use renewable sources of energy, as well as increase the energy efficiency of their farm equipment. The federal government— partnering with state governments—can help America's agricultural industry secure our common defense of energy freedom.

INTERNATIONAL PARTNERSHIPS

All humanity is linked to Earth's biosphere. We all require fresh air and water and the harvest from the soil and the seas to stay alive. These basic needs connect us in sharing the world's resources. Our survival as a species, however, is put at risk if we go too far in damaging our biosphere's capability to sustain us. Climate change threatens this capability, as does damage from extracting fossil fuels from the earth. Our global industrial civilization is also imperiled as we approach the point in time when those fossil fuels peak and start their decline in production. These are sound reasons for America to seek and cultivate international partnerships as we shape our national security policy around the burgeoning clean-energy revolution.

When searching for innovative ways to achieve our nation's energy freedom, we must look closely at the quality of relationships that the United States has built with other nations of the world. Pushed by a growing awareness that we all share the same energy and climate-change challenges, Americans will increasingly see a shift in our national mind-set in the direction of cooperating with other countries. We know we must work together to combat climate change. This attitude adjustment will prove significant. Tremendous economic and business opportunities will open up for the United States across the global market once we start building new international energy partnerships. These partnerships will help spread the energy-freedom movement beyond our borders, thus sowing the seeds for democracy that, with care and nourishing, could begin blooming in other countries around the world. As these nations become more stable and their governments become more responsive to their citizens, they will pose less and less of a national security risk to America and that will make our nation more secure. During the next forty years, the United States can also take vigorous measures to use energy-efficiency and carbon-limiting projects to stabilize the political and social turmoil in hot spots around the world. For example, we can provide robust leadership in organizing United Nations humanitarian aid programs that promote the installation of solar-, biofuel-, and wind-powered generation plants in villages throughout the African continent. The electricity generated in these community power plants could improve medical services and farming methods.

ENERGY INNOVATION

Technological innovations created our American society's current dependence on fossil fuels. The creative impulse that leads to technological innovations in clean-energy products and systems will help us gain our independence from hydrocarbon fuels as well. To achieve a strong national security, our leaders must encourage and promote the development of clean-energy ideas. During the next forty years, new and yet-undreamed-of inventions in energy technologies will come into existence if we can make it a priority to improve America's educational system. We must provide high-quality education to all of our children to stimulate their minds to create the sophisticated energy products and systems as the clean-energy and green revolutions advance in the twenty-first century. Exciting innovations will also be achieved when financial investors see our elected officials giving clear legislative signals to accelerate businesses and industries toward fuel-cost savings and new clean-energy product development. We can quicken our achievement of energy freedom if we encourage the spirit of experimentation and invention that is an inherent part of our national character and a fundamental part of a free and fair market environment.

Among the most important key innovations in the early years of the energy-freedom movement will be the mass production of lighter and stronger industrial materials, such as the carbon fibers that can be used in manufacturing America's new cars and trucks. Nanotechnology—the science of building on a very tiny level—could play a huge role in achieving these material-science advances. It could also bring about better manufacturing methods for more efficient and less expensive solar panels and fuel-cell products. Spurred by research advances in artificial intelligence, sophisticated robotic systems could also enable America's factories to make dramatic cuts in their use of fossil-fuel energy when producing renewable-energy products and other goods. If successfully implemented in modern factories, the advances in robotic manufacturing we could see in the next forty years may earn the United States additional global respect for the overall high quality and low price of its energy-technology products.

Over the coming decades, the seeds of American innovation if encouraged to sprout and grow will bring about astounding technological advances in renewable-energy production—many of which will seem mind-boggling to us, here in the first decade of this century. For example, sophisticated virtual-reality telepresence systems now being developed in Silicon Valley might one day enable businesspeople to digitally "travel" and "meet" fellow workers and customers across town or even in other parts of the globe in specially equipped rooms in their own office sites. As the world continues its rapid trend toward globalization, this invention would save American employees considerable hours and dollars spent traveling to far-off places. It would also reduce the need for using increasingly expensive fossil fuels for transportation to distant locations.

Another exciting trend over the next forty years might be America's leading the development of efficient desalinization plants that use wind, solar, and ocean thermal energy conversion (OTEC) power to extract salt and other minerals from seawater. Providing freshwater from these plants to human population centers around the world will play a crucial role in the energy-freedom movement. Besides sustaining urban areas and agricultural production for food and biofuels in the United States, much of this desalinized water could help grow crops and forests in arid areas and thus help to reduce the effects of global warming. Starting with the invention of Ben Franklin's stove and the American revolutionary leader's discovery of electricity, our nation's more innovative citizens have dreamed up many exciting ideas to more efficiently produce and use energy. No doubt in the coming decades, if properly motivated by our clean-energy leaders, we will come up with many more revolutionary energy innovations that will improve human life and society.

SECURING THE NEXT FORTY YEARS

As we have seen with the construction of the transcontinental railroad, the Panama Canal, the Interstate Highway System, and the Apollo missions that took astronauts to the moon and back, the spirit of innovation made the United States stronger in its economic, social, and defense security. Tapping into this spirit of innovation will stimulate us to achieve energy freedom not only for ourselves now but also for future generations of Americans. From its birth in 1776, the United States has always been the land of larger-than-life ideas. Many times throughout our history, Americans have taken hold of an ambitious idea and worked as one nation to turn into reality what was once considered an impossibility. This characteristic can especially be witnessed in our national drive to make new paths to new places. Whether it was creating the Oregon Trail for pioneers to travel from east to west, or building the Internet for digital information to travel from computer to computer, Americans have long been trailblazers. We are at our best when we focus on a daring vision that revolutionizes the world. That's why the energy-freedom movement is a bold concept that fits well with our national trait of doing things on a heroic scale.

With an optimistic eye toward the next forty years, we see that on the Fourth of July in the year 2050, Americans will stand tall and feel proud of the energy-freedom movement started today. If the people of the United States choose now to define their journey to energy freedom, and take action to reach that destination for the security of our nation and the preservation of our planet, all of humanity in the midpoint of the twenty-first century will be able to enjoy a world of increasing peace and prosperity. To achieve this happy outcome, we simply need to start today to take steps together on the journey to securing America's energy future.

CHAPTER 15

The Power of Leadership

Many Americans might be surprised to learn that George Walker Bush started one of America's most successful clean-and-green energy programs. In mid-1996, Texas Governor Bush had his monthly chat with Pat Wood, then the chairman of the state's Public Utility Commission. They were discussing the expansion of the state's power transmission grid. As Wood started to leave the governor's office that day, Bush shouted out from his desk, "Pat, we like wind." The astonished Wood responded with the question, "We what?" Bush answered, "You heard me. Go get smart on wind."[1]

The Texas public was polled on its opinion of what was, at the time, an unconventional idea: harvesting energy from the breezes that swept across the plains. The commissioners discovered that people in a state famous for having such a prominent oil industry were indeed willing to pay a little extra on their electricity bill if it meant they would receive renewable energy. Under Bush's orders, the utility commission began working with the energy companies and environmentalists to develop a statewide wind-energy program to be included in the 1999 industry restructuring law. That program, the Texas Renewable Portfolio Standard, gave the state's power companies a deadline of the year 2009 to produce 2,000 megawatts of electricity from sustainable sources. After its adoption, individuals and companies sensing economic opportunity rushed to begin building wind turbines to meet the mandate's goal. So successful was the state government's prompting that the objective was met in 2005, four years ahead of schedule. The next year, Texas surpassed California in wind-energy production. By the end of 2007, Texas wind-power capacity exceeded 4,370 megawatts—an electricity supply large enough to power 1.2 million homes a year.[2] Thanks to Governor Bush, the Lone Star State is now the number-one producer of wind power in America.

As the story behind Governor Bush's promotion of Texas's wind-energy industry proves, the power of leadership can push people to take a chance and build themselves a sustainable-energy economy and society. A major component of this power is the use of effective communication to drive action for real change. Leaders must provide a clear vision for a clean-energy future. Effective communication that enables Congress and the American president to connect with the hearts and minds of the majority of citizens is often not easy to find in a land with as many diverse views and opinions as the United States. However, if we are to create a better tomorrow for ourselves and for future generations of Americans, we need to use effective communication and share an inspiring vision in our quest to become a clean-energy nation.

THE AMERICAN CLEAN ENERGY AND SECURITY ACT

We as a nation can learn many important lessons about the power of leadership from the challenges the House of Representatives faced in 2009 when going through the process of passing the groundbreaking American Clean Energy and Security Act (also known by its acronym ACES). The bill was designed to benefit all Americans by gradually transitioning our nation to a clean-energy economy by the year 2050. It would create clean-tech jobs, reduce our dependence on foreign oil, and limit the emission of greenhouse gasses now changing our global climate. The story of the congressional struggle involved in trying to make this historic bill into a law demonstrates the difficulty of getting clean-energy legislation over the high hurdles of Washington's political system.

On March 31, 2009, Representatives Henry Waxman of California, the chairman of the House Committee on Energy and Commerce, and Edward Markey of Massachusetts, the chairman of the Energy and Environment Subcommittee, submitted a discussion draft of ACES to the House Committee on Energy and Commerce. The draft was the result of years of preparation by Waxman, Markey, other members of the committee, and the committee staff. Many previous bills tackling climate change were used as the basis for the overall ACES bill. In a series of hearings, committee members listened to the testimony of various experts on the pros and cons of creating a federally mandated cap-and-trade system of controlling carbon emissions to manage climate change. Testimony came from officials and scientists in the energy industry, the manufacturing industry, and environmental groups. The most dramatic hearing debates came from former Vice President Al Gore and former Speaker of the House Newt Gingrich. Gore advocated that the United States must take an assertive clean-energy stand in combating climate change. Gingrich plainly stated he believed the real energy problem facing America was that we were not drilling enough domestic oil. The cap-and-trade mandates were a major discussion in the overall series of testimony. There was considerable argument over the issue of the federal government's mandating a limit—or a "cap"—on the emission of carbon dioxide, which would create a market-driven trading mechanism to reduce the quantity of this greenhouse gas released into our atmosphere over the next several decades. After a month and a half of intense discussion, the House Committee on Energy and Commerce introduced a final version of the bill to the House on May 15, 2009. ACES was assigned the bill number H.R. 2454.

In the House and across the nation, the merits and defects of ACES received considerable debate. Leaders were well aware that ACES was a comprehensive energy bill for the United States. It would impact every American citizen if made into law. It included a section on Renewable Electricity Standards, which would require utility companies to produce 20 percent of their electricity by the year 2020 from renewable-energy sources such as solar, wind, and geothermal and from energy-efficiency savings. It also contained provisions to invest in American clean-energy technologies and energy efficiency by providing $90 billion in new subsidies by the year 2025. Innovations to promote the American clean-tech industry, which would help stimulate our national economy, would come by investing $20 billion in basic research and development done by scientists. The Environmental Protection Agency (EPA) foresaw that the bill would have "a relatively modest impact on U.S. consumers," and cost households about the amount of one postage stamp per day. The Congressional Budget Office analyzed the financial impact of the carbon allowances used in a cap-and-trade system and estimated that ACES would "raise federal revenues by $873 billion over ten years and increase direct spending by $864 billion, resulting in a net $9 billion reduction in the federal budget deficit."

In the grueling process of lawmaking, amendments were proposed by both Democratic and Republican representatives. Representative Kathy Castor of Florida provided an amendment that would let the states adopt "feed-in tariffs" for renewable-energy sources. Representative John Dingell of Michigan placed into the bill an amendment that would establish a financial system that would more effectively provide loans for clean-energy improvements. Countering the proposed clean-energy policy bill, opponents of ACES intent on defeating its passage attempted to place "poison pill" amendments into it, such as an amendment that would kill the bill unless the governments of India and China established similar energy strategies for their nations.

As with most significant and controversial legislation, a process of give-and-take was required to accommodate the divergent interests within the House of Representatives. Compromises were made with the intent of getting sufficient support to pass ACES. Most Republicans opposed the bill, but there were also several blocks of Democrats representing coal-mining states who were concerned about the bill's impact on jobs and energy prices for their constituents. Democrats from heavy manufacturing regions worried about the impact cap-and-trade carbon pricing would have on industry competitiveness and wanted to safeguard the jobs of workers. Democrats from petroleum-producing states wanted allocations for oil refining. The section in ACES on agriculture was designed to give significant jurisdiction over the bill's enforcement to the U.S. Department of Agriculture instead of to the EPA. This was done to get the support and endorsement of Representative

Collin Peterson, the chairman of the Agriculture Committee. Peterson's support would bring in votes from other representatives who came from rural districts with farm industries. During the compromise stage of the debate, 85 percent of carbon allowances would be given free to energy-intensive businesses in the early years to help them adjust to the clean-energy transition. These giveaways would taper off after ten years, when most of the allocations would then be auctioned.

Many amendments and changes were made to ACES through the heated process of House debate. The bill passed by a close vote of 219 to 212. During the debate and after passage, Americans began discussing the pros and cons of ACES. Certain Republicans saw the value in climate-change legislation. The group Republicans for Environmental Protection (REP) supported passage of ACES. After its House passage, David Jenkins, vice president for government and political affairs at REP, said in a press release, "Doing nothing is not an option. The costs and risks of failing to limit greenhouse gas emissions are too high. We owe it to our country and to our country's future citizens to take action. Today, the House looked to the future and did the right thing for our economy, security, and environment."[3]

There has been considerable discussion about how much compromise was necessary to obtain final House passage of ACES, but this is a minor point compared to the importance of what Congress accomplished. The remarks of ranking member Joe Barton should be examined more closely. He mourned the passing of the days when no cost was imposed for exploiting resources. He was right: The old model did create wealth and helped propel America to international economic dominance. But regrettably, it also created an extreme inequity in the distribution of wealth, as well as enabled tyranny in developing countries. On the other hand, moving expeditiously to establish energy freedom through bills similar to ACES would move us toward economic stability. Passage of the legislation was truly remarkable, especially in the current political climate. Congressional Democrats were able to cobble together a coalition of members of Congress to point to a new way of doing business that would, if passed into law, lead the rest of the world into a sustainable future. Unfortunately, as broad as the House legislation that finally passed became, it was not broad enough to attract any Republicans in the Senate. Much like their House counterparts, they were absolutely determined to prevent passage of ACES. However, the political significance of the American Clean Energy and Security Act is that it shows how determined leadership can overcome immense obstacles. ACES points to what form future legislation might take to tackle the problem of global warming. The threat of human-made climate change or other global threats *can* be addressed. We are not at the mercy of forces beyond our control. Humankind has the ability to stand up, assess long-term threats, and change the direction of history toward sustainability and harmony.

Even though our nation's leaders failed to make the American Clean Energy and Security Act of 2009 a law, the bill can still serve us by providing important lessons to aid the passage of similar legislation presented to Congress in the future. One lesson we must gain from ACES is the importance of all elected officials' never giving up on providing the American people with a solid national energy policy that supports the overall good of the nation. Another lesson is the significance of listening to valid points of view coming from all interests impacted by a clean-energy bill. With ACES, members of the House of Representatives heard the information and opinions of businesspeople and environmental leaders who supported the legislation, as well as businesspeople and environmental leaders who opposed it. This process of communication helped build trust among the various leaders involved in passing the bill in the House.

The most crucial lesson learned from ACES was how vital it is to get the support of the American people in creating effective energy legislation. If the United States is to have a chance to pass a bill similar to ACES in the future, its citizens must understand the magnitude of such a law for improving their lives. And they must actively voice their support for clean-energy lawmaking. Without a vision for creating a clean-tech economy and society, the American people will never back efforts to transform the United States into a nation run on clean energy. We all must work together to create and communicate this vision. By far, however, the leader who holds the chief responsibility for sharing this vision with the people is the president of the United States.

THE POWER OF THE PRESIDENCY

The American people have placed in the office of the president many great leaders. Throughout the more than twenty-three decades our venture in representative democracy has been proceeding, we've seen many men who have headed our national government and enabled our American family to make significant gains in our freedoms. We can use many of these presidential leaders as role models in our quest to become a clean-energy nation. Certainly among the greatest to fulfill the responsibility of the presidency, we include President George Washington, who set the standard high as our first national head of state. Washington ranks as a man of integrity who worked hard to merge the band of often bickering American states into one union under a banner of red, white, and blue. He also warned against the dangers of our nation becoming too divided by the dispute of warring factions—a warning our energy leaders would be wise to heed. Abraham Lincoln, our nation's first Republican president, also can serve as a role model for America's clean-energy leaders. He held office during the days of our nation's darkest war, when brother fought brother over the question of whether or not humans can be owned like animals and forced to labor against their will. Somehow, despite all the odds, Lincoln's leadership kept the nation united, although at a cost of more than 600,000 American lives. His political pragmatism, and also the spirit of compassion he possessed for showing "malice toward none" of the citizens of the vanquished South, has made The Great Emancipator a man many historians consider to be our greatest presidential leader.

The twentieth century is the period when the United States made the transition to world superpower. We were lucky to have at the very start of the last century the energetic leadership of Theodore Roosevelt. A progressive Republican president who pressed our nation forward in building up our naval strength for national defense, Roosevelt brought forth peace and reconciliation between Russia and Japan, and helped boost global trade and made America's national defense stronger by the construction of the Panama Canal. Roosevelt would no doubt be keen for our twenty-first-century

United States to make the transition to a clean-energy nation. He worked on preserving America's capitalist heritage by trust-busting the unfair monopolistic actions of John D. Rockefeller's Standard Oil Company. He also spent much of his dynamic energy on conserving the environment across much of our nation, as well as on protecting the health and physical well-being of the American people by the creation of the Food and Drug Administration. Woodrow Wilson, a Democratic president, proved to be an effective leader during his term in office as he set America to achieve the outcome of bringing peace—although a temporary peace—to the feuding nations in Europe during the First World War. His vision to preserve that peace by the creation of a League of Nations was, unfortunately, not approved by the U.S. Senate in 1919. The world thus lost the opportunity to prevent the Second World War. Wilson's unfulfilled dream to unify the world's nations in a spirit of harmony can now serve the United States in teaming with other nations to also encourage the worldwide transition to clean energy. Democratic President Franklin D. Roosevelt also can serve as a leadership model for achieving our energy freedom. Through his famous "fireside chats" on the radio, his inspiring messages helped citizens feel that they could play a role in the national vision of getting ordinary Americans back to work after the worst economic calamity the world has yet seen. Despite dealing daily with physical paralysis from polio, FDR proved himself to be a war hero. Serving as commander-in-chief, he led the American people to transform our national industry and armed forces to achieve victory over fascism in Europe and Asia. We need leaders with President Roosevelt's motivational skill to galvanize our patriotic citizens to make the small sacrifices necessary to re-create America as a clean-energy nation.

The responsibility of handling America's transition into the cold war era was placed in the hands of President Harry Truman, who took on the presidency at FDR's death in 1945. A highly pragmatic politician, and a man of strong vision, the Democratic Truman understood the necessity of being proactive in building a modern infrastructure in Japan and Europe so that the world would not repeat the mistakes of the Treaty of Versailles. The Marshall Plan of 1947 provided $17 billion to rebuild Western Europe, stimulating economic prosperity for the people there by creating more efficient factories and manufacturing sites, as well as modern transportation systems. Furthermore, the North Atlantic Treaty Organization (NATO) developed alliances with European countries to defend against aggression. Truman provides an example of how America can take the lead in creating alliances with other nations in moving forward to a clean-energy world. Following Truman, Republican President Dwight Eisenhower proved himself a true leader with vision in implementing the Interstate Highway System over several decades. This program, funded for the purposes of national defense, unified our nation by building a network of modern roads that have enhanced commerce and tourism in America. These highways created a positive ripple effect for our national economy that we continue to benefit from. Eisenhower's far-reaching vision can also be seen in his creation in 1958 of the National Aeronautics and Space Administration (NASA) to counter the Soviet Union in the space race. The "*Sputnik* crisis" also spurred Eisenhower to promote the improvement of our schools and universities through a $1 billion education fund. These investments in our nation's future paid off many times over through the new communication, information, and transportation technologies that benefit us today. We can use the visionary programs that came from Eisenhower's leadership to inspire us to pave new roads of innovation that lead to a clean-energy tomorrow and thus will benefit ourselves and future generations.

In the 1960s, the charismatic Democratic President John F. Kennedy learned hard-won lessons from the disastrous Bay of Pigs invasion of Cuba. He put these lessons into practice when he provided sound leadership (often going against the advice of military experts) during the Cuban Missile Crisis of October 1962, when Americans feared a nuclear Armageddon might bring an end to humanity. Kennedy showed true leadership when he set the United States on a mission to the moon, giving us an end-of-the-decade deadline to accomplish this exciting journey. His example demonstrates that leaders in the clean-energy movement need to be courageous and aggressive in setting challenging but achievable goals within a specific timeframe. With Kennedy's assassination, Democratic President Lyndon Baines Johnson came to office, focusing on an agenda of improving life for all Americans through his Great Society, the War on Poverty, and the promotion of civil rights. Johnson proved to be a pragmatic politician in implementing his domestic policies. Unfortunately for America, Johnson unwisely let his fear of being seen as weak in foreign-policy matters push him to escalate the war in Vietnam. The resulting social unrest and cost of the war severely impaired his Great Society promise. Johnson provides us with a valuable lesson that our national leaders must not let our clean-energy movement be distracted by conflict with other nations.

Despite the fact that his reputation will long be tainted by the Watergate scandal, Republican President Richard Nixon provides the clean-energy movement with another example of visionary leadership in the White House. Nixon has gone down in history as an effective foreign-policy leader. He set aside his cold-war warrior ideology to initiate communication and open the door to diplomatic relations with China and détente with the Soviet Union. Nixon provides clean-energy nation leaders with two important leadership lessons. The first is that we must be able to turn off our ideological biases if we wish to work in partnership with people we once considered enemies. The second lesson comes from Nixon's Watergate crisis. We can learn from Nixon that our leaders must show a high standard of integrity, or else risk letting scandal take us off course in achieving a clean-energy nation. In the 1980s, Republican President Ronald Reagan also demonstrated excellence in leadership with his extraordinary skill in connecting with the people of America and in providing a sense of optimism for a brighter tomorrow. Like Nixon, Reagan learned how to set aside his cold-war warrior ideology and closely work in partnership with Soviet Union leader Mikhail Gorbachev to bring an end to the tyranny of communism that had enslaved millions of people in Russia and Eastern Europe. "The Great Communicator" shows our clean-energy nation leaders how vital it is to be able to clearly present a vision for a better world. Reagan also demonstrates how politicians can gain ground in achieving their energy policy goals by setting aside their prejudices toward those who might oppose their opinions and to treat them as fellow human beings.

Twentieth-century American history also presents our clean-energy nation leaders with two presidents who failed in providing a clear and inspiring vision for the United States. The first is President Herbert Hoover, a Republican who had the bad luck to come into the White House shortly before the infamous Wall Street crash of 1929 brought on the Great Depression that severely damaged our national economy. Hoover had made his reputation as a humanitarian, providing relief to the people of Belgium in the aftermath of World War I. Unfortunately during his presidency, he failed to provide the American people with an inspiring vision that would unite them to take action to rebuild our nation's economy. Half a century later, Democratic President Jimmy Carter would serve in the Oval Office during the turbulent times of the energy crisis of the 1970s. Carter's micromanaging approach in running his administration and his sometimes dour communication style impaired his ability to provide an inspiring vision for the American people. His infamous "Crisis of Confidence" speech on energy in 1979 disheartened the American people during a time when they hungered for national leadership that would stir them into action. Despite some very positive policy initiatives, his lack of leadership in the White House slowed America's ability to repair itself from the energy crisis that started with the OPEC embargo of 1973. Both presidents Hoover and Carter provide lessons to our clean-energy nation leaders that they must communicate a clear and optimistic vision to the American people to unite us all in creating a more empowering fuel future.

A PATRIOTIC PARTNERSHIP

Great American leaders at all levels of government know the necessity of moving beyond their ideology to achieve great outcomes. Far too often in recent years, we've seen the American political system become a Punch-and-Judy Show in which people with opposing ideologies attack each other to score publicity points. A long-held tradition of democratic government is to promote lively argument in which opposing sides verbally joust with each other over the issues important to the times. A healthy and open debate is an excellent activity in encouraging the competition of ideas and policies produced by elected officials. Real and effective debate, however, becomes imperiled when our political system turns into a win-at-all-cost game for the prize of power. Instead, we must work together in a spirit of cooperation—in a patriotic partnership—to benefit all the people of the United States.

We can see this spirit of cooperation among leaders exhibited in the heated debate over American independence that took place among members of the Second Continental Congress in 1776. The Committee of Five responsible for penning the Declaration of Independence consisted of determined and pragmatic men. Among other important leaders of the American Revolution was a Pennsylvania lawyer named John Dickinson, one of the wealthiest men in the American colonies. He argued for reconciliation with Britain, representing the viewpoint of the conservative-minded people in the colonies, a group that some historians estimate equaled about 20 to 30 percent of the population. These Loyalists (also called "Tories," "Royalists," and "King's Men") believed that resisting the sovereign rule of King George III was morally wrong. Unfortunately, John Dickinson too often does not receive the credit he deserves in the telling of our American story. He provided the opposing argument, the contrasting view, and thereby gave a high degree of validity and legitimacy to America's leaders' declaring our nation's independence.

The balanced disagreement by Dickinson and other conservative members of the Continental Congress confirmed to the world that America's leaders considered both sides of the argument. Dickinson's opposition to Thomas Jefferson, John Adams, Benjamin Franklin, and others in Congress proved to the British people that the American people were not embarking on this revolutionary quest for self-government without seriously thinking about the consequences. In declaring our own independence from the tyranny of fossil fuels, we would be wise to remember the example of our Founding Fathers and strive for a balanced and evenhanded debate. When we move beyond the limited philosophy of our respective ideologies, we realize that we are not "Democrats" or "Republicans." We are Americans. We are all participating in a patriotic partnership called democracy. A key component of effective leadership in creating a clean-energy nation is to ensure that all values and views are freely expressed and heard in a fair and fact-based argument. As we saw with the story of Governor Bush's moving the state of Texas in 1996 to develop its wind-energy resources for the greater public good, the power of leadership can encourage us to go beyond our ideologies and give us a clear and inspiring vision to reap tremendous rewards and riches for ourselves and for future generations of Americans.

Beyond the immediate need for climate-change legislation, our nation, and indeed every nation, needs a vision for the future that will result in a sustainable-energy economy. It is probably not possible to entirely end our dependence on petroleum and fossil fuels, but we can certainly enact programs that give the proper incentives to become more energy efficient and to consume fewer natural resources so that our use of fossil fuels has a smaller impact on our living environment.

Throughout this book we've explored the relation between energy generation and consumption on different aspects of our civilization. We have seen that a vast array of technology is available at our disposal to become highly efficient and produce clean energy. We know from history that we as a people are capable of rising up and changing the direction of history when the need arises. Now is the time for such change. Moving forward in a deliberate and well-delineated path toward energy freedom that generates increasing economic activity and meaningful employment will bring a true sense of security to our nation and the world. Human beings have the capacity to plan ahead and prepare for the future like no other creature known to us. Let us use this capacity to look ahead and envision a future that drives us forward toward creating clean, secure, and prosperous lives for more and more people. And then, let us reach out and make that future happen.

CHAPTER 16

The Other Road

I n the spring of 1787, America stood at a crossroads. Inside the Pennsylvania State House in Philadelphia, in the same assembly room where the Declaration of Independence had been argued over more than a decade earlier, fifty-five representatives of twelve of the thirteen states met one May morning to begin a debate over the course the new nation would take after achieving political independence from Britain. Led by George Washington, these uniquely talented men deliberated for the next several months on the issue of how to successfully administer the complex management of their new country. Striving to find the best method of sharing power between the states and a federal government, they created the Constitution of the United States of America. With that great document, they sought to achieve something never before seen in all of human history. The framers of the Constitution understood that the words they penned would have a deep impact on the lives of millions of Americans who would follow in their footsteps. In their preamble, they stated their vision "to secure the blessings of liberty to ourselves and our posterity." Those words set all Americans on a course compelling us to preserve and protect our rights and freedoms and to ensure that the Founding Fathers' great legacy passes down to future generations of our republic. American citizens have long and successfully safeguarded their inheritance of independence. Our history has seen several key moments of crisis in which it seemed in high doubt if the experiment of American independence might continue. But with an instinctive desire that democracy and freedom must never perish from this nation, the people of previous eras struggled against adversity and made the momentous sacrifices necessary to keep liberty's flame lit.

Now, we as a nation face another point of crisis in our history. The legacy of liberty stands at stake. The question of achieving our energy freedom will likely be one of the most significant issues the American people will tackle in the twenty-first century. Because of the magnitude of the matter and how it will impact the future course of American democracy and prosperity, we would be wise to acknowledge that we have a moral responsibility to face this challenge. The task set before us of successfully answering this question will not be an easy one. It will require everyone who is a stakeholder to take part and contribute to upholding the sacred gift given to us in the founding of our nation. This responsibility requires us to maintain America's rights and freedoms so that future generations can savor the benefits that these ideals bring forth.

Unfortunately, far too many Americans do not fully comprehend how our lives, our families, our values, and our fortunes are jeopardized by our continued dependence on fossil fuels. They do not truly see the dangers we must deal with in the coming decades, from the national security threat; the economic threat of competing with other nations for dwindling petroleum resources; and the humanitarian threat of disease, poverty, and climate change. All of these dangers are directly influenced by the course we decide to take in our journey to energy freedom.

A CLEAN-ENERGY NATION

From the start of the American story, our people have traveled on a journey of heroic magnitude. We have long traversed on a continuous quest as we follow new paths to enrich our lives with liberty. From our current vista point, we look at the panorama of our vast history and see that our people have always been striving for something better, something beyond mere mortal existence. We have long sought the other road, the road untrodden. Our never-ending journey along this road has never been an effortless one. History always demands an arduous struggle in the pursuit of the prize all humans wish to win: freedom. Often, we have battled at war with ourselves in the struggle to secure this great prize. At our nation's very birth one hot and humid July day in Philadelphia, we fought each other over the words of a document that declared our independence from the tyranny of monarchy. In writing the Constitution, the supreme law of our land, we fought each other on the issue of the division of authority between state and federal governments. In the middle of the nineteenth century, we fought each other over the question of granting freedom to people who were shackled by the bondage of slavery because of the color of their skin. In the twentieth century, we fought each other over the issues of expanding voting rights to women, desegregating our society, and protecting our natural world from the exploitation of industry. The fight for freedom, we always found, was well worth the struggle.

Now, we face a fight for the future. The battle to win our freedom from fossil fuels is one we must not lose. The survival of our human civilization depends on our winning this war. We as a people must be tougher on ourselves to achieve a better energy tomorrow. We need to have a clear and compelling national goal to use energy freedom to make real a more peaceful and prosperous America. We Americans must give ourselves challenging yet achievable goals—such as reducing our national carbon output by at least 20 percent by the year 2020 and 80 percent by the year 2050. We will share up-front costs in striving for these milestones. The financial riches saved from energy efficiency, along with the social, economic, health, and defense rewards we will gain from our financial investment, will be well worth our sacrifices and efforts. Because the people of other nations look to the United States as the world's foremost leader, we must also develop a planetwide vision of energy freedom to enable the entire human family living in our global community to achieve widespread prosperity and lasting peace. We can and must open a new chapter of cooperation in human history. The stakes relating to energy freedom are immense for our species. That is why it is vital that we as a nation prove that we possess the moral courage to carry out our ambitious task.

The spirit of 1776 requires all Americans to commit themselves to be part of this new energy-freedom movement. Through our system of democratic government, every individual can contribute in creating better energy opportunities for our nation. We can all lend a hand to shape the course through history that this nation will take in coming years. American democracy, however, can operate effectively only if we the people choose to actively participate in the procedures of a legitimate representative government. If we citizens truly wish to secure the blessings of energy freedom for ourselves and our posterity, we are obliged to directly take active roles in the governing of our lives and resources. One of the most powerful ways to do this is for every person who has been blessed with the right to vote to play his or her part and follow through on this basic obligation for sustaining our freedoms. We must educate ourselves on the political issues and candidates we have the opportunity to decide upon during an election season. The patriotic spirit of 1787 requires all Americans to cast their ballots.

Our nation's people must become passionate about taking actions toward solving our energy challenges. Real passion is contagious. When a critical mass of people possess this quality of passion, they can transform our nation to achieve the potential greatness we are destined to reach. We Americans need to inspire our population and unify our nation to take steps toward achieving our energy freedom. We need leadership on all levels that will invite us to make the necessary and noble sacrifices to realize our goal. As Winston Churchill once said, "We make a living by what we get, but we make a life by what we give." The spirit of America compels all its citizens to give value back to their nation.

Our citizens should take an active role in shaping the clean-energy movement by sharing a vision of the kind of future they want for themselves and their children. To effectively promote energy freedom, the American people must make their voices heard. Through written correspondence and oral communication, they must express their ideas and opinions about our energy challenges with their elected city, county, state, and federal officials. The louder and clearer our citizens ring the bell of energy freedom, the more our nation will feel pressed to pursue the goal of gaining our fuel freedom.

In a broad sense, America has always been about rebuilding itself as a new and improved people. During the course of our nation's life, we have often reinvented ourselves in better ways when we faced moral and ethical challenges. We have found we can produce surprising results when we establish a clear and worthwhile purpose that people will unite around. Achieving our energy freedom now provides us with that purpose. It is a goal that all patriotic Americans can believe in. By laboring hard together to transform our lives and preserve our freedoms, we can heal the rift that has divided our people in recent decades and make the United States truly united once again as a clean-energy nation.

TOWARD A BETTER WORLD

The American people desire a change for the better. They want to be able to wake up in the morning and have no cause to worry that today there might be no usable energy to let them live their lives as they are accustomed to living. And when they recognize that it is an act of honor and patriotism for them to take personal steps and make small sacrifices to help the United States achieve true energy freedom, most of our nation's citizens should be indeed eager to join with their friends and neighbors and work for the greater good.

That joining together to bring about a common good has always been a cornerstone of America's success. Throughout our many yesterdays, we have innately understood and practiced that core value of cooperation. This value has made us special as a people in the chronicles of human history. Americans know that real change only comes when people collaborate and focus on a worthwhile purpose. Combining our talent and leadership influence, we as a people can achieve greatness. As Americans, we must ignite our innate can-do attitude and target it toward a better world. We must join together to adopt a bright and shining national intention of transforming our economic infrastructure to a new energy model that will create new patterns of financial reward. This great and moral cause will unite us. The results will be spectacular, worthy of the sacred trust bequeathed upon us by those previous generations of Americans who toiled and sacrificed to build our great nation. We hold a vision of hope and beauty, a vision of economic and spiritual growth, that future generations will marvel over, praising the foresight of our times. On the other hand, if we fail to act, any future civilization will be harshly judgmental of our era.

When the framers of the Constitution gave a groundbreaking government to the American people in 1787, they had no proof that their experiment in a democratic system of managing public affairs would succeed. Those fifty-five leaders took a monumental risk in creating something new in the world as they sought to use the ideals of representative democracy "to form a more perfect Union, establish justice, insure domestic tranquility, provide for the common defense, promote the general welfare, and secure the blessing of liberty to ourselves and our posterity." Those men expected that the generations of Americans who would follow them would value those aspirations enough to guard them from abuse or neglect. We must not fail them. And more important, we must not fail the generations of Americans who follow us.

Like America's Founding Fathers did at the birth of our nation, we stand today at the crossroads. We have journeyed down a path that has led us to the tyranny of fossil-fuel addiction. Now, destiny has given us an opportunity to rise up and realize a new freedom never before seen in all of human history. Here at the junction of one road leading to oblivion and another road leading to hope, we must make the wise choice for our future. For the sake of preserving America's values, let us now begin traveling toward a better world. Let us choose the other road. Let us journey together.

ACKNOWLEDGMENTS

For America to achieve its energy independence will require the teaming up of many people who will provide their unique talents and skills to a most worthy cause. So, too, is this book a collaboration of many people who provided their time and talent to its creation. There are many people who helped in the process, but the authors would like to especially thank Carole Berglie and Karen Brogno (for excellent copyediting); Mike Cox (Anaerobe Systems); Swanee Edwards (South Valley Democrats); Holly Fairbank (proofreader); David Gerard, Ph.D. (Right Management); Jennifer Holder (AMACOM); Nick Holder (Congressman McNerney's Chief of Staff); Charmaine Jabr (South Valley Democrats); Christopher James (Synapse Energy Economics); Paul Johnson (San Joaquin Valley Clean Energy Organization); Ginger Legato (interior book design); Deborah Morton-Padilla (who provided great editing advice); David Paxson (World Population Balance); Paul Peterson (Synapse Energy Economics); Barry Richardson (AMACOM); Rich Rosen (Tellus Institute); Lora Schraft (for the author photo); Greg Sellers (StablSolar); Erika Spelman (AMACOM); Andy Stone and John Varela (who both provided content advice); Stan Wakefield (AMACOM); and Kevin Wolf (Wind Harvest International). The authors would like to give special thanks to literary agent Sharlene Martin of Martin Literary Management for her exceptional dedication to this project and her encouragement throughout the entire process.

Introduction: A Declaration of Energy Independence

1. *Resolution of Independence*, moved by Richard Henry Lee for the Virginia Delegation, June 7, 1776.

2. George F. Will, "An Inconvenient Price," *Newsweek*, Oct. 22, 2007, 68.

3. American Wind Energy Association, "New Poll Shows Overwhelming Bipartisan Support for National Renewable Electricity Standard," press release, Nov. 13, 2007.

Chapter 1: The End of the Fossil-Fuel Age

1. A Tribute to M. King Hubbert, "Hubbert's Speech," www.mkinghubbert.com/speech/prediction.

2. M. King Hubbert, "Nuclear Energy and the Fossil Fuels," paper presented to the American Petroleum Institute, San Antonio, TX, March 8, 1956, www.energybulletin.net/13630.html.

3. Kenneth S. Deffeyes, *Hubbert's Peak: The Impending World Oil Shortage* (Princeton, NJ: Princeton University Press, 2001), 2–3.

4. "Hubbert, Marion King," *The Handbook of Texas Online*, www.hubbertpeak.com/hubbert/bio_doel.htm.

5. Tribute to M. King Hubbert, "Hubbert's Speech."

6. A Tribute to M. King Hubbert, "Post-speech Fallout," www.mkinghubbert.com/speech/postspeech.

7. Deffeyes, *Hubbert's Peak*, 3.

8. A Tribute to M. King Hubbert, "U.S. Oil Peak," www.mkinghubbert.com/speech/usoilpeak.

9. M. King Hubbert, testimony to the Subcommittee on the Environment and the Committee on Interior and Insular Affairs, United States House of Representatives, June 6, 1974, available at www.energybulletin.net/3845.html.

10. Noel Grove, "Oil: The Dwindling Treasure," *National Geographic*, June 1974, 821.

11. Deffeyes, *Hubbert's Peak*, 12.

12. Roger Bezdek and Robert Hirsch, *Peak of World Oil Productions: Implications, Opportunities, and Pitfalls* (presentation), 16, http://www.mkinghubbert.com/files/Candidate%20Briefing.pdf.

13. Walter Youngquist, "Shale Oil—The Elusive Energy," *Hubbert Center Newsletter*, Oct. 1998.

14. Maria Dickerson, "Will Mexico Soon Be Tapped Out?" *Los Angeles Times*, July 24, 2006, available at www.energybulletin.net/18505.html.

15. Elizabeth Shogren, "The Future of Fuel: Turning Dirty Coal into Clean Energy," National Public Radio Report, Morning Edition, April 25, 2006, www.npr.org/templates/story/story.php?storyID=5356683.

16. Matthew L. Wald, "Science Panel Finds Fault with Estimates of Coal Supply," *New York Times*, June 21, 2007.

17. Committee on Coal Research, Technology, and Resource Assessments to Inform Energy Policy, National Research Council, "Coal: Research and Development to Support National Energy Policy" (Washington, DC: National Academies Press, 2007); The National Academies, "Major Increase in Federal Research Needed to Determine Size of U.S. Coal Reserves and Meet Increasing Challenges in Mining Safety, Environmental Protection," press release, June 20, 2007.

18. Richard Heinberg, "Peak Coal: Sooner Than You Think," *Energy Bulletin*, May 21, 2007, www.energybulletin.net/299919.html.

19. Energy Watch Group, "The Capacity of Coal Is Significantly Overestimated," press release, March 3, 2007, http://www.energywatchgroup.org/fileadmin/global/pdf/EWG_Press_Coal_5-3-2007.pdf.

20. B. Kavalov and S. D. Peteves, "The Future of Coal" (Brussels: Directorate-General Joint Research Centre, European Commission, Feb. 2007).

21. Al Gore, *An Inconvenient Truth: The Planetary Emergency of Global Warming and What We Can Do About It* (Emmaus, PA: Rodale, 2006).

22. Samuel W. Matthews, "Under the Sun—It's Our World Warming," *National Geographic*, Oct. 1990, 19–20.

23. Union of Concerned Scientists, "Common Sense on Climate Change: Practical Solutions to Global Warming," Sept. 30, 2005, http://www.ucsusa.org/assets/documents/global_warming/climatesolns.pdf.

24. James M. Inhofe, floor statement, U.S. Senate Committee on Environment and Public Works, July 28, 2003.

25. Naomi Oreskes, "Beyond the Ivory Tower: The Scientific Consensus on Climate Change," *Science*, Dec. 3, 2004.

26. Kate Ravilious, "Extreme Global Warming Fix Proposed: Fill the Skies with Sulfur," *National Geographic News*, Aug. 4, 2006, http://news.nationalgeographic.com/news/2006/08/060804-global-warming.html.

27. Public Broadcast System, NOVA episode transcript: "Dimming the Sun," first broadcast on April 18, 2006, http://www.pbs.org/wgbh/nova/transcripts/3310_sun.html.

28. James E. Hansen, "Dangerous Human-Made Interference with Climate," testimony to the Select Committee on Energy Independence and Global Warming, United States House of Representatives, April 26, 2007, http://www.columbia.edu/~jeh1/2007/Testimony_20070426.pdf.

29. "Earth's Climate Approaches Dangerous Tipping Point," *Environment News Service*, June 1, 2007, http://www.ens-newswire.com/ens/jun2007/2007-06-01-01.asp.

30. Hansen testimony, April 26, 2007.

Chapter 2: How to Become Dependent on Fossil Fuels

1. Stanford Solar Center, "The Sun's Vital Statistics," www.solar-center.stanford.edu/vitalstats.html; NASA World Book, "Sun," www.nasa.gov/worldbook/sun_worldbook.html; International Solar Terrestrial Physics Program, "Some Interesting Facts About the Sun," http://www-istp.gsfc.nasa.gov/istp/outreach/workshop/thompson/facts.html.

2. "The Goldilocks Zone," *Astrobiology Magazine*, April 28, 2007, www.astrobio.net/news/article2314.html.

3. Estrella Mountain Community College, "Photosynthesis," http://www.emc.maricopa.edu/faculty/farabee/BIOBK/BioBookPS.html.

4. Description of the origin of fossil fuels is derived from Christine Pulliam, "Astronomers Create Chart to ID Life-Bearing Planets in Distant Star Systems," *Smithsonian Inside Research* 15 (Winter 2007), http://www.si.edu/opa/insideresearch/articles/V15_IDchart.html; Chapter 8: Fossil Fuels—Coal, Oil, and

Natural Gas, in *Energy Story* (Sacramento: California Energy Commission), www.energyquest.ca.gov/story/chapter08.html; and Janet Marinelli, "Power Plants—The Origin of Fossil Fuels," *Plants & Gardens News*, Brooklyn Botanic Garden newsletter 18, no. 2 (2003).

5. The Coal Resource, World Coal Institute, www.worldcoal.org; Education for a Sustainable Future: Environmental Project, "Fossil Fuel Formation," www.ESFEP.org; and National Ocean Industries Association (NOIA), "About Natural Gas," www.noia.org/website/article.asp?id=128.

6. Michael Schirber, "Asteroid Impact Fueled Global Rain of BBs," *Space.com*, www.space.com/scienceastronomy/050328_asteroid_impact.html; and Martin Jehle, "Paleocene Mammals of the World," www.paleocene-mammals.de/.

7. Chapter 8: Fossil Fuels, *Energy Story*.

8. William E. Brooks, "Coal and Cremation in Ancient Peru," *Geotimes*, Feb. 2004, www.geotimes.org/feb04/resources.html.

9. Chapter 8: Fossil Fuels, *Energy Story*; NOIA, "About Natural Gas."

10. Details of the early human history of fossil fuels are from Jeff Goodell, *Big Coal: The Dirty Secret Behind America's Energy Future* (New York: Houghton Mifflin, 2006), 11; Chapter 8: Fossil Fuels, *Energy Story*; W. E. Butterworth, *Black Gold: The Story of Oil* (New York: Four Winds Press, 1975), 13; and National Energy Technology Laboratory, "Secure and Reliable Energy Supplies— History of U.S. Coal Use," www.netl.doe.gov/KeyIssues/historyofcoaluse.html.

11. Details of the story of James Watt's role in creating the modern fossil-fuel age are taken from *Biographies: The Inventors of the Industrial Revolution*, www.blupete.com/Literature/Biographies/Science/Inventors.htm; British Broadcasting Company, "Historic Figures: James Watt (1736–1819)," www.bbc.co.uk/history/historic_figures/watt_james.shtml; and History Learning Site, "Great Britain 1700 to 1900: Industrial Revolution: Coal Mines," www.history learningsite.co.uk/coal.htm.

12. "Abraham Gesner: Inventor of Kerosene Oil, Founder of Modern Petroleum Industry, and Saver of Whales," *National Chemistry Week*, www.ncwsnc.cheminst.ca/articles/1999_gesner1_e.htm.

13. Virtual American Biographies, "Abraham Gesner," www.famousamericans.net/abrahamgesner; "Abraham Gesner," *National Chemistry Week*.

14. Butterworth, *Black Gold*, 23–26.

15. Explore PA History, "Striking Oil," www.explorepahistory.com/story.php?storyID+12&chapter=3.

16. Scott Canfield, "Tales of Destruction . . . Pithole, Oilfield Ghost Town," www.logwell.com/tales/pithole.html.

17. The story of John D. Rockefeller and big oil is from Public Broadcasting System, "American Experience: The Rockefellers," http://www.pbs.org/wgbh/amex/rockefellers/; and Joseph Kahn, "Big Oil: The Old Dynasty; An Oil Giant Would Lack a Rockefeller," *New York Times*, Dec. 3, 1998.

18. The story of Edison and Tesla and their roles in "electrifying the world" is from several sources: Public Broadcasting System, "The American Experience: Timeline of Thomas Edison's Life," www.pbs.org/wgbh/amex/edison/timelines/indext.html; IEEE Virtual Museum, "Pearl Street Station: The Dawn of Commercial Electric Power," www.ieee-virtual-museum.org/collection/event.php?id=3456876; Norman Bolotin and Christine Laing, *The World's Columbian Exposition: The Chicago World's Fair of 1893* (Champaign: University of Illinois Press, 2002), vii; and Public Broadcasting System, "Tesla: Life and Legacy—War of the Currents," www.pbs.org/tesla/11/11_warcur.html.

19. Automotive History Online, "Ford Motor Company—1903–Present," www.automotivehistoryonline.com/Ford.htm; The Henry Ford Museum, "The Life of Henry Ford," www.hfmgv.org/exhibits/hf/; and The Frontenac Motor Company, "The Ford Model T: A Short History of Ford's Innovation," http://www.modelt.ca/background-fs.html.

20. The story of Patillo Higgins and Texas oil is derived from several sources: Eugene Kim and Daryl Mazzanti, "Texas Oil and Gas," www.beg.utexas.edu/mainweb/services/pdfs/giddings.pdf; Free Enterprise Land, "The Gusher," www.freeenterpriseland.com/BOOK/GUSHER.html; "Spindletop Oilfield," *The Handbook of Texas Online*, www.tshaonline.org/handbook/online/articles/SS/dos3.html; and The Paleontological Research Institution, "Spindletop, Texas," www.priweb.org/ed/pgws/history/spindletop/spindletop.html.

21. "Oil and Gas Production: History in California," ftp://ftp.consrv.ca.gov/pub/oil/history/History_of_Calif.pdf; and Earthguide, "Rise of Oil Production," www.earthguide.ucsd.edu/fuels/production.html.

22. Grant Smith and Mark Shenk, "Al-Naimi Sees $60 Minimum; OPEC Supply Cut Unlikely (Update2)," *Bloomberg.com*, March 3, 2008, http://www.bloomberg.com/apps/news?pid=20601087&sid=aS7yUeT0CwNA&refer=home; and American Association of Petroleum Geologists, "'73–74 Was a Dark, Fateful Winter," www.aapg.org/explorer/2004/03march/embargo.cfm.

Chapter 3: The Dawn of a New Energy Era

1. Various facts on "sun power" are from Greenpeace and European Photovoltaic Industry Association (EPIA), "Solar Generation: Solar Electricity for Over One Billion People and Two Million Jobs by 2020," Sept. 2006, 4, www.epia.org/fileadmin/EPIA_docs/publications/epia/EPIA_SG_IV_final.pdf; Union of Concerned Scientists, "Clean Energy: How Solar Energy Works," www.ucsusa.org; Worldwatch Institute, "Solar Power Set to Shine Brightly," news release, May 22, 2007, www.worldwatch.org/node/5086; Solarbuzz, "Fast Solar Energy Facts: Global Performance," www.solarbuzz.com/Fast FactsIndustry.htm; and "Growing Number of Americans Think That Solar Electricity Should Be Offered on All New Homes," *Renewable Energy World*, May 31, 2007, www.renewableenergyworld.

2. Solar Navigator, "Archimedes 287 BC–211 BC," www.solarnavigator.net/inventors/archimedes.htm.

3. Solcomhouse, "Solar Power: How Does Solar Power Work?" www.solcomhouse.com/solarpower.htm.

4. David Shukman, "Power Station Harnesses Sun's Rays," *BBC News*, May 2, 2007, www.newsbb.co.uk/2/hi/science/nature/6616651; and David Mills and Rob Morgan, "Solar Thermal Electricity as the Primary Replacement for Coal and Oil in U.S. Generation and Transportation" (Palo Alto, CA: Ausra Inc., March 6, 2008).

5. Green Trust, "Solar Pond," www.green-trust.org/solarpond.htm; "Nanotechnology Advances the Efforts to Achieve Artificial Photosynthesis," *Nanowerk*, Dec. 5, 2006, www.nanowerk.com/spotlight/spotid=1098.php.

6. Martin I. Hoffert and Seth D. Potter, "Beam It Down: How the New Satellites Can Power the World," *Spacefuture.com*, Oct. 1997.

7. "Whatever Happened to Wind Energy?" *LiveScience.com*, Jan. 14, 2008; and Canadian Wind Energy Association, "Understanding Wind Energy: How Wind Is Produced," www.canwea.ca.

8. Mark Z. Jacobson and Gilbert M. Master, "Energy: Exploring Wind Versus Coal," *Science*, Aug. 24, 2001.

9. Mick Sagrillo, "Putting Wind Power's Effect on Birds in Perspective," http://www.renewwisconsin.org/wind/Toolbox-Fact%20Sheets/Birds.pdf.

10. Mohamed Bazza, "Overview of the History of Water Resources and Irrigation Management in the Near East Region," *Water Science and Technology: Water Supply* 7, no. 1, 201–9, http://www.iwaponline.com/ws/00701/01/default.htm.

11. Sandra M. Alters, *Energy: Supplies, Sustainability, and Costs* (Farmington Hills, MI: Thomson Gale, 2007), 86–87.

12. U.S. Department of Energy, Energy Efficiency and Renewable Energy, "How a Microhydropower System Works," www.eere.energy.gov.

13. U.S. Department of Energy, Energy Efficiency and Renewable Energy, "Ocean Wave Power," www.eere.energy.gov.

14. Description of tidal power projects comes from U.S. Department of Energy (DOE), Energy Efficiency and Renewable Energy, "Ocean Tidal Power," www.eere.energy.gov; DOE, "Ocean Tidal Power"; and Suzanne Pritchard, "Renewed Promise for Severn Power," *International Water Power and Dam Construction*, April 3, 2008, www.waterpowermagazine.com.

15. U.S. Department of Energy, Energy Efficiency and Renewable Energy, "Ocean Thermal Energy Conversion," www.eere.energy.gov; and Ocean Energy Council, "OTEC Energy," www.oceanenergycouncil.com/index.php /Ocean-Thermal-OTEC/OTEC.html.

16. Biofuel facts from American Coalition for Ethanol, "How It's Made," http:// www.ethanol.org/index.php?id=73&parentid=73; Renewable Fuels Association, "Ethanol Facts: Engine Performance," www.ethanolrfa.org/resource /facts/engine; and "Rudolf Diesel," DieselVeg, Ltd., www.dieselveg.com /rudolf_diesel.htm.

17. "Fibrominn Key Facts," Fibrowatt LLC, www.fibrowattusa.com.

18. U.S. Department of Energy, Energy Efficiency and Renewable Energy, "What Is Biogas?" www.eere.energy.gov.

19. John Sheehan et al., "A Look Back at the U.S. Department of Energy's Aquatic Species Program: Biodiesel from Algae" (Golden, CO: National Renewable Energy Laboratory, July 1998), http://www1.eere.energy.gov/biomass/pdfs /biodiesel_from_algae.pdf.

20. Deane Morrison, "Back to the Future: Prairie Grasses Emerge as Rich Energy Source," University of Minnesota news release, Dec. 8, 2006.

21. World Nuclear Association, "The Nuclear Fuel Cycle," www.worldnuclear .org/info/inf03.html; "Researchers Describe How Natural Nuclear Reactor Worked in Gabon," *SpaceDaily.com*, Nov. 1, 2004; and World Nuclear Association, "The Fuel Cycle in Brief," http://www.world-nuclear.org/how /fuelcycle.html.

22. Statistics on the nuclear-power industry are from the International Atomic Energy Agency (IAEA), "50 Years of Civilian Nuclear Power," press release,

May 2004, www.iaea.org; European Nuclear Society, "Nuclear Power Plants, Worldwide," http://www.euronuclear.org/info/encyclopedia/n/nuclear-power-plant-world-wide.htm; Alters, *Energy*, 65; World Nuclear Association, "Nuclear Power Reactors and Uranium Requirements," reactor data to March 20, 2008; and IAEA, "Nuclear Power's Changing Future," press release, June 26, 2004.

23. "About Uranium," Xemplar Energy Corp., http://www.xemplar.ca/uranium_about.php.

24. Federation of State PIRGs (Public Interest Research Groups), "The High Cost of Nuclear Power: Why Maryland Can't Afford a New Reactor," March 6, 2007, www.uspirg.org.

25. Nathan E. Hultman et al., "What History Can Teach Us About the Future Costs of U.S. Nuclear Power," *Environmental Science and Technology*, April 1, 2007, 2089, 2091.

26. Robert S. Mueller, testimony at the Senate Committee on Intelligence, February 16, 2005, http://www.fbi.gov/news/testimony/global-threats-to-the-u.s.-and-the-fbis-response-1.

27. Paul Leventhal, "Nuclear Power Reactors Are Inadequately Protected Against Terrorist Attack," testimony to the House Committee on Energy and Commerce's Subcommittee on Oversight and Investigations, Dec. 5, 2001.

28. Dr. Werner Zittel, "Uranium Resources and Nuclear Energy" (Berlin: Energy Watch Group, Dec. 2006), 13; and Energy Watch Group, "Energy Watch Group Warns: Depleting Uranium Reserves Dash Hopes for Atomic Energy Supply," press release, Nov. 29, 2006.

29. International Atomic Energy Agency, "Analysis of Uranium Supply to 2050" (Vienna: IAEA, 2001), 4; and James Hopf, "World Uranium Reserves," Nov. 2004, www.AmericanEnergyIndependence.com/uranium.html.

30. National Renewable Energy Laboratory Geothermal Technologies Program, "About Geothermal Electricity," www.nrel.gov/geothermal/geoelectricity.html; and California Energy Commission Renewable Energy Program, "Geothermal Electricity," http://www.energy.ca.gov/2005publications/CEC-300-2005-007/CEC-300-2005-007-FS.pdf.

31. James M. Taylor, "Geothermal Power Would Harm California, Claims Lawsuit," *Environment News*, July 1, 2004, www.heartland.org/Article.cfm?artID=15261.

32. U.S. Department of Energy, Energy Efficiency and Renewable Energy, "Hydrogen, Fuel Cells, and Infrastructure Technologies Program: Electrolytic

Processes," www1.eere.energy.gov; and Fuel Cells 2000, "Fuel Cell Basics: How They Work," www.fuelcells.org/basics/how.html.

33. Examples of hydrogen as an energy medium are taken from Prachi Patel-Predd, "Hydrogen from Algae," *Technology Review*, Sept. 27, 2007; Brookhaven National Laboratory, "Using Microbes to Fuel the U.S. Hydrogen Economy," www.bnl.gov; and Jennifer Chu, "Making Fuel from Leftovers," *Technology Review*, Nov. 26, 2007.

Chapter 4: Energy and Good Government

1. Laton McCartney, *The Teapot Dome Scandal: How Big Oil Bought the Harding White House and Tried to Steal the Country* (New York: Random House, 2008).

2. "Big Oil, Big Influence," Public Broadcasting Service "NOW" episode broadcast on the week of August 1, 2008, http://www.pbs.org/now/shows/347/oil-politics.html.

3. Dana Milbank and Justin Blum, "Document Says Oil Chiefs Met with Cheney Task Force," *Washington Post*, Nov. 16, 2005, A1; and Michael Abramowitz and Steven Mufson, "Papers Detail Industry's Role in Cheney's Energy Report," *Washington Post*, July 18, 2007, A1.

4. Charles Lane, "High Court Backs Vice President," *Washington Post*, June 25, 2004, A1.

5. Seth Borenstein, "Bush Changes Pledge on Emissions," *Philadelphia Inquirer*, March 14, 2001.

6. Union of Concerned Scientists (UCS) and the Government Accountability Project, "Atmosphere of Pressure: Political Interference in Federal Climate Science" (Cambridge, MA: UCS Publications, June 30, 2007).

7. James Hansen, "Political Interference with Government Climate Change Science," testimony to the House Committee on Oversight and Government Reform, March 19, 2007.

8. Andrew C. Revkin, "Bush Aide Edited Climate Reports," *New York Times*, June 8, 2005.

9. Memorandum, "Full Committee Hearing on Political Interference with Science: Global Warming, Part II," House Committee on Oversight and Government Reform, March 19, 2007, 1.

10. Andrew C. Revkin, "Bush Aide Softened Greenhouse Gas Links to Global Warming," *New York Times*, June 8, 2005.

11. U.S. House of Representatives Committee on Oversight and Government Reform, "Committee Report: Political Interference with Climate Change Science Under the Bush Administration," December 2007, http://oversight .house.gov/images/stories/documents/20071210101633.pdf.

12. Rick Piltz, "Hearing on Allegations of Political Interference with the Work of Government Climate Change Scientists," testimony to House Committee on Oversight and Government Reform, Jan. 30, 2007; and Rick Piltz, "Censorship and Secrecy: Politicizing the Climate Change Science Program," *ClimateScienceWatch.org*, June 8, 2005.

13. Information on Cooney's academic background and employment with ExxonMobil is from Center for Media and Democracy/Sourcewatch, "Philip A. Cooney," www.sourcewatch.org.

14. Union of Concerned Scientists (UCS), "Smoke, Mirrors, and Hot Air: How ExxonMobil Uses Big Tobacco's Tactics to Manufacture Uncertainty on Climate Science" (Cambridge, MA: UCS Publications, January 2007).

15. Greenpeace/Exxon Secrets, "Factsheet: William O'Keefe," www.exxon secrets.org.

16. Oliver Burkeman, "Memo Exposes Bush's New Green Strategy," *Guardian* (Manchester, England), March 4, 2003; and "Frank Luntz Memorandum to Bush White House, 2002," http://www2.bc.edu/~plater/Newpublicsite06 /suppmats/02.6.pdf.

17. "California Sues EPA for Delaying Global Warming Waiver," *Environmental News Service*, Nov. 8, 2007; and Office of the Governor, "Governor Schwarzenegger Announces Lawsuit Against U.S. EPA for Failing to Act on California's Tailpipe Emissions Request," press release, Nov. 8, 2007.

18. David Ehrlich, "U.S. EPA Chief May Have Ignored Advice on Emissions," *Cleantech.com*, Feb. 27, 2008; and Frank Davies, "EPA Chief Ignored Advice on Emissions," *San Jose Mercury News*, Feb. 27, 2008, A5.

19. John M. Broder and Felicity Barringer, "EPA Says 17 States Can't Set Emission Rules," *New York Times*, Dec. 20, 2007.

20. Frank Davies, "EPA Explains Waiver Denial," *San Jose Mercury News*, March 1, 2008, A7.

21. "Senator Boxer Bashes EPA Head: 'I've Never Seen Anything Like It,'" *The DailyGreen.com*, video, Jan. 25, 2008, www.thedailygreen.com/environmental-news/latest/boxer-EPA-global_warming-490125.

22. Associated Press, "EPA's Johnson Defense Actions," May 20, 2008.

23. Union of Concerned Scientists (UCS), "Hundreds of EPA Scientists Report Political Interference over Last Five Years," press release, April 23, 2008; and "Voices of EPA Scientists Survey: Human Health and the Environment Depend on Independence Science" (Cambridge, MA: UCS Publications, 2007).

24. Thomas Jefferson, letter to the Republican Citizens of Washington County, Maryland, 1809.

Chapter 5: Energy and National Security

1. James R. Reckner, *Teddy Roosevelt's Great White Fleet* (Annapolis, MD: Naval Institute Press, 1988), 155.

2. Nick Turse, "The Military-Petroleum Complex," *Foreign Policy in Focus*, March 24, 2008, www.fpif.org/fpifxt/5097.

3. Dr. Gal Luft, "America's Oil Dependence and Its Implications for U.S. Middle East Policy," testimony to the Senate Foreign Relations Subcommittee on Near Eastern and South Asian Affairs, Oct. 20, 2005.

4. Gibson Consulting, "Some Interesting Oil Statistics," www.gravmag.com/oil.html.

5. Stuart Levey, Under Secretary Office of Terrorism and Financial Intelligence for the U.S. Department of Treasury, testimony to the Senate Committee on Banking, Housing, and Urban Affairs, July 13, 2005.

6. Senator Kay Bailey Hutchison, "Stability and Democracy in Latin America" (speech, U.S. Senate, Washington, DC, March 14, 2007), www.senate/gov/~hutchison/speech550.html.

7. Natural Resources Defense Council, "Safe, Strong, and Secure: Reducing America's Oil Dependence," www.nrdc.org/air/transportation/aoilpolicy2.asp.

8. Jad Mouawad, "OPEC Gathering Finds High Oil Prices More Worrisome Than Welcome," *New York Times*, Nov. 17, 2007.

9. Milton Copulos, "The Hidden Cost of Oil: An Update" (Arlington, VA: National Defense Council Foundation, January 2007).

10. Alyeska Pipeline Service Company, "Pipeline Facts," www.alyeska-pipe.com/pipelinefacts.html.

11. Brian Whitaker, "Tank Blast Was Work of Terrorist," *Guardian* (Manchester, England), Oct. 17, 2002.

12. Louisiana Offshore Oil Port, "LOOP Receiving Tanker Shipments of Crude Oil," press release, Sept. 2, 2005.

13. Peter Schwartz and Doug Randall, "An Abrupt Climate Change Scenario and Its Implications for United States National Security," Oct. 2003, http://www.gbn.com/GBNDocumentDisplayServlet.srv?aid=26231&url=/UploadDocumentDisplayServlet.srv?id=28566.

14. General Gordon R. Sullivan (ret. U.S. Army) et al., "National Security and the Threat of Climate Change" (Alexandria, VA: CNA Corporation, April 2007).

15. Dan Smith and Janani Vivekananda, "A Climate of Conflict: The Links Between Climate Change, Peace, and War," *International Alert*, Nov. 2007.

16. Donald F. Fournier and Eileen T. Westervelt, "Energy Trends and Their Implications for U.S. Army Installations" (Vicksburg, MS: U.S. Army Engineer Research and Development Center, Sept. 2005).

17. CNA's Military Advisory Board, "Powering America's Defense: Energy and the Risks to National Security," May 2009, http://www.ncoc.net/index.php?tray=content&tid=top12&cid=2gp13.

18. John M. Amidon, "America's Strategic Imperative: A 'Manhattan Project' for Energy," *Joint Forces Quarterly*, no. 39 (2005), 68–77.

19. Military branches using clean-tech passage come from various sources: Peter Hoy, "The World's Biggest Fuel Consumer," *Forbes*, June 5, 2008; Alexandra Zavis, "Military Embraces Green Energy, for National Security Reasons," *Los Angeles Times*, April 26, 2009; "Navy, Army Push to Meet Renewable Energy Goals," *Environmental Leader*, March 18, 2010; "Military Seeks Fuel Efficiency with Ships and Electric Vehicles," *Environmental Leader*, May 21, 2009.

20. Jephraim P. Gundzik, "Solid Foreign Relations to Underpin Strong Economic Growth in Venezuela," *Power and Interest News Report*, Oct. 20, 2006, www.pinr.com; "Deal for Oil Fields Extends China's Quest for Energy," *New York Times*, March 15, 2010; "China Fuels Global Growth in Oil Demand," *Procurement Leaders*, March 17, 2010; Dr. Gal Luft, "Fueling the Dragon: China's Race into the Oil Market," *IAGS Spotlight* (Institute of the Analysis of Global Security), n.d., http://www.iags.org/china.htm; and Gal Luft and Anne Korin, "The Sino-Saudi Connection," *Commentary Magazine*, March 2004.

21. Luft, "Fueling the Dragon."

22. Luft, "America's Oil Dependence and Its Implications for U.S. Middle East Policy."

Chapter 6: Energy and the Environment

1. Peter Thomas and Donna Thomas, "A Trans-California Ramble: Rewalking John Muir's 1868 Trip from San Francisco to Yosemite: April 2–May 14, 2006," www.johnmuir.org/walk/indext.html.

2. John Muir, "The Treasures of the Yosemite," *The Century Magazine* 40, no. 4 (1890).

3. Deepwater Horizon material comes from various sources: "Investigating the Cause of the Deepwater Horizon Blowout," *New York Times*, June 21, 2010; Jessica Resnick-Ault and Katarzyna Klimasinska, "Transocean Rig Sinks in Gulf of Mexico as Coast Guard Looks for Survivors," *Bloomberg News*, April 22, 2010; "BP Leak the World's Worst Accidental Oil Spill," *London Telegraph*, Aug. 3, 2010; "Obama Blasts Oil Execs for Gulf Spill Finger-Pointing," National Public Radio, May 14, 2010; "Spill Costs Tally to $11.2 Billion for BP," *Forbes*, Oct. 1, 2010; "BP's Hayward Takes a Day Off for Yacht Race, Infuriating Gulf Residents," *Washington Post*, June 20, 2010; Henry Fountain, "U.S. Says BP Well Is Finally 'Dead,'" *New York Times*, Sept. 19, 2010; Gerald Herbert, "Has the Gulf Oil Spill Changed U.S. Attitudes?" Associated Press, Sept. 30, 2010.

4. Kristen Hays and Tom Fowler, "BP Will Plead to Felony in Plant Blast," *Houston Chronicle*, Oct. 26, 2007; "Prices Climbing After Oil Field Shutdown: BP Regrets 'Drastic Action' of Shutdown," *CNN.com*, Aug. 9, 2007; and U.S. Public Interest Research Group (PIRG) Educational Fund, quoting the Alaska Department of Environmental Conservation, in "Saving America's Arctic: Dispelling Myths About Drilling in the Arctic National Wildlife Refuge" (Washington, DC: U.S. PIRG Education Fund, Sept. 2005).

5. Stuart Hertzog, "Oil and Water Don't Mix: Keeping Canada's West Coast Oil Free" (Vancouver: David Suzuki Foundation, March 2003).

6. "Oil—Environmental Concerns About Oil Transportation," Library Index, www.libraryindex.com/page1505/Oil-Environmental-Concerns-About-Oil-Transportation.

7. Sierra Club, "Oil and Gas Drilling Is Dirty Business—Hurricane Risks," www.sierraclub.org/wildlegacy/bigoil/factsheet.asp; and "In Katrina's Wake," *Environmental Health Perspectives* 114, no. 1 (2006), www.ehponline.org/members/2006/114-1/focus.html.

8. Derek R. Lovley, "Bioremediation: Anaerobes to the Rescue," *Science*, Aug. 24, 2001, 1444–46.

9. Energy Information Administration, "China Energy Data, Statistics, and Analysis—Oil, Gas, Electricity, Coal," www.eia.doe.gov/emeu/cabs/Chiana/Coal.html.

10. James Russell, "Coal Use Rises Dramatically Despite Impacts on Climate and Health" (Washington, DC: Worldwatch Institute, 2008), www.worldwatch.org/node/5508; and "China's Mercury Flushes into Oregon's Rivers," *Oregonian*, Nov. 24, 2006.

11. The National Academies, "Coal: Research and Development to Support National Energy Policy" (report prepared for a briefing to Congress, June 18, 2007).

12. Union of Concerned Scientists, "Biofuels: An Important Part of a Low-Carbon Diet," Nov. 2007, www.ucsusa.org/clean_vehicles/vehicles_health/biofuels-low-carbon-diet.html.

13. Gary Braasch, *Earth Under Fire: How Global Warming Is Changing the World* (Berkeley: University of California Press, 2007).

14. David Adam, "Loss of Arctic Ice Leaves Experts Stunned," *Guardian* (Manchester, England), Sept. 4, 2007, http://www.guardian.co.uk/environment/2007/sep/04/climatechange.

15. "Arctic Ice Revealed," *NASA Science News*, Aug. 22, 2000, http://science.nasa.gov/headlines/y2000/ast22aug_1.htm.

16. Jane G. Ferrigno et al., "Coastal Change and Glaciological Map of the Palmer Land Area, Antarctica 1947–2009," United States Geological Survey report, Feb. 2009, http://pubs.usgs.gov/imap/i-2600-c/.

17. Description of global warming's impact on Antarctica is from Public Broadcasting System, "Antarctic Almanac," *NOVA*, www.pbs.org/wgbh/nova/warnings/almanac.html; National Snow and Ice Data Center, "Larsen B Ice Shelf Collapses in Antarctica," March 18, 2002, www.nsidc.org/iceshelves/larsenb2002/; and "Warming to Cause Catastrophic Rise in Sea Levels?" *National Geographic*, April 26, 2004, http://news.nationalgeographic.com/news/2004/04/0420_040420_earthday.html.

18. "Marine Plants Die in Warmer Oceans, Speeding Climate Change," *Environmental News Service*, Dec. 7, 2006.

19. Scott C. Doney and Naomi M. Levine, "How Long Can the Ocean Slow Global Warming? How Much Excess Carbon Dioxide Can the Ocean Hold

and How Will It Affect Marine Life?" *Oceanus*, Nov. 29, 2006, www.whoi .edu/oceanus/; and James C. Orr et al., "Anthropogenic Ocean Acidification over the Twenty-First Century and Its Impact on Calcifying Organisms," *Nature*, Sept. 29, 2005, 681–86.

20. National Science Foundation, "Hurricanes Growing More Fierce over Past 30 Years," press release, July 31, 2005; "The Increasing Intensity of the Strongest Tropical Cyclones," *Nature*, Sept. 2008, www.nature.com/nature/journal/ v455/n7209/full/nature07234.html.

21. United Nations Population Division, "The World at Six Billion," http://www .un.org/esa/population/publications/sixbillion/sixbilpart1.pdf.

22. Joseph A. McFalls, "Population: A Lively Introduction," *Population Bulletin* 62, no. 1 (2007).

23. Natalia Shakhova et al., "Extensive Methane Venting to the Atmosphere from Sediments of the East Siberian Arctic Shelf," *Science*, March 5, 2010. (Go to http://www.sciencemag.org/content/327/5970/1265.2.full to hear a podcast on the study.)

24. University of Leeds, "Climate Change Threatens a Million Species with Extinction," press release, Jan. 7, 2004; "The Day the Seas Died: What Can the Greatest of All Extinction Events Teach Us About Climate Change?" *Daily Galaxy*, Aug. 10, 2007; and American Museum of Natural History, "National Survey Reveals Biodiversity Crisis—Scientific Experts Believe We Are in Midst of Fastest Mass Extinction in Earth's History," press release, April 20, 1998, www.well.com/~davidu/amnh.html.

25. James Lovelock, "Nuclear Power Is the Only Green Solution," *Independent* (U.K.), May 24, 2004.

26. Jan Willem Storm van Leeuwen and Philip Smith, "Can Nuclear Power Provide Energy for the Future; Would It Solve the CO_2-Emission Problem?" Oct. 12, 2004 (available at http://www.greatchange.org/bb-thermochemical-nuclear_sustainability_rev.pdf).

27. Judy Pasternak, "A Peril That Dwelt Among the Navajos," *Los Angeles Times*, Nov. 19, 2006.

28. Helen Caldicott, *Nuclear Power Is Not the Answer* (New York: New Press, 2006), 9.

29. Description of nuclear reactor safety issues comes from Edwin S. Lyman, Ph.D., senior scientist with the Global Security Program, Union of Concerned Scientists, testimony to the U.S. Senate Subcommittee on Clean Air, Climate Change, and Nuclear Safety Committee on Environment and Public Works,

May 26, 2005; and National Research Council, National Academies, "Safety and Security of Commercial Spent Nuclear Fuel Storage" (Washington, DC: National Academies Press, 2006).

30. Statistics on radioactive waste disposal come from People for a Nuclear-Free Australia, "PNFA Fact Sheet: Medical Hazards of Radioactive Waste," www .pnfa.org.au/pdf/pnfa_fs3.pdf; and U.S. Department of Energy, "How Much Nuclear Waste Is in the United States?" www.ocrwm.doe.gov.

31. William Poole, "Gambling with Tomorrow," *Sierra Club Magazine*, Nov./Dec. 1992; and State of Nevada, Agency for Nuclear Projects, "Earthquakes in the Vicinity of Yucca Mountain," www.state.nv.us/nucwaste/yucca/seismo01 .htm.

32. Organization for Economic Cooperation and Development (OECD), International Atomic Energy Agency, and Nuclear Energy Agency, "An International Peer Review of the Yucca Mountain Project TSPA-SR: Total System Performance Assessment for the Site Recommendation" (Paris: OECD Publications, 2002).

33. Kenny C. Guinn, testimony to the Committee on Transportation and Infrastructure, Subcommittees on Railroads and Transportation and Hazardous Materials, United States House of Representatives, April 25, 2002.

34. Elizabeth A. Thomson, "Fusion Energy May Be Here by 2050, MIT Physicist Predicts," *MIT Tech Talk*, Feb. 27, 2002; and David L. Chandler, "No Future for Fusion Power, Says Top Scientist," *NewScientist.com*, March 2006.

Chapter 7: Energy and the Economy

1. Union of Concerned Scientists, "Current and Future Energy Trends," www .ucsusa.org/clean_energy.

2. Joseph Coton Wright, "Oil: Demand, Supply, and Trends in the United States," ca. 2006, http://dr.berkeley.edu/pdfs_to_post/OIL_OVERVIEW _OF_5DECADE_HISTORY_AND_TODAYS_CHALLENGES -1.pdf.

3. Statistics cited are from InflationData.com, "Historical Crude Oil Price (Table)," updated Jan. 16, 2008; and "Oil Sets New Trading Record Above $147 a Barrel," *ABCNEWS.go.com*, July 11, 2008, http://abcnews.go.com/ Business/PainAtThePump/wireStory?id=5353919.

4. Frank Ackerman and Elizabeth A. Stanton, "The Cost of Climate Change: What We'll Pay if Global Warming Continues Unchecked," National Re-

sources Defense Council, May 2008, http://www.nrdc.org/globalwarming/cost/fcost.pdf.

5. Sir Nicholas Stern, "The Stern Review: The Economics of Climate Change" (report prepared for Her Majesty's Treasury Department, London, Oct. 30, 2006), http://www.hm-treasury.gov.uk/independent_reviews/stern_review_economics_climate_change/stern_review_report.cfm.

6. Zachary Coile, "'Cap-and-Trade' Model Eyed for Cutting Greenhouse Gases," *San Francisco Chronicle*, Dec. 3, 2007.

7. U.S. Department of Energy documents: "Overview of the Electric Grid," www.energetics.com/gridworks/grid.html; "U.S. Power Grids," www.eere.energy.gov/de/us_power_grids.html; and "Gasification Technology R&D," www.fossil.energy.gov/programs/powcrsystcms/gasification/index.html.

8. Sean Casten, "Generate Energy Locally, Recycle Whenever Possible," *Grist Environmental News & Commentary*, April 23, 2008.

9. Brian Kingham, "Wide-Area Power Quality Analysis System for Utility Grid Applications" (Schneider Electric, 2006); and Joseph McClelland, "The Cyber Threat to Control Systems: Stronger Regulations Are Necessary to Secure the Electric Grid," testimony to Committee on Homeland Security's Subcommittee on Energy Threats, Cybersecurity, and Science and Technology, United States House of Representatives, Oct. 17, 2007.

10. Jon Wellinghoff, cited in Brian Bergstein, "Smarter Electric Grid Could Be Key to Saving Power," Associated Press, May 4, 2008.

11. U.S. Department of Energy, Office of Electricity Delivery and Energy Reliability, "The Electricity Delivery System," Feb. 2006, www.electricity.doe.gov; and Marsha Freeman, "U.S. Electric Grid Is Reaching the End Game," *Executive Intelligence Review*, Sept. 22, 2006.

12. Descriptions of the modernization of the electric power grid come from Electric Power Research Institute, "The IntelliGrid Consortium: Leading the Drive to Transform the Power Delivery System," www.epri.com; Campaign for Great Green Jobs, "Creating Jobs, Saving Money, Enhancing Security and Environmental Protection Through Energy Efficiency," www.GreatGreenJobsforPA.org; and Jean Elliott, "The Electric Slide, Fixing America's Power Grid," *Research Magazine*, Summer 2006, http://www.research.vt.edu/resmag/2006Summer/Slide.html.

13. MSNBC News Service, "Is Wal-Mart Going Green?" Oct. 25, 2005.

14. Lee Scott, "Twenty-First Century Leadership" (speech given at Walmart

meeting, Jan. 23, 2008); Michael Barbaro and Felicity Barringer, "Wal-Mart to Seek Savings in Energy," *New York Times*, Oct. 25, 2005.

15. Malika Worrall, "Green Energy Makes Money: Venture Investments in American Clean Technology Firms Reach a New High," *Fortune*, Nov. 29, 2007.

16. Cleantech Group LLC, "Clean Technology Venture Investment Totaled $5.6 Billion in 2009 Despite Non-binding Climate Change Accord in Copenhagen, Finds Cleantech Group and Deloitte," press release, Jan. 6, 2010, www .cleantech.com/about/pressreleases/20090106.cfm.

17. Deborah Gage, "Kleiner Perkins Bets Big on Green Tech Firms," *San Francisco Chronicle*, May 2, 2008; and Fred Krupp, "Climate Change Opportunity," *Wall Street Journal*, April 8, 2008, A20.

18. Brita Belli, "Welcome to Green-Collar America: Does the Future of the American Middle Class Lie in Sustainable Business?" *Emagazine.com*, Nov./Dec. 2007.

19. Daniel M. Kammen et al., "Putting Renewables to Work: How Many Jobs Can the Clean Energy Industry Generate?" report of the Renewable and Appropriate Energy Laboratory, Goldman School of Public Policy, University of California at Berkeley, Jan. 31, 2006.

20. Robert Pollin, James Heintz, and Heidi Garrett-Peltier, "The Economic Benefits of Investing in Clean Energy," University of Massachusetts, Amherst, and the Center for American Progress, June 2009, www.americanprogress. org/issues/2009/06/pdf/peri_report.pdf.

21. United States Geological Survey, Fact Sheet 0028-01: Online Report, "Arctic National Refuge, 1002 Area, Petroleum Assessment, 1998, Including Economic Analysis," http://pubs.usgs.gov/fs/fs-0028-01/fs-0028-01.htm.

22. Roger H. Von Haefen, "Can Ethanol End Our Oil Addiction?" *NC State Economist*, March/April 2007.

Chapter 8: Energy and Transportation

1. Statistics cited come from the Surface Transportation and Policy Project, "Transportation and Climate Change," www.transact.org/library/factsheets /climate.asp; and Brookhaven National Laboratory, "Ridesharing Benefits," www.bnl.gov/rideshare/benefits.asp.

2. "Traffic Facts and Figures: How Does Traffic Affect Us? A List of Facts and Figures to Put It in Perspective," *ABCNews.com*, Feb. 23, 2005.

3. Mile-per-gallon numbers for the United States, Japan, and Europe are from U.S. Department of Transportation, Bureau of Transportation Statistics, "Average Fuel Efficiency of U.S. Passenger Cars and Light Trucks," www.bts .gov/publications/national_transportation_statistics/html; and Bilal Zuberi, "A Drive Toward Fuel Economy," *Boston Globe*, Aug. 13, 2007.

4. Statistics cited are from American Association of State Highway and Transportation Officials, "Transportation: Invest in Our Future," www.transporta tion1.org/tif1report/glance.html; and Center for Transportation Excellence, "All Factoids," http://www.cfte.org/factoids/default.asp.

5. "California's Rough Pavement Puts State at Top of Worst Road List . . . Again, Transportation California Says," *The Auto Channel*, www.theautochannel .com/news/2008/03/12/080633.html.

6. Mark Clayton, "Safe Cars Versus Fuel Efficiency? Not So Fast," *Christian Science Monitor*, June 12, 2007.

7. Marc Ross and Tom Wenzel, "An Analysis of Traffic Deaths by Vehicle Type and Model," University of Michigan and Lawrence Berkeley National Laboratory, March 2002, http://www.lbl.gov/Science-Articles/Archive/assets /images/2002/Aug-26-2002/SUV-report.pdf.

8. Mackinac Center for Public Policy, "The Great Race: The Technological Challenges of More Fuel-Efficient Vehicles," Aug. 8, 2007, www.mackinac .org/article.aspx?ID=8869.

9. "GM Pulls Plug on Electric Car, Automaker Spent $1 Billion on Program; Never Sold One," *CBSNews.com*, March 11, 2003.

10. "Hybrid Battery Toxicity," *HybridCars.com*, April 8, 2006, www.hybridcars .com/battery-toxicity.html.

11. State of California, "Governor Schwarzenegger Announces the California Hydrogen Highways Network," press release, April 20, 2004; and Paul Rogers, "Hydrogen Highway Hits Roadblock," *San Jose Mercury News*, March 31, 2008.

12. Philip Reed and Mike Hudson, "Fuel Economy: We Test the Tips: What Really Saves Gas? and How Much?" *Edmunds.com*, Nov. 22, 2005, www .edmunds.com/advice/fueleconomy/articles/106842/article.html.

13. Joanne Helperin, "Driving Tips: Commuter Carpools Save Time, Money, and Stress," *Edmunds.com*, Oct. 4, 2005, www.edmunds.com/owernship /driving/articles/107371/article.html; and U.S. Census Bureau, "Most of Us Still Drive to Work—Alone," press release, June 13, 2007.

14. Minnesota Work-Life Champions, "The Advantages of Telecommuting," www.worklifechampions.org/practices_resources/documents/TheAdvant agesofTelecommuting_000.pdf.

15. Various statistics are from American Public Transportation Association (APTA), "Historical Ridership Trends," May 5, 2008, www.apta.com /research/stats/ridership/ridetrnd.cfm; APTA, "Public Transportation and Petroleum Savings in the U.S.: Reducing Dependence on Oil," Jan. 9, 2007; and Center for Transportation Excellence, "All Factoids."

16. Eric Young, "BART to Test Using Cell Phones as Tickets," *San Francisco Business Times*, Jan. 11, 2008.

17. John Semmens, "Public Transit: A Bad Product at a Bad Price," *Heritage Foundation*, Feb. 13, 2007, www.heritage.org/research/smartGrowth/wm213.cfm.

18. American Association of State Highway and Transportation Officials, "Transportation Revenue Needs: Current Federal Highway Trust Fund Revenues," www.transportation1.org/tif2report/trans_revenue.html; and John M. Brode, "Obama's Bid to End Oil Subsidies Revives Debate," *New York Times*, Jan. 31, 2011.

19. Smart Growth America, "What Is Smart Growth?" www.smartgrowthamerica .org/whatisg.html.

20. Examples of fuel consumption in the trucking industry come from "TRIP Report Finds Need for National Freight Policy: Safety and Mobility at Risk with Coming Surge in Truck Traffic," *BusinessWire.com*, Feb. 10, 2004; "Independent Truck Drivers Struggle to Survive as Diesel Prices Soar," Associated Press, April 1, 2008; Con-way Freight, "Con-way Freight Turns Back Speed Governors on Trucking Fleet," press release, March 10, 2008; "Low-Drag Trucks: Aerodynamic Improvements and Flow Control System Boost Fuel Efficiency in Heavy Trucks," *ScienceDaily*, Jan. 10, 2005; Clean Air Power, "Dual-Fuel Technology," www .cleanairpower.com/duel-technology.php; and FedEx, "Hybrid Electric Vehicle," www.fedex.com/us/about/responsibility/environment/hybridelec tricvehicle.html.

21. National Atlas, "Overview of U.S. Freight Railroads," www.nationalatlas .gov/articles/transportation/a_freightrr.html.

22. Michael Kanellos, "Sail-Powered Cargo Ship Test Results In: It Cut Fuel by 20 percent," *CNetnews.com*, March 19, 2008.

23. Jennifer Waters, "Say Goodbye to Cheap Flights, Maybe Peanuts, Too," *Market Watch.com*, April 8, 2008.

24. Andrew C. Revkin and Heather Timmons, "Branson Pledges to Finance Clean Fuels," *New York Times*, Sept. 22, 2006.

Chapter 9: Energy and Agriculture

1. Katherine Ainger, "Gleanings: The New Peasants Revolt," Rodale Institute, www.newfarm.org/depts/gleanings/0503/peasantrevolt.shtml.

2. Statistics on fossil fuel use in agriculture are from Worldwatch Institute, "State of the World 2004 Special Focus: The Consumer Society" (Washington, DC: Worldwatch Institute, Jan. 2004); Wisconsin Foodshed Research Project, "Food and Energy: Another Way to Count Calories," www.cias.wisc.edu/foodshed/pubsntools/meal1.htm; Tom Starrs, "The SUV in the Pantry," *Solar Today*, July/Aug. 2005, www.solartoday.org/2005/july_aug05/chairs-cornerJA05.htm; Stan Cox, "Hunger for Natural Gas," *AlterNet*, Oct. 12, 2005, www.chlseagreen.com/2004/items/highnoon/AssociatedArticles; and Ford B. West, "The High Price of Natural Gas and Its Impact on the U.S. Fertilizer Industry," testimony to the U.S. Senate Appropriations Interior and Related Agencies Subcommittee, Oct. 25, 2005.

3. Various statistics in this paragraph are from International Fertilizer Industry Association, "Greenhouse Gas Emissions, Sequestration, and Agriculture," http://www.fertilizer.org/ifa/Home-Page/LIBRARY/Publications.html/Global-Estimates-of-Gaseous-Emissions-of-NH3-NO-and-N2O-from-Agricultural-Land.html, citing data from the Organization for Economic Cooperation and Development; Laura Sayre, "New Finding: Organic Farming Combats Global Warming . . . Big Time," Rodale Institute, Oct. 10, 2003, www.newfarm.org/depts/NFfield_trials/1003/carbonsequest.shtml; and Associated Press, "World Fells Trees at 'Alarming' Rate, Expert Says," Feb. 3, 2008, citing the United Nations, "State of the World's Forests" report.

4. Juliet Eilperin, "More Frequent Heat Waves Linked to Global Warming: U.S. and European Researchers Call Long Hot Spells Likely," *Washington Post*, Aug. 4, 2006; and Intergovernmental Panel on Climate Change (hereafter IPCC), "Climate Change 2007: Impacts, Adaptation, and Vulnerability," April 6, 2007, www.ipccinfo.com/midwest.php.

5. David Lobell et al., "Prioritizing Climate Change Adaption Needs for Food Security in 2030," *Science*, Feb. 1, 2008, 607–10.

6. IPCC, "Fourth Assessment Report," Feb. 2, 2007.

7. Scientific research cited in this section comes from the Food and Agriculture Organization of the United Nations, "Dimensions of Need—Global Warming,"

www.fao.org/docrep/U8480E/U8480E0y.htm; Daniel R. Taub et al., "Effects of Elevated CO_2 on the Protein Concentration of Food Crops: An Analysis," *Global Change*, March 2008, 565–75; Lancaster Farming, "Research Shows Climate Change Could Bring More Weed Problems," April 4, 2008, citing research by the Weed Science Society of America, www.lancasterfarming.com/node/1179; United States House of Representatives, Select Committee on Energy Independence and Global Warming, "Health," www.globalwarming.house.gov/issues /globalwarming?id=0006; Larry J. Schweiger, "Global Warming: Is Time Running Out?" *National Wildlife Magazine*, Aug./Sept. 2006, www.nwf.org; and Civil Society Institute, "Experts: U.S. Agriculture, Food Supply Face Major Dangers and Some Opportunities from Global Warming," press release, Sept. 29, 2003, www.resultsforamerica.org/media/press_030929.php.

8. "Ocean Acidification Due to Increasing Atmospheric Carbon Dioxide," *Royal Society*, June 2005, www.royalsoc.ac.uk.

9. Union of Concerned Scientists, "Fact Sheet: Farming the Wind: Wind Power and Agriculture," http://www.ucsusa.org/assets/documents/clean_energy/ agfs_wind_2003.pdf; and U.S. Department of Energy, Office of Energy Efficiency and Renewable Energy, "Wind Powering America," May 2001, http:// www.nrel.gov/docs/fy01osti/29895.pdf.

10. Sustainable Agriculture Research and Education, "Smart Water Use on Your Farm or Ranch," www.sare.org/publications/water/water_10.htm.

11. "Study: Ethanol Production Consumes Six Units of Energy to Produce Just One," *Science Daily*, April 1, 2005, www.energybulletin.net/5062.html.

12. David Tilman and Jason Hill, "Biofuel Best for Ethanol Is Right at Home on the Range," *Washington Post*, March 24, 2007.

13. Emma Marris, "Putting the Carbon Back: Black Is the New Green," *Nature*, Aug. 10, 2006.

14. Janis Mara, "Dairies Convert Waste into Biogas for PG&E," *Oakland Tribune*, Nov. 6, 2007.

15. National Science Foundation, "From Farm Waste to Fuel Tanks," press release, Feb. 16, 2007.

16. Kazuhisa Miyamoto, ed., "Renewable Biological Systems for Alternative Sustainable Energy Production," FAO Agricultural Services Bulletin-128 (Rome: Food and Agricultural Organization of the United Nations, 1997), http://www.fao.org/docrep/w7241e/w7241e0g.htm.

17. Rainer Kalscheuer et al., "Microdiesel: *Escherichia coli* Engineered for Fuel Production," *Microbiology*, June 26, 2006.

18. "Energy Tech: Using Pond Scum to Fuel Our Future," *SpaceDaily.com*, Feb. 5, 2007; Mark Clayton, "Algae—Like a Breath Mint for Smokestacks," *Christian Science Monitor*, Jan. 11, 2006; and Sarah H. Wright, "Up on the Roof, Algae Appetites May Transform Waste into Energy," Massachusetts Institute of Technology news release, Aug. 9, 2004, http://web.mit.edu/newsoffice/2004/algae.html.

Chapter 10: Energy and Public Health

1. Details of Los Angeles from South Coast Air Quality Management District website, "The Southland's War on Smog: Fifty Years of Progress Toward Clean Air," May 1997, www.aqmd.gov/news1/Archives/History.marchcov.html.

2. Clean Air Task Force website, "Children at Risk: How Air Pollution from Power Plants Threatens the Health of America's Children," May 2002, www.catf.us/publications/reports/Children_at_Risk.pdf.

3. Environmental Defense Fund, "Coal-Fired Power Plants Are Big Contributors to Sooty Particle Pollution in Eastern States," April 24, 2007, www.edf.org/article.cfm?ContentID=3842.

4. National Academy of Sciences, "Reporter Examines Hidden Health and Environmental Costs of Energy Production and Consumption in U.S.," press release, Oct. 19, 2009, http://www8.nationalacademies.org/onpinews/news item.aspx?RecordID=12794.

5. Statistics cited are from the Clean Air Task Force, "Cradle to Grave: The Environmental Impacts from Coal," June 2001, http://www.catf.us/publications/reports/Cradle_to_Grave.pdf; American Heart Association, "Air Pollution, Heart Disease, and Stroke," www.americanheartorg/presenter.jhtml?identifier=4419; Environmental Defense Fund, "All Choked Up: Heavy Traffic, Dirty Air, and the Risk to New York," March 2007; Alice McKeown, "Burning Coal: Our Nation's Power Plants," June 2007, *Sierra Club Magazine*, p. 9; and OMB Watch, "Coal Miners Experience Unusual Occurrences of Black Lung Disease," www.ombwatch.org.

6. Ecomall, "Study Says Coal Plant Pollution Kills 30,000 a Year," www.ecomall.com/greenshopping/cleanair.htm; and Union of Concerned Scientists, "Fact Sheet: Healthy Children, Healthy Communities, and Healthy Economy in the San Joaquin Valley Act of 2005 (SB 999)," www.ucsusa.org/assets/documents/clean_vehicles/SB_999_Fact_Sheet.pdf.

7. Natural Resources Defense Council, "Sneezing and Wheezing: How Global Warming Could Increase Ragweed Allergies, Air Pollution, and Asthma," Oct. 2007, www.nrdc.org.

8. Center for Health and the Global Environment, "Experts: Childhood Asthma 'Epidemic' Among Inner-City Youths Seen in Absence of Steps to Curb Global Warming, Fossil Fuel Use," press release, April 29, 2004.

9. Jonathan A. Patz, "Impact of Regional Climate Change on Human Health," *Nature*, Nov. 17, 2005, 310–17.

10. Jose A. Suaya, et al., "Cost of Dengue Cases in Eight Countries in the Americas and Asia: A Prospective Study," *American Journal of Tropical Medicine and Hygiene*, May 2009.

11. Jonathan M. Gregory, "Threatened Loss of the Greenland Ice-Sheet," *Nature*, April 2004, 616; and Dr. Richard Podolsky, "Bright Lights, Big Ocean," International Dark-Sky Association information sheet #193, June 2003, www.darksky.org.

12. Central Ohio Public Information Network for Pandemic Flu, "History—Pandemic Influenza in the United States," www.columbuspandemicflue.com/history.html.

13. Climate Institute, "Human Health—Impacts of Natural Disasters," www.climate.org/topics/health.html; and "Katrina-Ravaged Gulf Coast Struggling 2 Years Later," *CNN.com*, Aug. 29, 2007, www.cnn.com/2007/US/08/29/katrina.day/index.html.

14. Climate Institute, "Human Health"; and Natural Resources Defense Council, "Consequences of Global Warming: Unless We Act Now, Our Children Will Inherit a Hotter World, Dirtier Air and Water, More Severe Floods and Droughts, and More Wildfires," www.nrdc.org/globalWarming/fcons.asp.

15. John Everett, Fishery Resources Division, Ocean Atlas, "Human Health, Harmful Algal Blooms, and Pollution," www.oceansatlas.org/world_fisheries_and_aquaculture/html.

16. U.S. Environmental Protection Agency, "Climate Change—Health and Environmental Effects," www.epa.gov/climatechange/effects/health.html.

17. Everett, "Human Health, Harmful Algal Blooms, and Pollution"; and Scott Doney, "Effects of Climate Change and Ocean Acidification on Living Marine Resources," written testimony presented to the U.S. Senate Committee on Commerce, Science and Transportation's Subcommittee on Oceans, Atmosphere, Fisheries, and Coast Guard, May 10, 2007, http://www.whoi.edu/page.do?pid=8915&tid=282&cid=27206.

18. Dan Bednarz, "Peak Oil and Healthcare," The Healthcare Blog, Dec. 31, 2006, www.thehealthcareblog.com/the_health_care_blog/2006/12/policy_peak_oil .html.

19. Howard Frumkin et al., "Peak Petroleum and Public Health," *Journal of the American Medical Association*, Oct. 9, 2007.

Chapter 11: Energy and Education

1. Norman R. Augustine et al., "Rising Above the Gathering Storm: Energizing and Employing America for a Brighter Economic Future," statement prepared by National Academy of Sciences' Committee on Science, Engineering, and Public Policy for the Committee on Science, United States House of Representatives, Oct. 12, 2005.

2. National Center for Education Statistics, "U.S. Performance in Mathematics Literacy and Problem Solving," Dec. 6, 2004, www.nces.ed.gov/surveys/ pisa/pisa2003highlights_2.asp; "Highlights from PISA 2009: Performance of U.S. 15-Year-Old Students in Science and Mathematics Literacy in an International Context," Dec. 4, 2007, www.nces.ed.gov/pubsearch/pubsinfo .asp?pubid=2008016; "Highlights from PISA 2006: Performance of U.S. 15-Year-Old Students in Science and Mathematics Literacy in an International Context," Dec. 7, 2010, www.nces.ed.gov/pubsearch/pubsinfo.asp?pubid= 2011004; and June Kroholz, "Economic Time Bomb: U.S. Teens Are Among the Worst at Math," *Wall Street Journal*, Dec. 7, 2004.

3. Center on Education Policy (CEP), "Choices, Changes, and Challenges: Curriculum and Instruction in the NCLB Era" (Washington, DC: CEP, Dec. 2007).

4. Augustine et al., "Rising Above the Gathering Storm."

5. Innovations in Civic Participation, "Legislative Update: The GIVE Act, Summer of Service, and the Energy Conservation Corps," www.icicp.org /ht/d/sp/i/1988/pid/1988.

6. Derrick Z. Jackson, "Green Energy Meets Jobs," *Boston Globe*, Sept. 29, 2007.

7. Kevin Coyle, "Environmental Literacy in America" (Washington, DC: National Environmental Education and Training Foundation, Sept. 2005).

Chapter 12: Energy and Two Valleys

1. Office of Mayor Chuck Reed, "San José's Green Vision," Oct. 5, 2007, http:// www.sanjoseca.gov/mayor/goals/environment/greenvision/san%20jose's%20 green%20vision%20fnl.pdf.

2. "Google Says, 'Here Comes the Sun,'" *msnbc.com*, Oct. 17, 2006, http://www
.msnbc.msn.com/id/15301514.

3. Niki Fenwick, Global Communications and Public Affairs, Google Inc.,
e-mail correspondence with author, April 23, 2008.

4. "Our Story," Calera website, http://www.calera.com/index.php/about_us/
our_story.

5. Adobe Systems Inc., "Adobe Headquarters Awarded Highest Honors from
U.S. Green Building Council," press release, Dec. 5, 2006; and Katherine Conrad, "Platinum Is the New Green: Adobe Takes Triple Kudos for
Healthy Downtown Buildings," *San Jose Mercury News*, Dec. 6, 2006, business section.

6. Electric car information comes from various sources: "About Tesla," Tesla
website, http://www.teslamotors.com/about; Tom Abate and David R.
Baker, "Tesla Joins with Toyota to Reopen NUMMI Plant," *San Francisco Chronicle*, May 21, 2010; Better Place website, http://www.betterplace
.com; "Government Lists Solar, EV, Digital Grid Projects Among 100
'Changing America,'" *Sunplugger.com*, Sept. 17, 2010, http://sunpluggers
.com/news/government-lists-solar-ev-grid-projects-among-100-changing
-america-0932.

7 SolarTech, "Creating a Solar Center of Excellence," June 2007, http://www
.solartech.org/STWP.pdf.

8. Information on Silicon Valley's solar power industry is from the various company websites.

9. Information on Republic Cloverleaf Solar is from Michael Moore, "County to
Be the First to Install Solar Highway," *Morgan Hill Times*, November 19, 2010,
http://www.morganhilltimes.com/news/270554-county-to-be-first-to-install
-solar-highway.

10. Rick Row, executive director, Sustainable Silicon Valley (SSV), e-mail correspondence with author, April 23, 2008; and SSV's "CO_2 Report 2007."

11. Marianne Kolbasuk McGee, "Data Center Energy Consumption Has Doubled Since 2000," *InformationWeek*, Feb. 15, 2007.

12. "About the Green Grid: Our Mission," http://www.thegreengrid.org/en/
about-the-green-grid/our-mission.aspx.

13. Matt Carter, "New Generation of Wind Farms at Altamont Pass," *Oakland Tribune*, March 31, 2005, http://findarticles.com/p/articles/mi_qn4176
/is_20050331/ai_n14615598.

14. "The National Ignition Facility: Ushering in a New Age for Science," NIF website, www.lasers.llnl.gov/about/nif.

15. Altamont Commuter Express, "History of ACE Passenger Railroad Service," http://www.acerail.com/about-ace/history-of-ace/history-of-ace.htm.

16. Jennifer Baldwin, "Manure Power: Dairies Harness Methane to Create Renewable Energy," *Bakersfield Express*, Nov. 11, 2009.

17. San Joaquin Valley Clean Energy Organization, "California's 25x'25 Commitment," http://www.25x25.org/storage/25x25/documents/summit2008/Summit 2008Presentations/rollie_smith.pdf.

18. Cleantech America, "KRCD Enters Long Term, Zero Emission Solar Power Plan," press release, July 6, 2007, http://www.cleantechamerica.com/Press Release/07-06-2007/9.

19. "Rx for Clean Air: Clean Energy," *Visalia Times-Delta*, Sept. 18, 2007; and Alcoa, "Photovoltaic Solar Power System at Alcoa's Kawneer Facility in California Begins Operation," press release, Aug. 23, 2007, http://www.alcoa.com/locations/alcoa_location/en/news/news_86.asp?code=86&strNumber=1.

Chapter 13: Energy and the World

1. Jill Jonnes, *Empires of Light: Edison, Tesla, Westinghouse, and the Race to Electrify the World* (New York: Random House, 2003).

2. International Energy Agency (IEA), "World Energy Outlook 2007" (Paris: IEA, 2007), http://www.worldenergyoutlook.org/2007.asp; and Keith Bradshet, "China to Pass U.S. in 2009 in Emissions," *New York Times*, Nov. 7, 2006.

3. Lascelles Linton, "Chery Has Huge Plans for Hybrids in 2008 and Beyond," Autoblog Green, posted on Nov. 16, 2007, www.autobloggreen.com; and "Chery to Go Hybrid Crazy by 2010," *China Car Times*, Nov. 16, 2007, www.chinacartimes.com.

4. "Heat for the Tubs of China: Cheap Solar-Powered Devices Bring Hot Water to Millions," *Wall Street Journal*, March 31, 2006, Marketplace section; and "The World's Billionaires, #396 Shi Zhengrong," *Forbes.com*, March 5, 2008, http://www.forbes.com/lists/2008/10/billionaires08_Shi-Zhengrong_EP46.html.

5. David McNeil, "Japan's Hybrid Train Hailed as the Future of Rail Travel," *Independent* (U.K.), Aug. 1, 2007.

6. Hiroko Nakata, "Fast Track to Controversy: JR Tokai Generates Friction with Costly Maglev Train," *Japan Times*, Feb. 27, 2008.

7. DeserTec, "TREC: Clean Power from Deserts," Jan. 15, 2008, http://www
   .desertec.org/downloads/summary_en.pdf.

8. Ian Traynor and David Gow, "EU promises 20% Reduction in Carbon Emissions by 2020," *Guardian* (Manchester, England), Feb. 21, 2007; and Leo
   Cendrowicz, "EU Aims to Choke Carbon Emissions," *Time*, Jan. 23, 2008.

9. Information on European-wide energy initiatives comes from Hjálmar W.
   Hannesson, "Climate Change as a Global Challenge," statement to the United
   Nations General Assembly, Feb. 8, 2007; Reuters, "Sweden Aims for Renew-
   able Sources of Half Its Energy," March 6, 2008; and Ida Kubiszewski and
   Cutler J. Cleveland, "Oedillo Font-Romeu, France," *Encyclopedia of the Earth*,
   June 14, 2007, www.eoearth.org/article/Odeillo_font-Romeu,_France.

10. European Wind Energy Association (EWEA), "Pure Power on the Hori-
    zon," press release, April 16, 2008, www.ewea.org; "UK Wind Power Reaches
    Milestone," BBC News, Feb. 9, 2007, www.news.bbc.co.uk; Danish Wind In-
    dustry Association, "Nysted Offshore Wind Farm," www.windpower.org/en
    /pictures/offshore.htm; and "Denmark to Increase Wind Power to 50% by
    2025," *Renewable Energy World*, Dec. 5, 2006.

11. Descriptions of energy independence projects under way in Britain are from
    "Shell Pulls Out of World's Biggest Wind Farm, Draws Criticism," *En-
    vironmental Leader*, May 5, 2008; Simon de Bruxelles, "Giant Wind Farm
    Planned for Bristol Channel," *Times* (London), May 18, 2007; Government of
    Hong Kong, Energy Efficiency Office of the Electrical and Mechanical Ser-
    vice Department, "Marine Renewables," http://re.emsd.gov.hk/english/other/
    marine/marine_tech.html; and "Cruachan Power Station," *Gazetteer for
    Scotland*, www.geo.ed.ac.uk/scotgaz/features/featurefirst2013.html.

12. Transport for London, "Congestion Charging," www.tfl.gov.uk/roadusers/
    congestioncharging/6741.aspx; and "Hydrogen Bus Trial," http://www.tfl.gov
    .uk/corporate/6585.aspx.

13. Western GeoPower Corp., "South Meager Geothermal Project," www
    .geopower.ca/meagerdescription.htm; and Enwave, "Our Vision," http://www
    .enwave.com/home.php.

14. "Nova Scotia Power . . . A Tidal Power Pioneer," *Electrical Line Magazine*,
    March/April 2002, 28–29.

15. Sandia National Laboratories, "U.S.-Mexico Renewable Energy Programs
    Help Farmers, Ranchers South of the Border," press release, Dec. 18, 2000.

16. Green Empowerment, "Renewable Energy for International Development:
    San Jose de Bocay," http://www.greenempowerment.org/home-mainmenu-

1/156.html?task=view; and "Renewable Energy for International Development: Ecuador," http://www.greenempowerment.org/projects-topmenu-28/ecuador-topmenu-35.html.

17. Adam Lashinsky and Nelson D. Schwartz, "How to Beat the High Cost of Gasoline. Forever!" *Fortune*, Jan. 24, 2006; Wan Imran Wan Chik, "The Ethanol Magic?" *Malaysian Business*, June 16, 2007; and Thomas L. Friedman, "The Energy Harvest," *New York Times*, Sept. 15, 2006.

18. Australian Government, Department of Environment, Water, Heritage, and the Arts, "Welcome to Australia's Solar Cities," www.environment.gov.au/settlements/solarcities.

19. Doug Kelly, "Renewable Energy for Micronesia," *Micronesian Counselor*, Sept. 2006.

20. U.S. Department of Energy, "Major African Environmental Challenge: Use of Biomass Energy," http://www.eia.doe.gov/emeu/cabs/chapter7.html.

Chapter 14: Securing America's Energy Future

1. Apollo Alliance, "Clean Energy Strategies for the Manufacturing Sector," www.apolloalliance.org.

Chapter 15: The Power of Leadership

1. Pat Wood III, e-mail comments to the author, May 9, 2008.

2. Ibid.

3. Republicans for Environmental Protection press release, "Passage of House Climate and Energy Bill a Step in the Right Direction," June 26, 2009, http://www.rep.org/opinions/press_releases/release09-6-26.html.

SUGGESTED READING

Braasch, Gary. *Earth Under Fire: How Global Warming Is Changing the World.* Los Angeles: University of California Press, 2007.

Brown, Lester R. *Plan B 3.0: Mobilizing to Save Civilization.* New York: W. W. Norton, 2008.

Caldicott, Helen. *Nuclear Power Is Not the Answer.* New York: New Press, 2006.

Deffeyes, Kenneth S. *Beyond Oil: The View from Hubbert's Peak.* New York: Farrar, Straus, and Giroux/Hill & Wang, 2005.

Goodell, Jeff. *Big Coal: The Dirty Secret Behind America's Energy Future.* New York: Houghton Mifflin, 2006.

Gore, Al. *An Inconvenient Truth: The Planetary Emergency of Global Warming and What We Can Do About It.* New York: Rodale, 2006.

Krupp, Fred, and Miriam Horn. *Earth: The Sequel: The Race to Reinvent Energy and Stop Global Warming.* New York: W. W. Norton, 2008.

Pearce, Fred. *With Speed and Violence: Why Scientists Fear Tipping Points in Climate Change.* Boston: Beacon Press, 2007.

Pfeiffer, Dale Allen. *Eating Fossil Fuels: Oil, Food, and the Coming Crisis in Agriculture.* Gabriola Island, Canada: New Society Publishers, 2006.

Richardson, Bill. *Leading by Example: How We Can Inspire an Energy and Security Revolution.* Hoboken, NJ: John Wiley & Sons, 2008.

Sandalow, David. *Freedom from Oil: How the Next President Can End the United States' Oil Addiction.* New York: McGraw-Hill, 2008.

Shah, Sonia. *Crude: The Story of Oil.* New York: Seven Stories Press, 2004.

INDEX

and national electric network, 134
and nuclear reactors, 122
Tesla, Nikola, 38, 39, 217
Tesla Motors, 149, 207
Texaco, 42
Texas, 42, 245–246
Texas Renewable Portfolio Standard,
245–246
"threat multiplier" effects, of global warming,
95
Three Mile Island nuclear accident, 67
tides, gravitational energy, 60–61
Tilman, David, 169
time factor, in Hubbert's curve, 18
Toyota, 72
Trans-Alaska Pipeline, 92, 107
Trans-Mediterranean Renewable Energy
Cooperation (TREC), 221
transportation
changes, 144
freight, 154–157
industry research on fuel efficiency, 236
in London, 224–225
"traveling wave" nuclear reactor, 124
truckers, fuel consumption, 154–155
Truman, Harry, 252–253
twentieth century, technological change, 47

Union of Concerned Scientists, 80, 82, 87, 110
United Arab Emirates, 44
United Kingdom, clean energy goals,
223–224
United States
crude oil foreign sources, 90
drought in Midwest and Southwest, 114
economic expansion in 1990s, 129
economic security, 234–237
education system, 188–189
generating capacity requirements, 134–135
goals, 261
government regulation over monopolies, 38
Hubbert graph of oil reserves, 13
Midwest dust storm, 159
nuclear reactors, 66
political system, 255–257
relations with China, 99–100
responsibility for greenhouse gases, 24
trade deficit with China, 100
University of Missouri in Columbia, 171
uranium, 65–66, 67, 120, 121
limited supply, 69

U.S. Army, transcontinental military convoy,
143–144
U.S. Constitution, 233
U.S. Defense Department, 234
U.S. Energy Department, 133, 234
Office of Petroleum Reserves, 16
projections on world coal consumption, 19
Wind Powering America, 168
U.S. Energy Information Administration,
17, 134
U.S. Environmental Protection Agency, 85,
132, 248
U.S. Geological Survey, 15
U.S. Green Building Council, 206
U.S. House of Representatives
Committee on Energy and Commerce, 247
Oversight and Government Reform
Committee, 80, 86
Select Committee on Energy Independence
and Global Warming, 22
U.S. Interior Department, 77
U.S. military, 89, 100–101
climate change and, 95
fossil fuel use reduction, 97–98
fuel consumption, 90, 96–97
leadership, 234
U.S. National Academy of Sciences, 122
U.S. Navy, emergency petroleum
reserves, 77
U.S. Nuclear Regulatory Commission, 68
U.S. President, 251–255
U.S. Senate
Environment and Public Works
Committee, 86
Foreign Relations Committee, 100
U.S. Supreme Court, 38
Utah State University, 172

Van Leeuwen, Jan Willem, 121
vehicles, 40–41
electric, 98, 149–150
fuel efficiency, 145, 148–152
hybrid, 155, 205
pollution from, 145
size vs. safety features, 147
wear and tear costs, 146
Vendant Power, 61
Venezuela, 44, 91
Caracas shantytown disaster, 180
trade relations with China, 99
veterans, education benefits, 196

CONGRESSMAN JERRY McNERNEY

I n the November 2006 election, the people of California's 11th congressional district (which includes parts of the Silicon Valley and San Joaquin Valley regions) elected Jerry McNerney to represent them in Washington, D.C. Reelected in 2008 and 2010, he is a member of the House Committe on Science, Space, and Technology; the Subcommittee on Energy and the Environment; and the Subcommittee on Investigation and Oversight.

McNerney was born in Albuquerque, New Mexico, and attended the University of New Mexico, where he studied engineering and mathematics, earning a Ph.D. in 1981. He served several years as a contractor to Sandia National Laboratories on Kirtland Air Force Base, working on wind energy and national security programs. In 1985, he accepted a senior engineering position with U.S. Windpower, Kenetech. In 1994, he began working as an energy consultant for Pacific Gas & Electric, FloWind, the Electric Power Research Institute, and other utility companies. During his career in wind energy, McNerney's work contributed to saving the equivalent of approximately 30 million barrels of oil, or 8.3 million tons of carbon dioxide—the main greenhouse gas—as well as other harmful pollutants.

McNerney and his wife of thirty-one years, Mary, make their home in Pleasanton, California. He is an avid reader, has written three unpublished novels along with numerous essays, and has also published several technical papers pertaining to wind energy.

MARTIN CHEEK

Martin Cheek has worked as a newspaper reporter and magazine writer for over two decades. He served as the European bureau chief for Edittech International, a news service that focuses on developments in science and the high-tech industry. At Edittech, he wrote more than 1,000 articles for magazines and newspapers in North America, Asia, Europe, and Australia. He has worked as a writer and an editor at *South Bay Accent Magazine*, *Triumph Magazine*, and *Defense Science Magazine*. He also regularly wrote articles for *San Jose Magazine*, profiling Silicon Valley's leading businesspeople. Several of his articles for this magazine won Peninsula Press Club journalism awards.

Cheek was born in Hollister, California; attended Palma High School in Salinas; and graduated in 1990 with a journalism degree from San José State University. He is the author of the first and second editions of *Moon Handbooks: Silicon Valley*, a travel guide to "the high-tech capital of the world." He is also the "City Expert" for the San José/Silicon Valley section of the travel-focused Home&Abroad.com website. His regular column, called "The Big Picture," is published in the *Morgan Hill Times*, the *Gilroy Dispatch*, and the *Hollister Free Lance*. It often discusses alternative energy issues in the Silicon Valley region.

He makes his home in Morgan Hill, California, where he is active in various nonprofit groups, such as the Friends of the Morgan Hill Library, the San Pedro Ponds Trail Volunteers, the Poppy Jasper Short Film Festival, and Leadership Morgan Hill. He also serves on the Morgan Hill Parks and Recreation Commission.